A Primer in Social and Sociological Theory

TOWARD A SOCIOLOGY OF CITIZENSHIP

KENNETH ALLAN

University of North Carolina at Greensboro

Los Angeles | London | New Delhi
Singapore | Washington DC

For information:

Pine Forge Press
An Imprint of SAGE
  Publications, Inc.
2455 Teller Road
Thousand Oaks, California 91320
E-mail: order@sagepub.com

SAGE Publications
  India Pvt. Ltd.
B 1/I 1 Mohan Cooperative
  Industrial Area
Mathura Road,
  New Delhi 110 044
India

SAGE Publications Ltd.
1 Oliver's Yard
55 City Road
London EC1Y 1SP
United Kingdom

SAGE Publications Asia-Pacific
Pte. Ltd.
33 Pekin Street #02-01
Far East Square
Singapore 048763

Printed in the United States of America

Library of Congress Cataloging-in-Publication Data

Allan, Kenneth, 1951-
A primer in social and sociological theory: toward a sociology of citizenship/Kenneth D. Allan.
      p. cm.
Includes bibliographical references and index.
ISBN 978-1-4129-6051-9 (pbk.)
    1. Sociology. 2. Sociology—Philosophy. 3. Sociologists. I. Title.

HM586.A437 2011
301—dc22   2009043871

This book is printed on acid-free paper.

10   11   12   13   14   10   9   8   7   6   5   4   3   2   1

Acquisitions Editor:	David Repetto
Editorial Assistant:	Maggie Stanley
Production Editor:	Carla Freeman
Copy Editor:	Teresa Herlinger
Typesetter:	C&M Digitals (P) Ltd.
Proofreader:	Andrea Martin
Indexer:	Rick Hurd
Cover Designer:	Gail Buschman
Marketing Manager:	Dory Schrader

Contents

Introduction

Is it possible that democracy can be a way of being in the world, not just a mode of governance circumscribed by corporate power and monied interests?

—West (1999, p. xx)

Democracy is a way of life controlled by a working faith in the possibilities of human nature . . . faith in the potentialities of human nature as that nature is exhibited in every human being irrespective of race, color, sex, birth and family, of material or cultural wealth.

—Dewey (1939/1988, p. 226)

The two quotes above are from men whose births were separated by almost a century of time and whose lives by the American racial divide. Yet they express the same sentiment, embody the same hope, and are the foundation upon which this book is built. As Cornel West and John Dewey claim, democracy isn't simply about voting; democracy is a way of existing, a way of being in the world that permeates our entire life. Democracy is present in our conversations, our daily practices, in the ideas and values that guide us, and in our collective efforts to define what it means to be human. Democracy is founded on a never-ending faith in human potential—it is a belief system that not only asks every person to take part, but is based on the idea that every part makes a difference and that collectively we can create an endless horizon of possibilities.

In this respect, this book is about authenticity. The democracy that West and Dewey are talking about is one where there is a vital connection between an individual's inner life and his or her practices. Yet because of what democracy entails—the extension of life, liberty, and the pursuit of happiness to all humankind—a person's inner life isn't simply an individual concern; it is a social, ethical issue. Please note that nowhere in this book will I ask you to conform to my ethics. Such an approach would be the exact opposite of democracy. In fact, I sincerely hope that we disagree; diversity and disagreement are touchstones for democracy. We need dissenting views. However, this book will ask you to examine your ethics and practices in light of the social world around you, and it will challenge you to do so using critical thinking and social theory. In a democracy, we need to be able to give a full and coherent account of our reasoning and practices. Critical thinking and social theory are the heart of just such an account.

This book is also based on the belief that the energies of a democratic life are urgently needed today, perhaps more than ever before. Our world is rapidly getting smaller, and it is a world filled with political tensions and violence laced with religious certainty; a world just beginning to come to grips with the possibility of environmental catastrophe; a world of nation building, diversity, and extreme poverty; and it's a world of mass media images, advertising, and commodities, for all their good and ill. Yet, while the need is great, democracy is also under assault—and the most significant problem is that most of us misrecognize the issue. While terrorism is undoubtedly a concern, there are more fundamental, more insidious, and longer-running attacks against democracy. To see these assaults, we must first understand and keep in mind the essential qualities of democracy: an educated citizenry actively pursuing freedom and equality for all peoples. Terrorists might attack our buildings and lives, but democracy isn't found in buildings, national boundaries, or security. Don't get me wrong—those are extremely important, especially the latter, but they do not define democracy. Take all of them away, and democracy would still exist. The true threats to democracy are those that arise from within. The threats originate in the dullness that consumerism brings, and in the insatiable quest for greater stimulation from mass media. They ferment in the sense that democracy is inevitable and complete in the United States and its economic partners; all that is needed is to modernize the rest of the world. They stand tall within the new American attitude that higher education is nothing more than a job placement program and can thus be held to economic standards of efficiency.

In the end, this book is an invitation and a challenge. Despite all my rhetoric up to this point, the purpose and design of the book are fairly simple. The purpose is to equip you to think critically and theoretically. The book is designed around nine ideas that generally form the basis of most contemporary social disciplines: modernity, society, self, religion, capitalism, power, gender, race, and globalization. The course of the book is set by the idea that modernity is based upon the desire to make human life better. Science was created to help meet this goal. Part of this modern project of bettering human life can be found in such sciences as medicine; other parts are found in the social and behavioral sciences. Social science, and social and sociological theories specifically, came about to study modern society, which by definition includes the idea of democratic nations and practices of citizenship.

The first chapter explains critical thinking and theory and how to practice them. Each of the subsequent chapters uses classic and contemporary thinkers to show how society, self, capitalism, and so forth fit into the project of modernity, especially as they were seen at the beginning of the modern age. However, as we move from chapter to chapter, and from classic to contemporary theory, we'll see that society, self, religion, capitalism, power, gender, race, and globalization all imply issues that require us to rethink the idea of modernity and perhaps participatory democracy. In other words, I'll be providing opportunities to use your critical thinking and theoretical skills in considering each of these major social issues. At the end of every chapter, there is a series of exercises called "The Craft of Citizenship." The exercises themselves will come out of the theories introduced in the chapters and will progressively equip you with higher levels of critical thinking and theorizing skills.

Ultimately, I want you to leave your reading of this book with more questions than answers. You'll learn theory; you'll learn the answers that different theorists give us about social things. But if that's all that happens, then I've missed the mark. Critical thinking and theory should actually unsettle you. You should begin to see things that you never noticed before, and you should begin to question things you never questioned before. I had a former student come into my office the other day and tell me that I need to warn all my students about this. She used an analogy from *The Matrix*. If you've seen the film, you might remember that the main character was offered two pills: one red (which would reveal the truth of the world) and the other blue (which would do nothing and allow life to carry on as before). My student told me that theory is like the red pill: "If you take it, really take it, everything changes." I hope she's right. As I said, theory should be unsettling—critical thinking, more so, especially when considering the implications of critical thought and theory for your craft of citizenship.

To be American is to raise perennially the frightening democratic question: What does the public interest have to do with the most vulnerable and disadvantaged in our society?

—West (1999, p. xix)

Acknowledgments

This is the book I've wanted to write for a good number of years, only I didn't know it. The ideas that formed the base from which this project emerged came through interacting with my theory students for the past 15 years and from my previous book projects with Pine Forge. To my students, I offer my thanks for making me think and teach better, for making me find reasons, and for their patience. To Pine Forge, thank you for giving me a creative atmosphere where new ideas can find a home and direction. My deep appreciation especially to Jerry Westby and Ben Penner, my first editorial team at Pine Forge; you guys were an inspiration that continues to stay with me. I also want to acknowledge my gratitude to Carla Freeman, for keeping me grounded, and Nancy Scrofano for making sure I stayed on track. Above all, my thanks to my copy editor, Teresa Herlinger. I'm always amazed at how thoroughly you check and the breadth of knowledge you bring, and, as always, my thanks for the questions and critical thinking—you see more than most. And, of course, my thanks to the following reviewers—my work is always improved by the comments and support of such colleagues.

Yaw Ackah
Delaware State University

Josh Adams
*State University of
New York–Fredonia*

Edward Crenshaw
Ohio State University

Stephen Groce
Western Kentucky University

Druann Heckert
Fayetteville State University

Ritchie Lowry
Boston College

Gerald M. Platt
*University of Massachusetts
Amherst*

Jeralynn Sittig
Mississippi State University

Kevin Wehr
*California State University,
Sacramento*

Modernity, Democracy, and the Making of a Civic Sociologist

With all historical time to develop in, sociology is only about a hundred years old.

—Martindale (1988, p. 3)

A number of years ago, I started asking my students how many of them were going on to become sociologists. As you can imagine, only a very few would raise their hands. I followed up by asking, "Then why are you here?" I used that occasion to invite students to consider theory as a way of understanding their lives: Max Weber's work actually gives us a pretty good explanation about why a college education is necessary to gain entry-level positions in a society such as ours. But just a few semesters ago I realized something. While my little exercise provided a way of understanding how theory could be important, I hadn't addressed the bigger issue: Why sociology? Or, to put it more broadly, why should you study society at all? The above quote by Don Martindale puts the same issue in a more historical context: Why did sociology develop when it did? The answers to why you should study society and why sociology was created are tied up together with what we call modernity.

The words *modern* and *modernity* are used in a number of different ways. Sometimes modern is used in the same way as contemporary or up-to-date. Other times it's used as an adjective, as in modern art or modern architecture. In the social disciplines, there has been a good bit of debate about the idea of modernity. Some argue that we are no longer modern, others that we never were, and still others that we are living in some different form of modernity, like liquid modernity. In the course of our time together, you'll find that there aren't any clear answers to these issues. But, rather than attempting to give answers, my hope is that this book will help you ask good questions about the time we live in and our society. In fact, I would be most happy if after reading this book you have more questions than you started with.

In this book, we're going to begin thinking about society and our place in it using a specific view of modernity, one that assumes a rational actor and an ordered world that can be directed. It's important to note that this approach to understanding modernity and knowledge is just one of many possibilities. So, this story of modernity is simply our beginning; it's our touchstone, the place from which to organize our thinking. As you move through the book, you'll find that many contemporary theorists, and even some classical ones, point to social factors and processes that make it difficult to be a reasoned social actor. There are also theories that indicate that the social world may not be ordered, but rather, is a kind of chaotic system. And, more fundamentally, the social world may not be objective, but may simply be a subjective attribution of meaning. Further, some critical theorists argue that the idea of scientific knowledge is intrinsically linked to power and is thus oppressive. That's why we are starting with this view of modernity and modern knowledge: It's the ideal, and it's the one that many people assume to be alive and well in modern democracy.

The Making of Modernity—Social Factors and Intellectual Ideas

As a historical period, **modernity** began in the seventeenth century and was marked by *significant social changes,* such as massive movements of populations from small local communities to large urban settings, a high division of labor, high commodification and use of rational markets, the widespread use of bureaucracy, and large-scale integration through national identities—such as "American" to unite differences like gender, race, religion, and so forth. In general, the *defining institutions* of modernity are nation-states and mass democracy, capitalism, science, and mass media; the *historical moments* that set the stage for modernity are the Renaissance, Enlightenment, Reformation, the American and French Revolutions, and the Industrial Revolution.

But modernity is more than a period of time; *it's a way of knowing* that is rooted in the Enlightenment and positivism. The Enlightenment was a European intellectual movement that began around the time Sir Isaac Newton published *Principia Mathematica* in 1686, though the beginnings go back to Bacon, Hobbes, and Descartes. The people creating this intellectual revolution felt that the use of reason and logic would enlighten the world in ways that fate and faith could not. The principal targets of this movement were the Church and the monarchy, and the ideas central to the Enlightenment were progress, empiricism, freedom, and tolerance.

The ideas of *progress and empiricism* are especially significant. Prior to the Enlightenment, the idea of progress wasn't important. The reason for this is that the dominant worldview had its basis in tradition and religion. Traditional knowledge is by definition embedded in long periods of time and thus resists change and progress. Religion is based upon revelation, which, again by definition, makes our learning about the world dependent upon God's disclosure and not upon us developing or advancing it. In order for the modern idea of progress to make sense, the universe had to be seen in a specific light. Rather than the world being a mix of the physical and the spiritual, as with religion or magic, it had to be understood as simply empirical, and our knowing of this world dependent upon our own efforts, our own observations using our five senses, and our own gathering of evidence. Traditional knowledge is valid if it stands the test of time; religious knowledge is valid if it is revealed by God; but modern knowledge is valid if and only if it is empirically tested and works.

The idea of progress is also tied up with what's called *positivism*. The basic tenet of positivism is that theology and metaphysics are imperfect ways of knowing and that positive knowledge is based upon facts and universal laws. The ideal model for positivistic knowledge is science: *Science* assumes the universe is empirical; that it operates according to law-like principles, and that human beings can discover these laws. Further, the reasons to discover these laws are to explain, predict, and control phenomena for the benefit of humankind. Scientific knowledge is built up or accumulated as theories are tested and the untenable parts discarded. New theories are built up from the previous and those in turn are tested, and so on. It's essential for you to note that this business of testing is one characteristic that separates positivistic knowledge from all previous forms: *The basis of accepting knowledge isn't faith but doubt.* It's this characteristic of positivistic knowledge that gives progress its modern meaning.

Modernity's Two Projects

Progress in modernity—and thus the intent of modern knowledge—is focused on two main arenas: technical and social. The technical project of modernity is generally the domain of science. In science, knowledge is used to control the universe through technology. While we've come to see science as the bastion for the technical project of modernity, the responsibility for the social project is seemingly less focused, at least in our minds today. Generally speaking, the institutional responsibility for the social project rests with the democratic state. Prior to Western modernity, the primary form of government in Europe was feudalism, which was based on land tenure and personal relationships. These relationships, and thus the land, were organized around the monarchy with clear social, hereditary divisions between royalty and peasants. Therefore, the experience of the everyday person in feudal Europe was one where personal obligations and one's relationship to the land were paramount. Every person was keenly aware of his or her obligations to the lord of the land. These were seen as a kind of familial relationship, with fidelity as its chief goal. The main type of political identity available in feudalism was the *subject*—subjects are placed under the authority, control, or dominion of the monarchy.

Modern democracy began with the American and French Revolutions. The U.S. Declaration of Independence captures this new type of government: "We hold these truths to be self-evident, that all men are created equal, that they are endowed by their Creator with certain unalienable Rights, that among these are Life, Liberty and the pursuit of Happiness." The social project of modernity, then, was founded on the belief in natural, human rights—rights that cannot be given to people by a government because they belong to every person by birth. A necessary implication of this belief is that government can only rule by consent of the governed; that is, modern government can only rule through democracy.

While the main identity available in feudalism was the subject, in a modern democracy it is the *citizen*. It's important for you to see the connection between modern knowledge and citizenship. Both science and citizenship are based on the idea of a new kind of person—the supreme individual with the power to use his or her own mind to determine truth and to use reason to discover the world as it exists and make rational decisions. This belief gave the Enlightenment its other name: the Age of Reason. This new idea, this reasoning person, obviously formed the basis of scientific inquiry; more importantly, for our purposes, it also formed the basis for the social project. Democracy is not only possible because of belief in the rational individual; this new person also *necessitates* democracy. The only way of governing a group of individuals, each of whom is capable of rational inquiry and reasonable action, is through their consent.

Defining the Demos

Part of what I'll be asking you to do in this book is to unpack (analyze) some of the things we take for granted. The democratic citizen is one of those ideas we will be looking at closely. Our word *democracy* comes from two Greek words: *dēmos,* which simply means "the masses" or "the people," and *kratos,* which is "strength" or "to rule." Democracy, then, means the strength to rule rests in the common people. Of course, there are assumptions in back of what we mean by the common people. As was mentioned, the main type of political person available in modern democracies is the citizen. But, as Shakespeare said, there's the rub. Just what exactly is a citizen? More precisely, what kinds of people qualify as citizens?

The Problem of the Citizen

This issue goes all the way back to ancient Greece and the first democracies. Plato had deep problems with democracy because he felt that it would lead to the rule of the poor and ignorant over the intelligentsia. There's a way in which the issue for Plato was really about public opinion versus authoritative opinion. The elite were well educated and disciplined in their personal lives, and thus ideal for making decisions regarding the public good. The masses, on the other hand, Plato saw as uneducated and living according to the dictates of their physical appetites rather than the soul or mind. This problem was compounded by the Sophists. The Sophists were a group of itinerant intellectuals who made their living by teaching courses on the nature of language, culture, virtue, and so on. More than any other group, they were the founders of *rhetoric*, the science and art of persuasion. Part of what they did was to sell their services to local politicians. In some sense, they were the first spin doctors. They taught politicians how to persuade a crowd to their own ends. The masses were susceptible to these speeches that were tuned by rhetoric. It was their lack of education and their responsiveness to persuasion that worried Plato about the masses.

The problem of the citizen has also been an issue in modern nations, but for different reasons. The history of the United States, for example, has to a large degree been defined by contentions over the meaning of "all men" in the U.S. Declaration of Independence. Initially, only white, property-owning, Protestant, heterosexual males over the age of 21 were intended. It's important to note that there are two different issues at stake between what the ancient Greeks were debating and what's usually seen as the problem in the United States. The latter is a legal issue of rights: What social groups will have the right to vote? This is the issue of universal suffrage. For the Greek philosophers, however, it was an issue of quality or responsibility: What kind of person is best qualified for civic responsibility?

The interesting thing is that in modern democracy, we usually assume that every voting member of the citizenry is capable of the kind of rationality needed—ironically, this is precisely what Plato was worried about: Under the tenets of natural rights and the autonomous individual, we believe every person by birth is capable of reasoned decision making and action, and this capability is seen as a right, whether exercised or not. Historically, we have focused on the legal issues of civil rights and universal suffrage. Over the past 200 years or so, U.S. citizens have decided that membership in a particular group is not a basis for determining who has the right to democratic participation. However, given the age in which we live, we ought to consider the implications of what modern democracy has simply assumed. Rather than glossing it over, let's take a moment and think about the characteristics a modern citizen ought to embody—the kind of person who is best qualified for civic responsibility.

Bringing together what we've already learned about the Enlightenment and knowledge, along with the projects of modernity, we can say that the modern citizen is assumed to be much like an itinerant scientist, with basically the same goals (explain, predict, control), using similar methods, with similar pragmatic ends. Further, the modern citizen has a mandate—indeed, an obligation—to think critically about democracy. After the U.S. Declaration of Independence talks about life, liberty, and the pursuit of happiness, it goes on to say the following:

> That to secure these rights, Governments are instituted among Men, deriving their just powers from the consent of the governed, That whenever any Form of Government becomes destructive of these ends, it is the Right of the People to alter or to abolish it. . . . [I]t is their right, it is their duty, to throw off such Government, and to provide new Guards for their future security.

It is thus the ethical duty of all democratic citizens to prepare themselves to the best of their abilities to continually hold the government up to scrutiny— much as a scientist doubts and tests—in order to give their best efforts in securing the social project of modernity for all people. This idea of the citizen as a "lay social scientist" is clearly related to the birth of sociology.

It's extremely important that you see the connection between modernity and the kind of person you can potentially and are expected to be, especially as it is related to knowledge. Because it's often difficult to understand ourselves as historically specific, I want to repeat what I said earlier: Science and citizenship are both based on a new way of knowing and a new type of person: an individual with the power to use his or her own mind to determine truth and make rational decisions. This belief gave the Enlightenment its other name: the Age of Reason. This new idea, this reasoning person, obviously formed the basis of scientific inquiry; more importantly for our purposes, it also formed the basis for the social project. Democracy is not only *possible* because of belief in the rational individual; this new person also *necessitates* democracy. Another way to put this is that modern democracy stands or falls based on this type of person.

It's also significant to note that the Enlightenment's view of the person included the idea of *the autonomous individual*. In large part, this notion owes its existence to the Protestant Reformation. Rather than receiving God's grace because of and through the Church, Protestantism separated out the individual and made him or her stand before God's judgment. Judgment was determined by faith, but it was the individual's decision that was the crux of the matter. According to Protestant doctrine, being baptized as an infant couldn't "save" a person because it wasn't based on the individual's decision to follow Christ. The Enlightenment's idea of the reasoning, deciding individual is clear in Protestant doctrine. It's also clear that the person's individuality is the result of birth. Remember these words from the Declaration of

Independence: People are "endowed by their Creator with certain unalienable Rights." Early modernity brought with it, then, this vision of the autonomous person: "the human person as a fully centered, unified individual, endowed with the capacities of reason, consciousness, and action, whose 'center' consisted of an inner core, which first emerged" at birth and continued to unfold "throughout the individual's existence" (Hall, 1996, p. 597).

America and the First Sociologists

Sociology was and continues to be one of the best disciplines for inquiry into modernity's social goals, precisely because it is the study of society. The first sociologists did not hold PhD's, nor did they go to school to study sociology. They were generally found among the "thousands of 'travelers,' . . . who came to [the United States] to observe how the new revolutionary system worked" (Lipset, 1962, p. 5). In the beginning phases of modernity, the United States was seen as the first and purest experiment in democracy. Unlike Europe, where modern government had to contend with and emerge from feudalism, America was born in democracy. People thus came to the United States not only to experience freedom, but also to observe how modern democracy worked.

Two of these itinerate sociologists were Alexis de Tocqueville and Harriet Martineau. Tocqueville was French and lived from 1805 to 1859. His best-known work is *Democracy in America,* a two-volume investigation of the United States published in 1835 and 1840. Harriet Martineau was British, lived from 1802 to 1876, and is well-known for several works. The first is her translation of Auguste Comte's *Positive Philosophy,* one of the foundation stones of science in general and sociology specifically—Comte is usually seen as the founder of sociology. Another of Martineau's important works is *How to Observe Morals and Manners,* published in 1838. The work was quite probably the first methodology book for the social sciences. It's important to note that this book is addressed to "travelers" and "tourists." Remember, modernity brought rapid increases in transportation and communication technologies; people were thus able to move about the globe in a way that was never before possible. Moreover, they were challenged and excited by the new idea of knowledge that modernity brought. Many thus set out to discover society, just as the founders of science did with the physical world.

Martineau wrote her methodology book because she was concerned: People were making observations of society haphazardly and were reaching conclusions with bias and with too little research—her concern was thus much like Plato's. To make her point, Martineau (1838/2003) asks the traveler if he or she would feel confident to answer if someone were to ask about the "geology of Corsica, or the public buildings of Palermo" (p. 14). She then takes the part of the traveler and answers this rhetorical question herself: "'Oh, I can tell you nothing about that—I never studied geology; I know nothing about architecture'" (p. 14).

Please notice clearly what Martineau is saying: People can and should observe, investigate, and discover society. But we cannot and should not take this endeavor lightly. Yes, everybody can observe, but everybody needs to be prepared: "Of all the sciences . . . [the study of society is] the most difficult in its application" (p. 15). Martineau wrote *How to Observe Morals and Manners* on her voyage to the United States, where she collected data for her subsequent three-volume work, *Society in America,* published in 1837. These two books obviously go hand-in-hand: *Morals and Manners* contains the methodology Martineau used to study American democracy. Martineau's basic method was to compare what America said it was going to do (morals) with what it was actually doing (manners). Today, the title might be *Ethics and Practices.* Thus, Martineau very clearly saw the American experiment as an ethical, moral issue. In her mind, then, the ethics of democracy are the most important causal force—practices should flow from ethics.

Martineau isn't alone among early sociologists in seeing this connection. Jane Addams (1860–1935), the first American woman to win the Nobel Peace Prize (1931), also understood this central issue. In the introduction to her book *Democracy and Social Ethics,* Addams (1902/2002) says, "It is well to remind ourselves . . . that 'Ethics' is but another word for 'righteousness,' that for which many men and women of every generation have hungered and thirsted, and without which life becomes meaningless" (p. 5). Further, Addams sees democracy not "merely as a sentiment which desires the well-being of all men, nor yet as a creed which believes in the essential dignity and equality of all men, but as that which affords a rule of living as well as a test of faith" (p. 7).

Practicing Democracy

As these early sociologists saw it, there are certain assumed practices that come with democracy. Two of the most important practices and ideas involve the association of the individual with the collective and emergent ethics. Something is said to *emerge* if it rises from or comes out of something else, as steam emerges out of water and heat. In this case, the ethical practices of democracy arise from specific kinds of associations between the individual and the living collective. In this way, democracy is intrinsically open-ended. It's an emergent, ongoing project. American democracy as it is set forth in the Declaration of Independence, the U.S. Constitution, and the Bill of Rights explicitly structures the system in this way. That's the reason why freedom of the press, freedom of speech, and the freedom to gather are among the rights of citizens.

Of our three sociologists so far, Addams had the clearest philosophical base for understanding the idea of emergence intrinsic in democracy. Addams was a pragmatist. Pragmatism is the only indigenous and distinctively American form of philosophy. Pragmatism rejects the notion that there are any fundamental truths and instead proposes that *truth* is relative to time, place, and purpose. Pragmatism is thus "an idea about ideas" and a way of relativizing ideology (Menand, 2001, p. xi), but this relativizing doesn't result in relativism. In fact, pragmatism is founded upon clear and strong ethical beliefs. However, rather than these ethics being based in some outside, preexisting force or system, *the ethical basis of pragmatism is the belief in human reason and consensus.* Thus, truth in pragmatism is specific to community: Human action and decisions aren't determined or forced by society, ideology, or preexisting truths. Rather, decisions and ethics emerge out of a consensus that develops through interaction.

Ethics and morality are thus social rather than individual and come out of experience, experimentation, and diversity. Addams specifically argues that democratic citizens are morally obligated to seek out interactions with people *unlike themselves,* because truly democratic ideals and practices cannot come out of interactions within a homogeneous group. This is a law of people and culture: Patterned and repeated interactions among individuals will create and sustain similar and particularized cultural beliefs. Democracy, which is fundamentally concerned with bringing freedom and equality to all humankind, must then seek diverse people and diverse interactions, out of which will come what Tocqueville calls the *moral majority.*

The Moral Majority

During the 1980s, there was a Christian political organization and movement called the Moral Majority. The organization, founded by Jerry Falwell, was responsible for creating the idea of the New Christian Right and is credited with significantly helping Ronald Reagan get elected president. The Moral Majority supported mass media censorship; American military strength; and a return to "family values," which included opposition to abortion, homosexuality, and the Equal Rights Amendment. Though the organization disbanded at the end of the eighties, Falwell brought the idea back to life for the twenty-first century in 2004 with the Moral Majority Coalition.

It's interesting to view Tocqueville's discussion of the moral majority alongside Falwell's. In doing so, my point isn't directed at any differences in belief; most of the issues that Falwell is concerned with were not on the national agenda in the 1830s. But there is a pronounced difference in foundations. For Falwell, the emphasis was on the moral beliefs of Evangelical Christianity. In contrast, Tocqueville's emphasis is on the *morality inherent in the democratic process of the majority*. The belief in back of this is the idea that "there is more enlightenment and wisdom in a numerous assembly than in a single man" (Tocqueville, 1835/1969, p. 247). The emphasis here is on diversity of thought. It is, as Tocqueville says, "the theory of equality applied to brains" (p. 247). The morality of the majority isn't found in a homogeneous belief system—quite the opposite. The moral majority is found when the greater part of the citizenry come together for political discourse where diverse ideas can clash and where reason can create consensus. Modern morality, then, isn't a static belief system; modern morality is the ongoing and public meeting of the minds of the majority of people. As Jane Addams (1902/2002) puts it, "Unless all men and all classes contribute to a good, we cannot even be sure it is worth having" (p. 97).

Modern Institutions

Modernity also brought with it new institutions and new institutional arrangements. In premodern society, social institutions overlapped quite a bit. One of the most important overlaps was between religion and government. In feudalistic Europe, for example, the right of kings to rule was legitimized by religion, and second and third sons of royalty were often trained clergymen. If we look back further in history, we can see that in almost every society, religion and government overlapped and legitimated one another.

Modernity, then, is unique in that it *intentionally separates church and state*. This separation is necessary because democracy cannot function under absolute truth and legitimation. Theocracy is the polar opposite of democracy. In a theocracy, the power to rule comes from the top (God) down; in a democracy, the power to rule goes from the bottom (citizens) up. However, it's also clear by looking at early social thinkers and sociologists that this separation did not necessarily mean that religion wasn't important or would go away. On the contrary, religion plays a key role in modernity; and we'll explore that role in Chapter 4. For now, let's think about the unique place that education holds in the social project.

Education and Democracy

Martineau (1838/2003) argues that in the history of humankind there are two great social powers—force and knowledge—and the story of human progress is the movement away from one and toward the other. Social relations began through physical force and domination and the idea that might makes right. Knowledge, as we understand it today, was of little worth. Rather, what was important in terms of knowledge was tradition. In such societies, the past is everything. Thus, by definition, traditional authority isn't critically examined and maintains the status quo; it "falls back upon precedent, and reposes there" (p. 45).

Modern knowledge, as we've seen, is clearly different. It values reason, progress, and change. The important point here is that Martineau sees a clear link between modern knowledge and government. Power in a modern state rests upon the people. The method through which democratic citizens are to exercise their power is through knowledge, which is why education is a keystone for modernity. Tocqueville (1835/1969) likewise sees education as the foundation of democracy: "The first duty imposed on those who now direct society is to educate democracy" (p. 12). And Jane Addams (1902/2002) tells us that democracy is based on belief in the power residing in each one of us, and that it is education that will unlock that potential: "We are impatient to use the dynamic power residing in the mass of men, and demand that the educator free that power" (p. 80).

Martineau (1838/2003) argues that two of the most important indicators of the relationship between education and freedom are the extent of free education and the position of the university. The *extent of free education* is an unmistakable measure of societal support of the ideas of equality and democracy. In modern countries, education is perceived as the legitimate way to get ahead. In other words, the kind of job and pay you get is initially based on your level of education. Martineau is saying that to understand the level of equality that society supports, one need only look at the kinds of job opportunities that free, public education provides. For example, if a society supports public education only through high school, it indicates that the level of equality the state is interested in supporting is only equal to the jobs that require a high school education.

On this point, Martineau's indictment of America is clear. While our moral says that we believe in equality of opportunity for all people, our manners (practices) say different. While Tocqueville's (1835/1969) focus isn't the same as Martineau's, his criticism is identical:

I think there is no other country in the world where, proportionately to population, there are so few ignorant and so few learned individuals as in America. Primary education is within reach of all; higher education is hardly available to anybody. (p. 55)

The second indicator of the place of education in society is the *regard given the university.* Martineau (1838/2003) claims that "in countries where there is any popular Idea of Liberty, the universities are considered its stronghold" (p. 203). The reason for this link between liberty and universities is precisely the connection that was made earlier: Democratic citizens are morally obligated to continually examine the state in terms of its progress in fulfilling the social goals of modernity. And this examination is to be insistent, assertive, and uncompromising. As Martineau puts it, "It would be an interesting inquiry how many revolutions warlike and bloodless, have issued from seats of learning" (p. 203).

Not only are the purpose, content, and environment of the university important, but so are its students, in particular their motivation for study. To the degree that students are motivated to obtain a university education for a job, to that degree is education for freedom compromised. Martineau (1838/2003) makes a comparison between students in Germany and those in the United States. German students are noted for their quest for knowledge: The German student may "remain within the walls of his college till time silvers his hairs." The young American student, on the other hand, "satisfied at the end of three years that he knows as much as his neighbors . . . plunges into what alone he considers the business of life" (p. 205). Obviously, in advanced capitalist society, getting a college education is important for economic success. But seeing and using education *primarily* as a method of credentialing and job placement sounds the death knell for democracy.

Civic Sociology and the Craft of Citizenship

To state the obvious, there is an intrinsic relationship between education and democracy. As a citizen, you need to be able to understand and use information and ideas to make reasoned decisions about the world around you. More than at any other time in our history, democracy matters, and being a citizen offers a horizon of possibilities. Today, democracy implies more—much more—than simply voting. It's my intent in this book to encourage you to practice your citizenship through civic sociology:

A civic sociology . . . evidences a desire to connect with people (citizens), their concerns and their biographical problems. It produces [writings and stories] that move people to action, works that promote serious discussion about democratic and personal politics. (Denzin, 1996, p. 747)

We'll see as we move through the book that there are new challenges to this type of participatory democracy. The words of C. Wright Mills (1959) have never been truer:

> What they need . . . is a quality of mind that . . . may be called the *sociological imagination*. . . . [T]he first lesson of the social science that embodies it—is the idea that the individual can understand his own experience and gauge his own fate only by locating himself within his period. . . . The sociological imagination enables us to grasp history and biography and the relations between the two within society. (pp. 5–6, emphasis added)

The sociological imagination and civic sociology begin with critical thinking.

Critical Thinking

The people who hold the power in society—in a democracy, that would be you and me—need to have informed opinions about how to guide society. Here's an analogy: If you've been diagnosed with cancer, whose opinion do you want, radio talk show personality Don Imus or a trained oncologist? Now, you may and probably should get several opinions, but if you have half a lick of sense, the people whose advice you seek will all be professionals trained in their discipline and not Imus. What you are looking for in choosing an oncologist over Imus is an *authoritative opinion* rather than personal opinion. Imus may have an opinion about cancer, but it would be a personal opinion, not a knowledgeable one. Everyone seems to feel entitled to an opinion, and that's fine. Having simple opinions about things like what music is worth listening to is okay, but not about things that inform our participatory democracy. I believe that the question of democratic participation is at least as important as finding a good oncologist to treat cancer. Consider this: If I don't get a good oncologist, I might die; if we don't participate democratically, tens of thousands of people could die, or be oppressed, or suffer needlessly, or the environment could be destroyed, and so on.

There are a number of elements that go into an informed opinion. One of them is, of course, knowledge. The oncologist knows more about cancer than does Imus. Yet there's more to this issue of knowledge than most people might think. Imus could go online and get quite a bit of information about cancer; but the oncologist would still offer the more knowledgeable opinion of the two because the medical doctor understands the information about cancer within the context of a knowledge base. This is an extremely important issue that most people today miss: There is a difference between information and knowledge. In previous times, information was only a piece of the learning process; equally important was the training of the mind. The computer and Internet have made information abundant, readily available, and ever-changing. Thus, most of us now think of knowledge as bits of information, able to exist and be consumed apart from any training of the mind. We are programmed by our culture and social relations to see things as disconnected and fragmented. But in doing so, we lose whatever cultural power we might have. One of the most important ways that we will be able to make a difference in this day and age is if we have the ability to use knowledge (not just information) effectively to analyze the social world around us and to create cohesive arguments about what we as a society ought to be doing.

There are at least two other important differences between authoritative and personal opinions: critical thinking and theory. Getting back to our oncologist example, if you're smart, you'll not only choose the oncologist over Imus, but will also get the opinions of several oncologists. This tells us something important about the nature of knowledge, something that you may have already begun to notice in your college experience: There are very few "right" answers, and there certainly aren't any simple ones about things that matter. What becomes important, then, is not only what you know, but also how you use what you know, and how you use what you know is based on critical thinking. (*Theory*, as we'll see, is a special type of critical thinking.)

Critical Thinking Attitudes

Without a doubt, critical thinking is necessary for a democracy to work. But what do we mean by critical thinking? There are a number of ways the word *critical* can be used, and it's important to understand how it is meant here. Some of the synonyms for critical include dangerous, significant, life-threatening, unfavorable, and analytical. In critical thinking, we most specifically mean analytical. But critical thinking may end up being significant, dangerous, or unfavorable as well. Critical thinking doesn't accept all opinions and every piece of information equally. Thus, by definition, it will be unfavorable to some ways of knowing. Critical thinking can also end up being significant or dangerous, but, again, not because it is inherently so. Critical thinking may be significant or dangerous because it challenges everything; nothing is simply accepted or taken for granted.

Critical thinking involves sets of attitudes and skills, with the attitudes defining a specific kind of person. The most basic attitude is that *the critical thinker takes responsibility for his or her own knowledge.* Your path in education should move from schooling to scholarship. In schooling, you are presented with information as facts, and your job is to conform. This is the kind of education that is characteristic of kindergarten through high school in the

United States. In higher education, however, your disposition should change from "Will that be on the test?" to "How can I be sure of that?" And your skill set should change from memorization and categorization to research.

Further, *the critical thinker believes*. This belief, however, isn't in a final truth. In fact, that type of belief is antithetical to critical thinking and democracy. To believe in a final truth, especially about democracy, is to believe a myth. It is a form of what Judith Butler (1993) calls "presentist conceit" (p. 228)—the belief that despite the lessons of human history, we have somehow achieved truth and perfection in our moment in time. This myth "allows the comfort of opinion without the discomfort of thought" (John F. Kennedy, quoted in Shenkman, 2008, p. 1). Myths and beliefs are comforting; democracy and critical thinking are unsettling. Critical thinking is always questioning, always moving. The belief that critical thinking is based on is the modern faith in human potential, not absolute truth. And because of this belief, *the critical thinker is curious and hungry to know*. C. Wright Mills (1959) once wrote about the "passionate curiosity about a great problem, the sort of curiosity that compels the mind to travel anywhere and by any means, to re-make itself if necessary, in order to find out" (p. 103). The critical thinker is one who is driven to find out, and who believes in the processes of insight and discovery.

The critical thinker is purposeful and goal directed. Most of the thinking we engage in is on automatic pilot or just sort of a meandering of the mind. Critical thinking, on the other hand, is alive and searching. One of the reasons that critical thinking is purposeful is that two of our most cherished values—the ability to decide and the freedom to act—are based on it. Neither the ability to decide nor the freedom to act exists freely; both must be critically examined in order to exist at all. Deciding without examining the basis and context of that decision is in truth not a decision at all. Some things can appear as decisions when they are little more than compliance. And, by its very nature, action implies purpose; that's the distinction between acting and reacting. Purposeful, critical thinking is about scrutinizing your decisions and actions. Further, as we've seen from our early sociologists, democratic decisions and actions are intrinsically ethical. So part of our purposeful thinking must entail a consideration of our ethics: What ethics inform your decisions and actions?

The critical thinker is clear and systematic in using reason and analysis. Not only is critical thinking mindful behavior, it's also behavior that is logical and systematic. *The critical thinker is decidedly open-minded.* Having an open mind can be frightening. With it, we may come in contact with people and ideas that challenge our way of life. A closed mind is satisfied with its version of truth and is closed to all others. However, thousands of years of human history should teach us one thing: We've always been wrong. To think we're right today and to be closed-minded is simply conceit. *The critical thinker is creative.* Critical thinking always sees beyond; critical thinking is driven to new insights. Critical thinking seeks to get out of the box. (A word to the wise: You must first know and understand the box in order to intentionally get out of it; otherwise, it's just an accident.) And, finally, *the critical thinker values thinking and is motivated to improve it.*

Critical Thinking Skills: The Basics

The fundamental critical thinking skill is the inclination and ability to ask questions—"we cannot be skilled at thinking unless we are skilled at questioning" (Elder & Paul, 2005, p. 3). Notice that there is both an attitude and a skill here. We must be inclined to ask questions as well as able to do so. Before going further, I have a side comment: Critical thinking is a valuable tool in almost every aspect of your life. You can use it to make decisions about what to buy, what classes to take, which news sources to listen to, and so on. My specific focus here will be on using critical thinking to understand arguments about society—what society is, how it works, and how we can be involved. But I also want to note that what you learn here about critical thinking will prove valuable in every other area of your life, because critical thinking attitudes and skills are generally the same. So practicing your skills here will prepare you to use critical thinking in your professional and personal lives as well.

Your first steps as a critical thinker involve asking **comprehension questions,** beginning with understanding the important ideas and concepts that are used by an author. You should read with a dictionary by your side, or use an authoritative online service like Merriam-Webster.com. Theory, however, uses a lot of specialized terms that can't be found in a standard dictionary. A word of caution: Some theoretical terms may appear to be in the dictionary. For example, you'll be able to find "religion," but the dictionary will not give you the theoretical definition of the concept. Most of the time, theoretical terms are defined in the particular text you are reading; even so, it's still a good idea to have and use reference books such as John Scott's *Sociology: The Key Concepts* (2006) or Allan G. Johnson's *The Blackwell Dictionary of Sociology* (2000).

Theoretical terms need theoretical definitions, and they aren't as easy or simple as you might imagine. Let's use a common table to help us see. Any specific table is there for everyone to see and touch. We can assess it using a standard of measurement. So, we can say, "That table is 48 by 24 inches." (Of course, it changes to 121.92 by 60.96 centimeters if we use the metric system.) But a definition of *table* must be general enough to be used to classify all tables, not just this one. Definitions describe ideas and concepts. How, then, do we know where the idea or category of table begins and ends? The only way to limit the idea of table is to specify it through a definition.

If I ask you to give me a definition for table, you might say something like, "A table is a wooden structure that has four legs." But is that general enough? No. Don't we call some metal things tables as well? And some things that count as tables have three rather than four legs. So, you might then say, "A table is a structure made out of any material that has three or more legs that has a flat surface upon which we can place objects." That's better, but is it good enough? Maybe, but this definition could also apply to chairs as well as tables. Obviously, we aren't usually this concerned about the definition of table. We all know what a table is, at least within practical limits, which is all we're really concerned with in everyday life. But I hope you can see the issue for critical thinking and theory: If all we have to build arguments and theory out of are concepts, then definitions become extremely important. They are the basic fodder for critical thinking and are the fundamental building blocks of theory and arguments.

Strong definitions will go beyond a simple description and will explain the conditions necessary for belonging to the concept/class being defined. We were working toward this kind of **stipulative definition** in our discussion of table. In our definitions, we want to fully explain the qualities that make something what it is and not something else. Merriam-Webster (2002) defines table as "a piece of furniture consisting of a smooth flat slab fixed on legs or other support and variously used (as for eating, writing, working, or playing games)." That strikes me as a fairly good definition. It's general enough to include tables with three, four, six, or eight legs, yet specific enough to exclude other similar objects like chairs (tables are used for "eating, writing, working, or playing games")—the definition *stipulates* the necessary conditions for a thing to be considered a table.

Sometimes definitions need to go further; this is especially true for **theoretical definitions**. One of the things that the Merriam-Webster definition includes is what a table does. When talking about tables, that doesn't seem all that interesting, but if we consider theoretical issues, its importance can more easily be seen. For example, the definition of *class consciousness* is the subjective awareness that class determines life chances and group interests. But what does class consciousness do? The answer is that class consciousness acts as one of the precursors to revolutionary social change. Another example is the definition of *money*: a generalized medium of exchange for goods and services. What does money do? Besides enabling you to buy things, money is actually one of the most powerfully acting forces in society. It creates higher levels of trust in government, trivializes meaning, increases the number of rational rather than ethical relationships among people, stretches out social networks across time and space, increases the diversity and number of available commodities and markets, and so on. What I want you to see here is that, because theories explain how something works or comes about, *good* theoretical definitions will include variability and effects. *Variability* explains how this concept came to exist and how there could be more or less of it; *effects* explain what the concept does, what it creates. The bottom line is that the definitions you write must be able to perform work in a theory or argument.

Understanding the concepts being used is our important first step in critical thinking. However, concepts don't exist in a vacuum; a concept must always be understood within its context or argument. Part of comprehension, then, is discovering the argument: You don't truly understand the chapter, book, theory, or article until you comprehend the argument. Whether you realize it or not, every book, chapter, and article that you read for school is presenting an argument. In fact, almost everything we come in contact with—such as advertisements, newspapers, magazines, news broadcasts, and so on—implicitly or explicitly carries arguments. Defining an argument is easy: An **argument** is a course of reasoning presented to persuade the reader/hearer of a specific conclusion. While defining an argument is easy, writing good arguments and critiquing others take a great deal of practice, which is one of the aims of this book.

There are certain things that you need to find out about the arguments you read or hear. The first issue is *the question* or main point that's driving the argument. Ask yourself, what is this chapter or theory about? What question is the author answering? You should be able to find this in either the introduction or the conclusion. If possible, you also want to find the *author's purpose* in writing or doing the research. It isn't hard to imagine that an article written by a scientist employed by a chemical company will, perhaps, be biased, and the author's purpose will likely be connected to that company's goals. Part of what we see about arguments is that they are strongly influenced by the *perspective of the author*. So an argument that addresses self-esteem will be different if the person writing is a sociologist rather than a psychologist. Always search for the assumptions, perspectives, and possible biases in the writing.

These issues—questions, purpose, assumptions, and perspective—frame arguments. Arguments themselves always have a specific conclusion or intent and are built by *logically linking together different premises*. We can think of premises as ideas or facts that lead to a specific conclusion. Usually, you'll understand the premises by defining the main concepts. But there's more to understanding arguments than simply comprehending the concepts and ideas. Arguments are specifically created through the way in which the concepts and premises are linked together. The ways that premises and concepts are related to one another form the structure of the argument or theory. This feature is extremely important, and the one with which most people have problems. To see the importance, consider this: What are the differences between 235 and 2 + 3 = 5? The numbers are the same, but they are structured differently and thus have entirely different meanings. As we'll see, this issue of how ideas or premises are put together is extremely important for theory.

Being able to evaluate and write arguments is paramount for critical thinking, because you must be able to give a full and coherent account of your thinking and reasoning; you must be able to *explain* your answer. Here's a simple example: Let's say you're in my theory course, and I ask you to write a theoretical definition of *class*. So you take a shot at it, and it sucks. You know it sucks; I know it sucks. So, I ask, "Can you make it better?" You say, "Yes." And I say, "How?" You then proceed to rewrite the definition—and that's where the problem begins. Let's say you write a better definition. It isn't hard with a definition that sucks. But *how* did you do it? What criteria did you use? Do you see the point? You may have an intuition you've picked up over your many years of schooling that you could use to make a definition better, but critical thinking demands that you be able to give an explanation—a full and lucid account of your thinking and reasoning, which always takes the form of an argument.

Critical Thinking Skill Set 1: Inference and Application

You don't fully understand concepts, arguments, or theories until you are able to apply them to the world around you. More importantly, civic sociology is dependent upon you doing just that—applying your knowledge of theory to the world around you. To *infer* is to derive by reasoning or implication, and by definition it is based on insight: Insight is seeing beyond or deeper than what is available on the surface. So always ask, what insights can be derived from this information, argument, or theory? How can I see the world differently because of this new knowledge? For example, in social theory, Émile Durkheim (1912/1995) gives a specific and unique definition of religion:

A religion is a unified system of beliefs and practices relative to sacred things, that is to say, things set apart and forbidden—beliefs and practices which unite into one single moral community called a Church, all those who adhere to them. (p. 44)

Thus, you can't infer Durkheim's definition of religion; he's already explicitly provided it. You can, however, infer from his definition. And using his definition of religion, you could deduce that sport in modernity is a form of religion.

Another example of an important but often neglected application question is at the core of citizenship and critical thinking: What are the implications of the things we believe and practice every day? One of the most difficult assignments I've ever given was to ask my "Sociology of Religion" students to examine the implications of their personal beliefs and practices. This was difficult because it asked students to (1) be reflexive, and (2) understand their individual lives in terms of social implications (e.g., to think sociologically). Also notice that inference assumes a thorough understanding of the ideas or practices at the core of the issue. In this case, the students had to understand the effects of religion generally in order to infer how their personal beliefs might impact society.

What's more, social theories must be applied to the social world. There are two areas here. First, theory is applied to the world through research methods. Theories aren't simply best guesses about how society works; they are meant to be tested over and over against empirical evidence. Each test sharpens our concepts and explanations. Empirical testing of theories is usually covered in research methods classes. But our theorizing may also be tested a second way. Rather than being tested against empirical evidence, critical theories are to be tested by the standard of social justice issues. This is where the value we place on our sociological work becomes important. If your purpose is to simply explain how society works, then applying the theory through research methods is all you need to do. On the other hand, if your goal is to change society, then the theory is also applied toward increasing social justice and equality; in short, theory can be applied to further the project of democracy.

Critical Thinking Skill Set 2: Interpretation, Analysis, Evaluation, and Synthesis

Your first jobs in critical thinking, then, are to discover the purposes and questions driving the author, comprehend the major concepts, find the argument (you'll see shortly that every theory is an argument), and think through the implications and social practices that the theory involves. After addressing these issues of understanding, there are several skills that move our thinking further ahead. The four skills in this set are nested within one another: Interpretation leads to analysis, analysis to evaluation, and evaluation to synthesis. **Interpretation** entails the ability to use diverse perspectives to think about and question events, arguments, situations, and so forth. Our word *perspective* comes from the Latin *perspectus,* and it literally means "to look through." Perspectives act like glasses—they bring certain things into focus and blur our vision of others. All perspectives are built upon *assumptions*—things that we suppose to be true without testing them. There's an old saying that goes like this: When you assume, you make an Ass out of U and Me. That saying is dead wrong. Human beings can't begin to think, let alone act, without making assumptions. What makes an ass out of you and me is when we don't acknowledge and critically examine the assumptions underlying our knowledge and actions.

There are **three basic assumptions used in social theory**: assumptions about human nature, the existence of society, and the purposes and goals of knowledge. *Human nature* may be seen as utterly social or egoistic, symbolic and flexible or genetically determined, rational or emotional, freely acting or determined, and so on. While there are a number of variations, the basic assumption about *society* is whether or not it exists objectively—as something that can act independently of the individuals that make it up. At one end of this continuum are those who assume that social structures are objective and strongly influence (or cause) human behavior. Theory that is based on this assumption seeks to explain and predict the effects of social processes using law-like principles. At the other end of the continuum are those who argue that society does not exist objectively outside of human interpretation and action. These kinds of theories don't try to predict human action at all; instead, they seek to understand and explain contextual social action. The assumption about *purpose* involves the value or ethics of theory and sociological work. At one end of this continuum are those that believe sociology should be value-free and only explain what exists. This is the ideal of science—knowledge for knowledge's sake. At the other end of the spectrum are those that believe the purpose of theory and sociological work is to critique society and bring about change.

To analyze something is to break it down into its parts. **Analysis** thus implies ordering: In breaking something down into its constituent parts, we understand it in an ordered manner. On one level, this is something we do every day without even thinking about it. We analyze, order, and break down our time according to the idea of the week. Weeks don't exist in nature; the concept of "Monday" is simply a social convention that allows us to organize our behaviors in certain ways. Analysis in critical thinking is similar in that it is based on taking a given perspective. It may surprise you to know that the Egyptians, Chinese, and French at one time used a 10-day week and the Mayans a 13-day week, and most of these different orderings of time (including our own 7-day week) are based on different religious perspectives. Thus, analysis always implies interpretation because it depends upon the use of a specific perspective in order to unpack something—how something is broken down into its parts, then changes depending on the way in which the thing is viewed. For example, human behavior looks very different if you use a sociological rather than a psychological perspective.

Having analysis in your critical thinking tool kit means that you take little if anything for granted—critical analysis begins by unpacking ideas and concepts that you take for granted. In sociology, your goal is to first understand the basic concepts of theory as well as social life. For example, what is gender? Is it genetic, or is gender an achievement of social interactions? Or perhaps gender is a function of social structures. You could ask the same kinds of questions about race, sexuality, religion, and so on. Analysis at this level begins with definitions: We're asking how gender, race, and religion exist— in answering, we're minimally stipulating the necessary characteristics to be such a thing (race, sexuality, etc.) and ideally how each concept varies and affects other issues.

Analysis usually leads to **evaluation**. Once we realize all analysis is interpretive to one degree or another, then evaluating the different analyses that diverse perspectives give is the next logical step. To evaluate means "to examine and judge concerning the worth, quality, significance, amount, degree, or condition of" (Merriam-Webster, 2002). Evaluation is always guided by perspectives and is preceded by analyses. It thus involves the capacity to compare and contrast the strengths and weaknesses of different definitions, theories, perspectives, arguments, information, and inferences, all of which are based on knowing the specific criteria in each perspective. Interpretation also involves evaluating the validity of your sources. For example, there are differences between the information available on the Internet and the knowledge found in research journals. You have undoubtedly run across this distinction in your college-level education, but do you know what those differences are? What makes certain kinds of knowledge better or more valuable? What criteria can be used in such an assessment?

Synthesis is creatively bringing two or more arguments or theories together to build a new, more robust whole. This is where your own personal work can really shine, because you're seeing something that the original authors did not. Synthesis begins with compare-and-contrast work and by analyzing and evaluating strengths and weaknesses of different theories, arguments, or information. This kind of work will lead you to see where one argument or theory may fit together with or complement another. All critical thinking skills and practices require explanation, but this is particularly true for synthesis—because this is your work! You will need to explain how these arguments or theories fit together, and you will have to convince your reader of this good fit through argumentation. In fact, a synthesis is by definition an argument.

Critical Thinking and Self-Evaluation

Self-evaluation is the inclination and ability to observe, critique, and change one's own thinking and conclusions. While this is listed last, it is essential to what Browne and Keeley (2007) call strong-sense critical thinking: "Weak-sense critical thinking is the use of critical thinking to defend your current beliefs. Strong-sense critical thinking is the use of the same skills to evaluate all claims and beliefs, especially your own" (p. 10). Unless we subject our own thinking, knowledge, and beliefs to critical thinking, we run the risk of becoming dogmatic and a hindrance to true democratic energies. The criteria you use to evaluate your own thinking, at least initially, are the attitudes and skills of critical thinking we just reviewed. Here are some samples:

- What is my purpose in thinking about this information, argument, or theory?
- What are my assumptions and biases? How are these influencing how I read, analyze, and evaluate information, arguments, or theories?
- What are my strengths and weaknesses as a thinker and writer? Am I continually working with course material? Can I summarize the information/arguments/ theories to this point? Do I continually evaluate and understand the implications of my way of thinking and the knowledge I hold? Can I write cohesive and persuasive arguments?
- What questions drive my curiosity? Do I know how to ask questions of courses, textbooks, arguments, information, and theories? Can I formulate questions about a subject using the various issues in critical thinking (analysis, interpretation, evaluation and synthesis, inference, implication, insight, explanation)?
- Can I write strong definitions of concepts that provide all the necessary and sufficient information?
- What diverse perspectives am I able to use to ask questions of my social world and personal actions?
- What skills do I need to find out about something? Am I improving my research skills? Are there better tools or ways to use the tools I have?
- What criteria do I use to evaluate my learning and thinking? Can I explain their relevance?

Theory

Theory is at the heart of modern knowledge and science, yet there's a line in pop culture that says, "It's only a theory." The truth of the matter is that apart from tradition and religion, theory is all we have. All scientific work is based on theory—science and technology in all its forms would not exist if it wasn't for theory. Theories aren't accepted on faith, nor are they time honored. In fact, the business of science is the continual attempt to disprove theories! Theories are accepted because they have stood up to the constant doubt and battering of scientists. Furthermore, "facts" are actually a function of theory: Scientific data is produced through testing and using theoretical perspectives and hypotheses. So, having "just a theory" is a powerful thing.

The first and most important function of theory is that it explains how something works or comes into existence—theory is a logically formed argument that explains an empirical phenomenon in general terms. I came across two statements that help illustrate this point. A recent issue of *Discover* magazine contained the following statement: "Iron deficiency, in particular, can induce strange tastes, though it's not known why" (Kagan, 2008, p. 16). There are many of these empirical observations in science and medicine. For example, it's not known why some people get motion sickness and others don't, nor is it known why more women than men get Raynaud's disease. Observations like these that simply link two empirical variables together are not theoretical.

The second statement appeared in an article about how exercise improves memory and may delay the onset of Alzheimer's. In linking these variables, the article says, "It works like this: aerobic exercise increases blood flow to the brain, which nourishes brain cells and allows them to function more effectively" (Redford & Kinosian, 2008, p. 26). Unlike the first statement, this one offers an explanation of how things work. This, then, is a theoretical statement. It describes how the empirical association between exercise and improved memory works. This function of theory is extremely important, especially for civic sociology. So in studying theory, always look for factors that, when connected, explain how something works or exists.

Theory is built out of assumptions, perspectives, concepts, and relationships. We've already talked about all of these building blocks. (As I said, theory is a special type of critical thinking.) Yet I do want to point out a couple of things. The general assumptions that theorists make are the ones we've already noted, about humans, society, and purpose or values. Keep these in mind as you go through the book; they'll be important for understanding the theories. There are many perspectives in sociology. Some of the ones we'll specifically cover are functionalism, symbolic interaction, dramaturgy, conflict theory, and critical theory. Each of these gives us a different way of seeing the social world and understanding our place in it. Assumptions and perspectives form the background work; actual theory is built out of concepts and relationships. Theoretical concepts are abstract, which is why definitions are so important. The more abstract a concept, the greater its *explanatory power*. In other words, abstract concepts allow you to explain more things.

Because theory explains how something works or came into existence, it is built by proposing specific *relationships* among various concepts. There are at least two concerns in spelling out theoretical relationships. The first is the direction of the relationship. There are two basic possibilities, positive and negative. A relationship is positive if the concepts vary in the same direction (either both increase or both decrease); relationships are negative if they vary in opposite directions (if one increases, the other decreases). Let's use a simple example—education and occupation. The relationship between these two concepts is positive (at least, that's your working hypothesis for being in school): Increasing years of education will produce higher-rated jobs for the individual. Notice that because the relationship is positive, it works the same in reverse: Lower years of education produce lower-rated jobs.

The second concern with relationships is more difficult: We need to explain the relationship. More years of education might equate to a better job, but how does that work? If you think about this a moment, you'll see that the theoretical task just grew tremendously. What is it about education that would affect jobs in that way? How does this relationship work? Historically, it wasn't always true that formal education and occupation were related. Why are they now? Many people in our society know that higher levels of education lead to better jobs, but most can't explain how that works. When you can do that, you're beginning to form authoritative opinions.

But theory can and should do more. Theory should inspire and give insight; it should make us see things we wouldn't otherwise. For example, when Marx says that capitalism breeds its own gravediggers, we see something that isn't possible when giving a technical explanation of the material dialectic. Or, when Durkheim says that the collective consciousness is so independent that it will often do things for its own amusement, our mind is captured in such a way that a technical explanation of social facts can't match. The same is true with Habermas' colonization of the lifeworld, or the idea that money is a pimp, or the notion of plastic sexuality, and many others. It's important to see that this function of theory isn't simply a matter of "turning a phrase." These kinds of theoretical statements get at the essence—they help us see into the core of a social factor or process. Both functions of theory are important, but they can easily overshadow one another. Theory should thus explain how something works or came about as well as inspire us to insight.

The Craft of Citizenship	Modernity, Theory, and Citizenship

The Basics: Comprehension and Explanation

- Construct a table or list of the critical thinking and theoretical issues and questions that this chapter raises. Move from the most basic to the most difficult. This list will be a critical thinking "cheat sheet" that will be an aid to help you work through issues.

  - ➤ *Helpful hints:* Such a list would begin with "Identify the central question" and end with "Synthesize this theory with others that address its weaknesses."

- What qualities go into making a theoretical definition, one that will work in a theory or argument? Put another way, what makes one definition theoretical and another not?

- Write a stipulative definition of modernity, paying particular attention to the type of knowledge.

  - ➤ *Helpful hints:* In the chapter, the terms in **bold** are the important concepts, and *italicized* words are ideas that help explain the important concepts. So, go back to the place in the chapter where modernity is in bold and then pay particular attention to the italicized ideas that surround it. Caution: You can't simply list the italicized words—they are only signposts.

- List the basic assumptions of social/sociological theory.
- Using the information in this book and one other source, define *theory*.
- Using the information in this book and one other source, define *critical thinking*.
- Using the information in this book and one other source, define *democracy* and *citizenship*.

Skill Set 1: Inference and Application

- Explain the place and importance of education in democracy. What are the implications of this for the way in which you are involved in your own education? What place does education have in your country?
- All the work you do for school is graded using explicit criteria. These criteria are the standards against which your work is compared. Part of being a critical thinker is being able to self-evaluate. To that end, I'd like you to use the material from this chapter to write the grading criteria for a theory paper. Start your thinking by filling in the blank: "A good theory paper needs to be/have _____." Another way to stimulate your thinking is to answer this question: What makes one paper theoretical and another not? Come up with at least four criteria.

(Continued)

(Continued)

- What does pragmatism infer about your democratic participation? Use Tocqueville's idea of the moral majority to analyze your democratic participation.

  > *Helpful hints:* Sometimes to answer one question you have to ask others. So, to answer these questions you must first ask, what is pragmatism and Tocqueville's idea of moral majority?

- What is civic sociology? What does the idea of civic sociology imply about your own practices and beliefs? In what ways do you use civic sociology?

Skill Set 2: Interpretation, Analysis, Evaluation, Synthesis

- Evaluate the following statement: "Without a doubt, critical thinking is necessary for a democracy to work."

2

Society

Imagine a group of early humans. There are about 25 to 30 members; they're nomadic, constantly moving in search of food; and they have an early form of speech but no writing. Would you say they have a society? If you answered yes, where is it? You can see them hunt and gather, hear their speech, and see them interact. Where do you see society? Maybe you'd answer by saying that all those things together make it a society. But be careful: What are the implications of such a definition? It would imply that every group of people that works and talks together forms a society. And this definition of society would mean that the staff on the morning shift at Denny's restaurant in Flagstaff, Arizona, is a different society from the crew of a shrimp boat in Bayou La Batre, Alabama. Most people today would probably shy away from defining society in terms of such small groups. However, if you answered no to my first question about whether or not the nomadic group is a society, then you are left with the problem of defining the point at which a group *becomes* a society. What would have to exist or be happening that would make you at one point say, "there's no society," yet at another proclaim, "now there's society"?

The word **society** came into the English language from the French and has a Latin base. The Latin root of the word means companion or fellowship, and up until the middle of the eighteenth century, it kept this basic meaning (Williams, 1983, pp. 291–292). Society thus initially referred to a group of friends or associates, like a legal or scientific society. But toward the end of the seventeenth and through the middle of the eighteenth century, the idea of society was seen in more abstract ways, referring to something that was bigger than face-to-face social interactions as well as an objective entity that could act independently. This is what Durkheim (1895/1938) means when he refers to society as a *social fact*, which "consists of ways of acting, thinking, and feeling, external to the individual, and endowed with a power of coercion, by reason of which they control him" (p. 3). These ideas began to give people a language they could use to talk about such things as religion, education, family, economy, and so on as separate parts of a larger entity called society. Notice that society not only became larger and more abstract, but was also seen in terms of a *system* of interrelated parts.

Along with these changes in the idea of society came an important shift in the use of the word *state*. In the thirteenth and fourteenth centuries, **state** was used to refer to any hierarchical order, such as the state of priests, the state of knights, and when referring to the monarchy. In time, the idea of state came to be used in the way we generally understand it today, in its political sense. The significance of this seemingly minor shift is that the state and society came to be seen by some as two different but related spheres: the state as the organization of power and society as an organization of free people. The ideas were further differentiated with the use of the term **civil society**, especially in the political discourse of the seventeenth and eighteenth centuries. Here, society is specifically seen as "of or belonging to citizens" (Williams, 1983, p. 57).

The three theorists in this chapter are specifically concerned with this idea of society as an objective, macro-level system. Herbert Spencer is the earliest of the three, publishing his work between 1843 and 1904. Spencer is one of the founding thinkers in what became known as **functionalism**. At the core of Spencer's functionalism is the *organismic analogy,* a way of understanding society as if it were an organism, like your body. There are four implications that come from this analogy. First, society is like your body in that both have *different structures designed to meet specific needs*—your body has distinct and specialized organs (like the stomach), and society has distinct and specialized institutions (like religion). Second, all of these *structures are interrelated,* and many form subsystems within the larger system. For example, in your body there is a digestive system, which needs and is related to the circulatory system, and in society there's the economic system, which needs and is related to the education system.

Third, there has been an *evolutionary progression* from single-celled to complex organisms (like your body), and from simple societies to complex ones (like modern societies). Fourth, complex systems suffer problems of coordination and control. Your body is a complex system that relies on certain subsystems, like the autonomic system, to coordinate all of its functions and movements. When one of these control systems is damaged, as in multiple sclerosis, problems of coordination and control will manifest. The same is true in society: Because different institutions tend to work in different ways and produce different results, there must be some system (like government or law) that coordinates the actions, outcomes, and interactions of these different structures.

Our second theorist is also a functionalist. In fact, Talcott Parsons is probably the most influential of all the functionalists. Parsons' first book, *The Structure of Social Action* (1937), has been described as a

> watershed in the development of American sociology in general and sociological theory in particular . . . [which] set a new course—the course of functional analysis—that was to dominate theoretical developments from the early 1940s until the middle of the 1960s. (Coser, 1977, p. 562)

Like Spencer, Parsons saw society as a system of interrelated structures. But Parsons focused more specifically on the question of integrating distinct parts, rather than how the parts evolved. Parsons argued that culture is most important for integration.

The third theorist we'll consider is Jeffrey Alexander; he began publishing in the 1970s and continues to this day. Like Parsons, Alexander considers culture to be extremely important, but he differs from both Spencer and

Parsons in significant ways. For our purposes, the most important distinction of Alexander's approach to functionalism is that he argues that culture is structured, yet meaning emerges out of interactions.

The Evolution of Society—Herbert Spencer

Herbert Spencer was born on April 27, 1820, in Derby, England, the eldest of nine children, and the only child to survive to adulthood. His father, George (a religious dissenter and Benthamite), was a schoolteacher and taught Herbert at home until he was 13, after which the boy continued his training with his Uncle Thomas. Part of his schooling was taken up with reading aloud from Harriet Martineau's *Illustrations of Political Economy*. At age 17, young Spencer decided he wasn't cut out for a university education and worked as a railway engineer for about 4 years. Afterward, he supported himself as a journalist and editor (at *The Nonconformist* and the *London Economist*) until his uncle died and left him some money. From that point on, Spencer lived as a private intellectual. Herbert Spencer was one of the most widely read writers of his time—his books sold somewhere between 500,000 and 1,000,000 copies in his day. These works formed the foundation of many intellectual disciplines, including biology, psychology, sociology, physics, and education. In sociology, Spencer's concern was to explain how societies change and function. After a lengthy illness, Spencer died on December 8, 1903.

Concepts and Theory: Structures, Functions, and Systems

The idea of **structure** is fundamental to the social disciplines, so let's take a moment to think about structures generally. There are two fundamental characteristics of structures: First, structures are made up of *connections,* and second, structures create and *sustain predictable patterns* and shapes. "Let me give you an example of the first characteristic." And I just did. The words within the quotations make sense because they were put together according to certain grammatical rules. Those rules structure the sentence, but you don't *see* the rules; you only see the effects. This sentence can also serve as an example of the second characteristic. Sentences are predictable and always fall into certain patterns. It's the grammatical *structure* that patterns our use of words.

We'll be coming back to this idea of structure time and again in this book, so hold onto this basic definition: Structures are sets of connections that to one degree or another influence the creation of patterns. When we are talking about *social structures,* especially in functionalism, we are referring to the way in which connections are made between social actors, which include individual persons, organizations, institutions, and systems.

Requisite Needs and Functions

The organismic analogy also helps us see that society doesn't usually create structures randomly—every structure does something for the whole, and there is a correspondence between the way the structure is made and what it does. For example, why are your stomach and lungs built differently? The answer is obvious: The cells in your stomach and lungs are structured differently in order to meet different needs that your body has (food and oxygen). Each structure is specialized and separate. When these structures do what they're supposed to do, we say that they are functional; that is, their effects function to meet the needs of the system. By analogy, the same is true for society.

In order to increase the explanatory power of their theory, many functionalists like Spencer propose sets of very general needs or functions that any system must meet—we call these **requisite functions**. In order to do this, Spencer must first make his concepts as abstract as possible, and then he must make inferences based on the organismic analogy. Let's try it. Take your stomach, for example: What does it do? The straightforward answer is that it digests food. Can we make "digests food" more general? Well, when the stomach is digesting food, what is it doing? Or let's approach this differently: Why is your stomach digesting food? The food contains nutrients that your body needs, and the stomach breaks down the actual food into usable substances. And from where does the actual food come? To keep this simple, let's just say that the food—the basic raw resources that your stomach converts—comes from the natural environment. So, generally speaking, what is your stomach doing? It's processing raw materials from the environment and creating usable substances that your body needs. Now we have a much more general explanation of what your stomach is doing. Is there another organ (structure) in your body that does the same thing but differently? Yes, your lungs remove carbon dioxide from the air and supply the body with oxygen. (Note that what I just walked you through, the process of making concepts more general, is a fundamental skill in theory.)

Spencer calls this the *operative function.* Every system, organic or social, must have ways to extract what it needs to exist from the environment. For a society, these needs could be cultural or material. The cultural needs of a society are met through institutions such as education; and the material needs are met through the economy. But, if you think about it, the operative function can't work alone. Once your lungs have filtered the oxygen out of the air, then what? Some other structure or system has to get the oxygen to the places it's needed. Spencer calls this the *distributive function*. It involves those structures that carry needed information and substances. In society, this function is fulfilled by the transportation (roads, railways, airlines) and communication (telephone, mail, and Internet) networks that move goods and information through society. Systems also need to be directed; and Spencer calls this the *regulatory function*. The structures in the operative and distributive systems have to be regulated so that they'll work together. In the human body, the big player in the regulatory function is the central nervous system. An example of a regulatory social structure is government or polity. Governments, both local and national, set and enforce laws that control relationships, whether between internal units (such as individuals or corporations) or between our society as a whole and other external systems (such as a foreign country).

Systems and Change

As you can already tell, the organismic analogy leads us to think about society as a **system**. There are two basic ideas in seeing things systemically. First, a system is defined as a complex unity or *whole that is made up of interrelated parts*. This quality of systems implies two very important issues: We must understand the different parts or structures in a system with reference to the whole, and the elements within a system influence one another. Let's use the body again as an analogy. If you eat foods that are high in cholesterol, you increase your risk of heart attack. The same sort of thing happens in society. Changes in the economy, for example, will produce changes in the family. The second idea basic to systems is that *they exist in environments*. The important thing here is to know that environments exert pressure on systems to change and adapt. This idea of environments exerting pressure is critical to understanding how systems change and fundamental to understanding globalization (Chapter 9). As the environment changes, systems (society, for us) change by creating different responses. Some of these are poor adaptations and won't help the system survive; others, however, are adaptive and naturally selected. *Natural selection* in evolution is like an invisible hand that chooses some forms to live and some to die out.

Concepts and Theory: Social Evolution

Spencer was one of the first evolutionists, and his central concern in sociology is to understand how societies evolve. One of the basic factors in evolution is

structural differentiation, the processes through which structures become different from one another and specialized. For example, the theory of biological evolution tells us that all organisms started from single cells called protozoa, and over time, cells built up to form structures and then systems of differentiated structures. As a result, there was an evolutionary movement from simple to complex organisms. One of the main reasons for these changes is adaptability: Complex systems are more adaptable to changing environments. There's a lot going on in structural differentiation, and we need to unpack (explain) it. Spencer tells us that structural differentiation happens through segmentation and specialization. In evolutionary theory, *segmentation* is the process through which structures divide from one another. Initially, government, education, and the economy were all wrapped up with family. But they separated and became distinct—each with different sets of roles, norms, values, and beliefs. The important insight here is that separate structures exist in separate environments and can change independently. Thus, complex systems, like modern societies, change rapidly. *Specialization* is the process whereby structures become dedicated to performing few or single tasks, so, for example, the things that education does today are not the things that the economy does. Notice something here: As structures differentiate and become separate and specialized, they also become increasingly interdependent.

According to Spencer, the most basic force in back of social evolution is **population growth**. Generally speaking, increased population growth increases the level of structural differentiation. There are two basic reasons why this happens: Size raises the demand for requisite functions (if there are more people, the system needs more food), and survival of the fittest pushes for efficiency (a system that simply replicates existing structures becomes inefficient). There are two ways a population can grow: A population can increase through a higher birth rate than death rate or by what Spencer calls *compounding* (the influx of large populations through either military or political conquest).

Integration and Power

So far, we've seen that society exists as a social system of structures that become different from one another through social evolution. But there are problems. Making structures and systems different from one another means that there will be **problems of coordination and control**. Think about religion and the economy. The functions of each and the way they connect people together are dissimilar; there are vast differences between priests and parishioners and line supervisors and workers. Yet religion and the economy are part of the same social system. How are those two very different structures coordinated so that they produce an undivided society?

Part of the answer is *structural interdependency*. Religion, for example, needs the economy to provide jobs for believers, and the economy needs workers who have ethical values that will keep them working. But interdependency isn't enough, especially in complex systems. If we think for a moment, we can see where a pressure to resolve control and coordination problems could be focused. What function stabilizes relationships between elements within the system? For Spencer, the answer is *increased regulation*. Thus, increases in structural diversity create pressures for increased levels and centralization of regulation, which in social systems is found in government. Together, mutual dependency and a strong regulatory subsystem facilitate structural integration. Centralized authority thus solves the problems of coordination and control, but *overregulation* in turn can create productive stagnation and resentments over excessive control. Overregulation also hampers the exchange of information, the flow of markets, and so forth. In contrast, low levels of control (greater freedom) encourage innovation. In the long run, then, a push–pull relationship develops between these pressures for increased regulation for integration and pressures against regulation due to stagnation.

Military and Industrial Cycles

As societies grow and become diversified and more complex, they go through cycles of regulation and deregulation. Spencer developed a **societal typology** to understand this cycle. There are two societal types in his scheme—militaristic and industrial—and they are defined around the relative importance of the regulatory (state) and operative (economy) functions. It's important to be aware that "militaristic societies" aren't necessarily at war, and "industrial societies" don't necessarily use machinery for production. What Spencer is capturing are different institutional configurations. In the *militaristic societies,* the state is dominant and controls all other sectors. For example, the economy's first mission in this type of society is to provide for military needs rather than consumer products. In militaristic societies, religion provides sets of ultimate values and beliefs that reinforce the legitimacy and actions of the state. The religious structure itself is rather homogeneous, as religion needs to create a singular focus for society. Information and media are also both tightly controlled. The status hierarchy in militaristic societies is highly pronounced, and the rituals (like bowing or using titles such as madam, lord, mister) surrounding status are clear, practiced, and enforced.

Industrial societies are less controlled by the state and are oriented toward economic freedom and innovation. Rather than the collective being supreme, the individual is perceived as the focus of rights, privileges, consumer goods, and so forth. Religion is more diverse, and there is a greater emphasis on individualistic reasons for practicing religion rather than collective ones. Individual happiness and peace are associated with salvation and religiosity. Education shifts to scientific and inclusive knowledge rather than increasing patriotism through selective histories and ideological practices (like the pledge of allegiance). Information flows freely from the bottom up.

All societies begin as militaristic, with top-down control, but there is an evolutionary tendency for societies to become industrial. Societies, however, can also **regress to militarism**. There are three main reasons why a society would, once it has become industrialized, move back toward the militaristic type. First, there is pressure in the system toward militaristic society originating from the *military complex* itself. A military complex is formed by a standing army and the parts of the economy that are oriented toward military production. It's a fact of evolution: Once an organism comes into existence, it will fight for its own survival; this is no less the case for social entities. Thus, a military complex will always find reasons for its continued existence by creating perceptions of threat. There are of course *legitimate threats,* and this is the second reason a society would regress—external or internal threats will always push a society back to militaristic configurations for its own survival.

The final reason why a society might revert is the presence of territorial subjects. A *territorial subject* is a social group that lives outside the normal geographic limits of the state, yet is still subject to state oversight. A current example of this kind of relationship for the United States is Puerto Rico—a commonwealth of the United States with autonomy in internal affairs, yet its chief officer is the U.S. president and its official currency is the U.S. dollar. The United States not only has a vested interest in Puerto Rico, it is also organizationally and politically involved. Issues of investments and responsibilities provide opportunity for military action and the creation of a militaristic society.

Culture and Society—Talcott Parsons

Talcott Parsons (1902–1979) was born in Colorado Springs, Colorado. Parsons began his university studies at Amherst (Massachusetts), planning to become a physician, but he later changed his major to economics. After receiving his BA in 1924, Parsons studied in Europe, completing his PhD work in sociology and economics at the University of Heidelberg, Germany.

After teaching a short while at Amherst, Parsons obtained a lecturing position in 1931 at Harvard and was one of the first instructors in the new sociology department. Parsons became department chair in 1942 and began
work on the Department of Social Relations—formed by combining sociology,
anthropology, and psychology. It was Parsons' vision to create a general science of human action. Parsons was a man with a grand vision. He wanted
to unite the social and behavioral disciplines into a single social science and
to create a single theoretical perspective. His desire, then, wasn't simply to
understand a portion of human action; he wanted, rather, to comprehend
the totality of the human context and to offer a full and complete explanation of social action. The department existed from 1945 to 1972 and formed
the basis of other interdisciplinary programs across the United States.

After 10 years of work, Parsons' first book was published in 1937: *The
Structure of Social Action.* More than any other single book, it introduced
European thinkers to American sociologists and created the first list of "classical" theorists. His other prominent works include *The Social System, Toward
a General Theory of Action, Economy and Society, Structure and Process in
Modern Societies,* and *The American University.* For much of the twentieth
century, Parsons was "the major theoretical figure in English-speaking sociology, if not in world sociology" (Marshall, 1998, p. 480). As Victor Lidz (2000)
notes, "Talcott Parsons . . . was, and remains, the pre-eminent American sociologist" (p. 388). Parsons died on May 8, 1979, while touring Germany on the
50th anniversary of his graduation from Heidelberg.

Evaluation, Synthesis, and Theory Building

Before we take a look at his theory, I want to point out that Parsons' work
gives us a good example of how critical thinking can be used in theory building, especially the work of synthesis. Parsons (1961) draws on three different theorists in order to elaborate his theory:

> For the conception of the social system and the bases of its integration, the
> work of Durkheim; for the comparative analysis of social structure and for the
> analysis of the borderline between social systems and culture, that of Max
> Weber; and for the articulation between social systems and personality, that of
> Freud. (p. 31)

Your being able to identify which portions of Parsons' theory come from
which of these other theorists isn't important right now. What is important
is that you see how Parsons used critical thinking, specifically evaluation and
synthesis, to form his theory.

Parsons sets up his argument by criticizing three specific elements in Spencer's theory. First, Parsons critiques the assumption of progressive evolution—the idea that society is constantly and irrevocably getting better. In contrast, Parsons (1949) wants us to consider the possibility that "contemporary society is at or near a turning point" (p. 4). Second, Parsons critiqued Spencer's conclusion that the progress of modern knowledge would reduce humanity's need for religion. The primary reason Parsons disagrees with this assessment of religion is the place that culture has in establishing social solidarity, and religion contains the strongest expression of culture. Third, Parsons tells us that Spencer was an "extreme individualist." According to Parsons (1949), there is a basic supposition about human nature at the heart of Spencer's theorizing—Spencer assumed that humans are by nature motivated by a "rational pursuit of self-interest" (p. 4). Self-interest and survival of the fittest go hand-in-hand for Spencer. This rational self-interest is one of the mechanisms through which survival of the fittest and natural selection operate in human society. As people try different responses to environmental changes, the automatic, self-regulating mechanism of natural selection ensures that "the pursuit by each individual of his own self-interest and private ends would result in the greatest possible satisfaction of the wants of all" (p. 4).

With these critiques in mind, Parsons builds on what we've already learned. Like Spencer, he sees society as a system of interrelated parts that function to meet the requisite needs of the system through structural differentiation and specialization; he agrees with Spencer's argument that structural differentiation leads to problems of integration. To that explanation, Parsons adds three specific issues: (1) Rather than purely rational self-interest, people engage in "voluntaristic action"; (2) rather than seeing power as centrally addressing the issue of integration, it's culture that plays a decisive role; and (3) rather than simple linear, progressive change, societies may change suddenly due to cultural issues.

Concepts and Theory: Voluntaristic Action

In thinking about humans, it's sometimes convenient to make the distinction between behavior and action: All living things behave; only humans have the potential to act. Action implies choice and decision, whereas behavior occurs without thought, as when a plant's leaves reach for the sun. Of course, humans behave as well as act; there are a lot of things we do on autopilot, but we have the potential for action. Theory that focuses on this issue is referred to as *action theory*, which has been an interest of philosophy since the time of Aristotle. Parsons' work on action theory draws from Max Weber, who argued that action takes place when a person's behavior is meaningfully oriented toward other social actors, usually in terms of meaningful values or rational exchange. *Voluntaristic action,* then, is never purely individualistic: People choose to act voluntarily within a context of culture and social situations in order to meet individual goals. And because human needs are met socially, people develop shortcuts to action by creating norms and by patterning action through sets of ends and means.

Parsons calls this context of action **the unit act.** There are a variety of factors in the unit act. The first, and in some ways the most important, are the *conditions of action.* There are of course occasions when we have some control over the initial context—for example, you may decide to go to the movies on Saturday or study for a test. But once the choice is made, the actor has little immediate agency or choice over the conditions under which action takes place. Parsons has in mind such things as the presence of social institutions or organizations, as well as elements that might be specific to the situation, such as the social influence of particular people or physical constraints of the environment. The second set of factors under which people act concerns *the means and ends of action.* Here we can see a fundamental difference between action and reaction: Action is goal oriented and involves choice. But for people to make choices among goals and means, the choices themselves must have different meanings. According to Parsons, the meanings and relationships between means and ends are formed through *shared value hierarchy.* Cultural values are shared ideas and emotions regarding the worth of something, and values are always understood within a hierarchy, with some goals and means more highly valued than others; otherwise it would be difficult to choose between one thing and another because you wouldn't care.

Because they are shared, value hierarchies stabilize interactions across time and situations. Action and interaction would be disorganized without the presence of a value system that organizes and prioritizes goals and means. Imagine a situation where you value education as a means of economic success, but your parents value thievery for the same goal, your best friend doesn't value economic success at all, half the students in your class value cheating on exams, your significant other decides to join a gang, and so on. Eventually, acting with others would become extremely difficult and utterly subject to chance. A shared value system thus structures and patterns our action, as do norms. *Norms* are actions that have sanctions (rewards or punishments) attached to them. So, for example, besides education being more highly valued by society to achieve economic success, there are also norms against using thievery or gang membership. All voluntary action thus takes place within units of action that are defined and ordered by different sets of values and legitimated means and ends. Further, all these elements are structured in specific patterns that are called institutions. For functionalists such as Parsons, *institutions* are enduring sets of roles, norms, status positions, and value patterns that are recognized as collectively meeting some societal need, which brings us back to the idea of function.

Patterning Action: AGIL

By giving culture a prominent place in the process of integration, Parsons gives us *four requisite functions*. Think for a moment: What can culture do to integrate society that governmental power and regulation can't? Let's use a simple story to help us think about this. In the United States, the speed limit on most highways that run through cities is 55 miles an hour. Though governmental regulation is essential, its drawback is that it depends on monitoring: You're less likely to speed if you see a cop than if you don't. Now, imagine a situation where you actually believed that it was wrong to speed. Chances are good that you wouldn't speed, even if you're not being watched. Notice the difference in the mechanism. The method through which governmental regulation works is external and requires both monitoring and power (the penal system) to back it up. In contrast, culture as a method of controlling actions is internal and works without being noticed.

Parsons calls this process of controlling and coordinating *latent pattern maintenance*. If something is latent, it's hidden and not noticed. Every system requires not only direct management, like that performed by a government, but also indirect management. Not everything that goes on in our bodies, for example, is directed through cognitive functions. Rather, some of these functions, like breathing, are managed and maintained through the autonomic nervous system, a subsystem that maintains patterns with little effort. Society needs the same thing. For this task, society uses culture and socialization (the internalization of society's norms, values, beliefs, cognitions, sentiments, etc.). The chief socializing agents in society are the structures that meet the requirement of latent pattern maintenance—structures such as religion, education, and family.

In addition to latent pattern maintenance, Parsons gives us three other requisite functions for a system: adaptation, goal attainment, and integration. You'll notice that the actual functions are quite similar to Spencer's; Parsons just divides them up differently. The *adaptation* function is fulfilled by those structures that help a system to adapt to its environment. Adaptation draws in resources from the environment, converts them to usable elements, and distributes them throughout the system. *Goal attainment* is like Spencer's regulatory function. It's the subsystem that activates and guides all the other elements toward a specific goal. In Parsons' scheme, *integration* refers to the subsystems and structures that work to blend together and coordinate the various actions of other structures. In society, the structure most responsible for this overt coordination is the legal system. Together, these four functions are referred to as AGIL: Adaptation, Goal attainment, Integration, and Latent pattern maintenance.

Cybernetic Hierarchy of Control

Parsons argues that every system can be analyzed using these four requisite needs. Based on this implication or assumption, Parsons uses this scheme to develop an overall model of how the systems surrounding human life integrate. The model is called the general system of action, or the **cybernetic hierarchy of control**. *Cybernetics* is the study of the automatic control system in the human body. The system is formed by the brain and nervous system, and control is created through mechanical-electrical communication systems and devices. In using the term cybernetic, Parsons tells us that control, and thus integration, are achieved primarily through information or culture.

Based on AGIL, there are four systems that influence our lives (and form the cybernetic hierarchy of control): the culture, social, personality, and organic systems. These systems are in descending order in terms of control. The *culture system* is at the top, indicating that control of human action and life is achieved through cultural information. And the *organic system*—in this case, your body—is at the bottom. The energy for the hierarchy comes from the bottom and moves up the systems. In other words, the entire system works due to your biological needs, but how those needs are met is controlled by the information that comes from the culture system down through the social and personality systems. Culture has no intrinsic energy and is dependent upon the lower systems. Culture is most immediately dependent on the *social system* (social institutions) for its existence. It is also dependent upon the *personality system,* because it's individual humans who internalize and enact culture. For Parsons, this hierarchy exists within a context, with ultimate meanings at the top and the physical environment at the bottom. However, Parsons never makes any comment about what ultimate reality is; he doesn't define it, but its understood existence is extremely important for the culture system. Parsons argues that our most important values are framed in terms of ultimate truths, and these truths are religious in nature. Parsons, then, sees religion as an important influence on the culture system in general, and in turn, on the social and personality systems.

Concepts and Theory: Revolutionary Change

One of the critiques that Parsons had of Spencer's work is his linear model of social change. Parsons accepts evolutionary change, but he also argues that societies can change suddenly due to factors other than population dynamics. Parsons argues that culture is the prime force bringing a differentiated society together through both latent pattern maintenance and integration (formal law is a part of culture). As society changes, as the structures become more differentiated and diverse, culture has to change as well. In order to integrate increasing diversity, culture must become more generalized. A prime example is the history of race in the United States. Initially, blacks were not included in the idea that "all men are created equal." But in response to structural and cultural changes, the idea of "all men" had to become more general, to include not only those of African heritage but also women.

However, the process of *culture generalization*, Parsons (1966) notes, may also bring about severe conflicts: "To the fundamentalist, the demand for greater generality in evaluative standards appears to be a demand to abandon the 'real' commitments" (p. 23). For example, in U.S. society, the call to return to "family values" is just such an issue. Societies that are able to resolve these conflicts move ahead to new levels of adaptive capacity through innovation. Others may "be so beset with internal conflicts or other handicaps that they can barely maintain themselves, or will even deteriorate" (p. 23). It is at this point that *revolutionary change* becomes more likely.

There are four conditions that must be met for a revolutionary movement to be successful. First, the potential for change must exist—this is the place where culture becomes the primary force driving revolution. Parsons refers to this potential as *alienative motivational elements*. That is, people become motivated to change the system as the result of value inconsistencies. These inconsistencies are inevitable and continually present in a modern society, particularly one that has been generalized to incorporate a number of diverse groups, such as in the United States. These strains are expansive, especially in a democracy—opening the door to equality to one disenfranchised group opens the possibility for others. Second, dissatisfaction with the system is not enough to begin a revolutionary movement; the subgroup must also become organized. The *social organization* of a group around a subculture enables members to evade sanctions of the main group, create solidarity, and create an alternative set of normative expectations and sanctions; it also enables expressive leadership to arise. Third, the organized group must develop an *ideology* that incorporates symbols of wide appeal and can successfully put forward a claim to legitimacy. The ability to develop an alternative claim to legitimacy is facilitated by two factors: Modern value systems are very general and can thus be used by diverse social movements, and, when the values of society aren't applied equally to all people, groups can question the legitimacy of the system as a whole.

The fourth condition that must be met is that a revolutionary subgroup must eventually *integrate the social system*. It is this connection that institutionalizes the movement and produces equilibrium. There are three issues involved in creating integration: (1) The utopian ideology that was necessary to create group solidarity must bend in order to make concessions to the adaptive structures of society (e.g., kinship, education)—in other words, the revolutionary group must meet the reality of governing a social system; (2) the unstructured motivational component of the movement must be structured toward its central values—the movement must institutionalize its values in terms of both organizations and individuals; and (3) out-groups must be disciplined vis-à-vis the revolutionary values that are now the new values of society.

The System of Civil Society—Jeffrey C. Alexander

Jeffrey C. Alexander received his PhD in 1978 from the University of California, Berkeley. He was a professor of sociology at the University of California, Los Angeles, from 1976 to 2001, where he is now emeritus. In 2001, Alexander took a professorship at Yale University and is currently the Lillian Chavenson Saden Professor of Sociology and codirector of the Center for Cultural Sociology. Alexander has also held numerous visiting appointments, including at the University of London, The London School of Economics, Konstanz University, and the Center for Advanced Study in the Behavioral Sciences. Among his more important works are *Twenty Lectures: Sociological Theory Since World War Two, Action and Its Environments: Towards a New Synthesis, Structure and Meaning: Relinking Classical Sociology, Neofunctionalism and After, The Meanings of Social Life: A Cultural Sociology,* and *The Civil Sphere.*

Alexander extends Parsons' work by incorporating elements from what is usually called "the linguistic turn." The term itself simply means a move to language, and it implies an approach to understanding human beings that emphasizes language above everything else. This emphasis brought two issues to the front stage for theory: meaning and structure. Meaning is usually seen as subjective and structure as objective. Yet language has structure and it also creates meaning. Alexander situates his theory at that apparent tension point and asks essentially the same question that Spencer and Parsons asked: How can complex and diverse societies hold together and act in concert? Alexander calls his approach a "strong program in cultural sociology."

Strong Program in Cultural Sociology

There are three elements to Alexander's **strong program in cultural sociology**. First, *culture needs to be understood meaningfully*. More than any other species on the planet, humans are oriented toward meaning. And meaning is never fixed or determined; it must be interpreted. If something is determined, interpretation isn't needed. You don't need to interpret an object falling on your head; it's determined by the law of gravity—yet the "American flag" has to be interpreted because its meaning varies. Cultural sociology thus places importance on interpretation. Alexander argues that for "most of its history, sociology . . . has suffered from a numbness toward meaning" (Alexander & Smith, 2001, p. 138). While Parsons emphasized culture, his theory did not incorporate meaning, in this sense of the word. In order to give meaning its proper place, Alexander advocates the use of what's called *thick descriptions*—minute descriptions of a social phenomenon. They provide the tiniest details of human interaction.

The second element in a strong program is that the relationships that culture has to other social factors need to be *analytically bracketed*. When we bracket something analytically, we just look at how it works, all by itself. Alexander isn't saying that culture is really separate; like Parsons, he sees all subsystems as nested within one another. However, if we tried to look at all the subsystems together, we would miss how each works individually. And this is particularly important for culture. Many sociologists argue that culture is simply a by-product, something that comes out of more fundamental and real processes like social organization and power. Alexander, however, is arguing that *culture is an autonomous sphere* and can act independently. Culture can act independently because it is structured. Remember our basic definition of structure: Structure is made up of explicit connections that impose themselves on other things, thus creating recognizable patterns. Alexander is arguing that culture has an intrinsic structure that operates as an independent variable with "relative autonomy in shaping actions and institutions, providing inputs every bit as vital as more material or instrumental forces" (Alexander & Smith, 2001, p. 136).

The third characteristic of a strong program in cultural sociology is the *explication of causal paths and mechanisms* that explain precisely how meaning (characteristic 1) and the structure of culture (characteristic 2) relate. As an illustration, think of the structured cultural value of education. Alexander always understands such things as coded in binary oppositions; like the idea of good and bad, one can't exist without the other. For the value of education, we could say that it is formed by <well informed and reasonable> versus <ignorant and dogmatic>. That's the cultural structure for our example.

Another part of this illustration is you. What does education mean to you? Meaning is subjective, so what education means to you may be something different from what it means to someone else. The third part of this example is the university you attend. That organization links you (meaning) to the cultural value of education (structure). The causal paths and mechanisms thus form bridges between the structure and meaning of culture. These causal mechanisms take the form of people, organizations, and institutions. Alexander uses this model for a strong program in cultural sociology to provide scaffolding for his theory of democracy in modern society. Alexander argues that, by definition, modern systems are not only complex and differentiated, as Spencer and Parsons tell us, but are also specifically democratic.

Concepts and Theory: Culture and the Civil Sphere

As we saw in Chapter 1, democracy requires certain kinds of institutions for it to exist. Collectively, these institutions and other social organizations form what Alexis de Tocqueville called **civil society**. We'll come across this idea of civil society a few times in this book. So, as with other important concepts, build your definition as we move through our theorists. Generally speaking, "Civil society refers to all the places where individuals gather together to have conversations, pursue common interests and, occasionally, try to influence public opinion or public policy" (Jacobs, 2006, p. 27). Beyond this general idea, Alexander shows us that what goes into making civil society has changed over time.

The *first idea of civil society* emerged during the birth of modernity. For Tocqueville, Martineau, and Addams, civil society initially included capitalism, voluntary or moderate religion, and education. Together, these provided both structural and cultural bases for democracy. The culture of civil society is particularly important, as it provides the moral, ethical force of democracy. Specifically important for Alexander are the ideas of the individual that accompanied early capitalism. Capitalism was seen as a system of individual possibilities; yet the individual within that system was a moral rather than self-serving person, one concerned with self-discipline and civic responsibility.

According to Alexander, *the second idea of civil society* emerged in the mid-nineteenth century, and the most important change involved capitalism. For it was at that time that people such as Karl Marx began to see the other side of this modern economic system. As capitalism grew and became more powerful, the instrumental and exploitive aspects became clear. The robber barons ruled, and the workers were manipulated and subjected to unsafe and unhealthy working conditions that often equated to little more than indentured servitude. For those on the political left, capitalism became the institution from which all wrong flowed. Nothing good could come out of capitalism, and only by capitalism's destruction—or at least control—could civil society again flourish. Of course, the right argued just the opposite: Defining human nature as intrinsically selfish, free market capitalism was seen as the path to the greatest social good. These discourses from the second age of civil society continue to inform contemporary debates, as do the ideals of the first.

In recent decades, renewed theoretical and political concerns for civil society have surfaced. Alexander argues, however, that this new thrust has thus far only attempted to revive previous concepts of civil society. But the ideas of people like Tocqueville, Martineau, and Addams can only hold in the type of social system that existed at that time, at the beginning of modernity and democracy. As Spencer and Parsons have shown us, societies in general tend to change as a result of structural differentiation, segmentation, and specialization, and these tendencies are exaggerated in the modernity of the twenty-first century. Thus, modern societies are much more complex and the people more diverse and fragmented than during the first age of civil society. We need, then, a different understanding of civil society, one that is more dynamic and complex than the dominant ideas of early modernity. In other words, civil society has changed in response to the new complexity of society and the democratic project.

Defining the Civil Sphere

To make the distinction, Alexander (2006) uses the term **civil sphere** rather than civil society and defines it as "a world of values and institutions that generates the capacity for social criticism and democratic integration at the same time" (p. 4). One of the reasons that Alexander uses the word sphere rather than society may be that he is clearly emphasizing the cultural component. The word *society* implies social networks of people or systems of structures, and while culture is part of these, it isn't given the central place that Alexander wants. As he says,

> We need a theory . . . that is less myopically centered on social structure and power distribution, and more responsive to the ideas that people have in their heads and to what Tocqueville called the habits of the heart. (p. 43)

An important implication of Alexander's definition is that where this sphere begins and ends isn't as clear as the social structures that Spencer and Parsons have in mind. The civil sphere is defined by a specific type of culture that overlaps and includes some portions of those social structures, as well as organizations, networks of people, and interactions.

Civil Values

The civil sphere is a **world of values,** a field of meanings and collective feelings that form a "secular faith," and thus, a moral or ethical sphere. The strongest feeling in the public sphere is *social solidarity.* There are three elements that define social solidarity: the subjective sense of individuals that they are part of the whole, the actual constraint of individual desires for the good of the collective, and the coordination of individuals and social units. These three elements can vary independently, which creates higher or lower social solidarity in a group. Alexander focuses on one specific aspect of solidarity—the feeling of connectedness to other members in a community. But the solidarity of the civil sphere isn't like that of particularized groups. For example, a woman may feel very connected to members of her sorority, but that isn't the solidarity of democracy. The feeling of connectedness that Alexander (2006) is referring to "transcends particular commitments, narrow loyalties, and sectional interests" (p. 43) such as sororities, teams, family, and even race and gender. The sense of connectedness in back of social solidarity is a *universal commitment to diversity,* based not so much on group identity as on a mutual identification with a set of democratic ethics, which in turn brings "democratic integration."

However, look at the definition of civil sphere that Alexander gives in the quote above. Notice that Alexander talks about integration, and in the same breath he says that the civil sphere creates the capacity for *social criticism.* Contemporary democracy is explicitly based on tensions that were only implicit in the beginning of civil society, such as "all men are created equal." In other words, most people back when those words were written didn't experience tension; most thought they were doing a good job of treating all men equal. However, that tension existed within the structure of the culture. And those cultural tensions in the long run provide the "value inconsistencies" and "alienative motivational elements" that Parsons talks about. In other words, culture itself is influencing the types of tensions we sense, the discussions we engage in, and thus the progress that democracy makes. Alexander argues that the democratic culture of the civil sphere is formed through **binary structures of purity and impurity.** These structures form and pattern the ideas, values, and discourses that democracy holds dear. Binary structures are found on three levels: motives, social relations, and institutions, which are then used to define in- and out-group members, civil and uncivil people. For example, the civil sphere includes people who are active and autonomous (purity) and excludes those who are passive and dependent (impurity). The kinds of relationships between people in the civil sphere are open (purity) rather than secretive (impurity), trusting and not suspicious, critical rather than deferential, and truthful instead of deceitful. And finally, civil institutions are rule regulated (purity) and anti-civil ones are arbitrary (impurity); civil institutions are built upon law and anti-civil ones upon power; and civil institutions are equal while the anti-civil are hierarchical. Notice that these pairs (binaries) are the values that an open democracy is founded upon.

We use these binary codes to build communities and rich narratives of democratic life. We use them when events or identities are contested—they form the basis of our criticisms and arguments. Some events and identities are so clearly "good or bad" that they obviously fall to one side or the other. Most, however, become part of the ongoing political argument of democracy. A clear example in recent history is the identity of Dr. Martin Luther King Jr. Although King was assassinated in 1968, the first celebration of Martin Luther King Jr. Day didn't occur until 1986. The path between those two dates saw people both for and against the King holiday use various parts of the binary structure to define and establish King's identity.

Civil Institutions

The civil sphere is also made up of civil institutions. **Civil institutions** are those social organizations and cultural practices that are most closely linked to the culture of the civil sphere. These institutions form boundary relations with non-civil society. Parsons and Spencer were also concerned with boundary relations—that's what the problem of coordination and control is about. Alexander is arguing that in this current period of modernity, this issue is most fully met by active democratic culture—the level of diversity present in this time mandates democracy as never before. Civil institutions, then, are those that are most closely associated with promoting democracy. They create norms, goals, rewards, and sanctions; they make exchanges, create demands, and so forth. Civil institutions express and implement the symbolic, binary codes found in the structure of democratic culture by persuasion and enforcement, specifically through communicative (persuasion) and regulative (enforcement) institutions.

Regulative institutions are made up of two broad arenas: civil power and law. Generally speaking, power in society has been and is linked to having control over collecting taxes, creating and controlling army and police forces, and building the administrative structure of society. In times past, this state power was controlled by aristocrats. The question in modern societies is whether or not an elite, moneyed class controls this power. To the degree that it does, "democracy doesn't exist" (Alexander, 2006, p. 109). In a democracy, political power should be based in civil power that is acquired through voting and political party conflict and participation. Civil power thus varies by the degree of class-based elite control and by the level of group-specific inclusion in the political process (like race, gender, religion, and so forth). The law of course enforces the demands of a society. Yet it is important for us to note that the law is a direct expression of the binary cultural codes of democracy. The motives (why we do things) in the civil sphere are based on our desire to be rational (pure) rather than irrational (impure), and the relationships and institutions are intended to be deliberative, not conspiratorial; rule regulated, not arbitrary; and impersonal, not personal. Thus, law is "not an external mechanism that coerces people but an expression of their innate rationality, mediating between truth and mundane events" (Alexander, 2006, p. 60).

Communicative institutions are made up of organizations and associations that create and circulate cultural meanings, and that influence our thoughts and feelings about the civil sphere. These institutions obviously communicate, but they particularly translate the abstract ideals found in the binary codes through specific events and people. The mass media—including television, movies, books, the Internet, news services, and so on—and public opinion polls are two particularly significant parts of communicative institutions. The mass media presents two kinds of narratives, fictional and factual. The importance of fictional mass media is that it has a greater cathartic impact. Fictional media can weave stories of heroism, sacrifice, and valor using the binary codes of democratic culture. And we respond with tears, laughter, pride, heart-felt concern, and belief. We're lifted up and energized by these stories. We are also energized against stories or characters that exemplify the impure side of the binary. Factual media is more immediately influential, as it reports such things as the news and, most importantly, public opinion.

The notion of public opinion is based on a kind of imagined community. The "public" doesn't really exist anywhere; it isn't based on face-to-face communion between people. Yet the public is more than an idea. Public opinion polls matter. They not only matter in terms of affecting politicians' actions; they also matter to us personally. We see ourselves in the public— an imagined community in which we can be seen and heard. It is this public that different conflict groups want to influence, because it is through the public that their agendas, formed around binary cultural structures, are given voice. And because this voice expresses an opinion, it concerns how the public feels about a given topic. Public opinion, then, inserts itself "into social subjectivity as a structure of feeling. . . . Public opinion is the sea within which we swim, the structure that gives us the feeling of democratic life" (Alexander, 2006, pp. 72, 75).

Concepts and Theory:
Movement Toward Universal Inclusion

The boundary between the civil and non-civil spheres is tense because of the nature of the binary structures that the civil sphere expresses. Binary discourses "simultaneously open up universalistic solidarity as a possibility and restrict it as a fact" (Alexander, 2006, p. 213). Alexander points out that tensions and conflicts aren't simply due to our shortsightedness—tension is structured through binary codes and is therefore inevitable. For example, the idea of freedom intrinsically carries with it its binary opposite. Thus, we regularly deny certain freedoms to individuals we label "felons." Just the idea of freedom means we must contend with the conditions under which we will deny that freedom. Here's another example: Modern democratic societies are built upon the idea of nations linked to territory, which automatically creates in- and out-groups (citizens and non-citizens). And this binary implied in *nation* means that this tension will inevitably enter our national discussion, as it is currently in the United States with the "problem of illegal immigrants." Because of the nature of these codes, tension is unavoidable in a democracy, and critical thinking is necessary. Critical thinking makes the conversation around the tensions reasonable, and it is the only way that these conflicts can lead to growth rather than schism and destruction.

This implies that the project of democracy is perpetually unfinished, yet a living democracy makes continual steps toward **universal inclusion**. According to Alexander (2006), this movement toward universal inclusion has thus far gone through three phases: assimilation, hyphenation, and multiculturalism. The process of *assimilation* is what is meant when America is characterized as a melting pot. All the important differences in identity are assimilated in one general identity. *Hyphenation* is a way of creating cultural identities that brings two or more types of identity together, like African American. *Multiculturalism* is unique among the three in that this belief system doesn't attempt to form single identities out of many; multiculturalism values different and distinct identities because of their diversity.

Note that all these modes can exist together; but which one is most prominent is historically specific. The most important difference lies between assimilation and hyphenation on one hand and multiculturalism on the other. In both assimilation and hyphenation, differences between in- and out-groups are seen as primordial or essential. In other words, people are seen as different because it's believed that they actually *are* different, and these inherent differences are hierarchical. Under assimilation and hyphenation, it is still better to be white than black, male than female, and heterosexual rather than homosexual. In both assimilation and hyphenation, inclusion into the main group occurs as the essential qualities of difference are shed and the person in one way or another becomes more like the dominant group. In these inclusion movements, the dominant group's nature is seen as more civilized, better in some real way.

Multiculturalism is distinct because difference itself becomes valued. Rather than differences being rejected automatically, in- and out-group members struggle to "resignify and experience" the differences (Alexander, 2006, p. 451). Thus, differences aren't automatically valued hierarchically. It isn't necessarily better to be white than black, or heterosexual than homosexual, for example. There is still struggle, however. Some groups or group characteristics may be seen as too different and thus stigmatized, which of course sets up another binary issue of exclusion. In multiculturalism, the universal value of human nature is seen as diverse, rather than being defined by the main group's identity. Moreover, incorporation and social solidarity are viewed as achievements of diversity rather than inclusion. The differences between groups of people "become reinterpreted as representing variations on the sacred quality of civility" (Alexander, 2006, p. 452). Rather than the recognition of difference leading to denigration and inhibition, as with assimilation and hyphenation, multiculturalism leads to a culture of authenticity that expands and shares cultural identities.

| The Craft of Citizenship | Society |

The Basics: Comprehension and Explanation

- Define functionalism.
- What are the main questions that drive the theorists in this chapter? Do you see these questions as important today? Why or why not?
- Identify and define the most important theoretical terms in Spencer's, Parsons', and Alexander's theories. Remember, the main concepts are in bold and supporting ones are italicized.

  > *Helpful hints:* Remember, some terms are best defined using the essential characteristics (stipulative definition), and for others you need to include the term's variability and effects (theoretical definition). For example, the definition for society should be stipulative rather than theoretical. It doesn't make sense to speak of having more or less society. Modernity, however, may in fact vary and thus needs a theoretical definition. And also remember, a theoretical concept must be defined in a way that allows you to analyze the social world.

- As in Chapter 1, there are a number of ideas that are generally significant, not just for the theorists, in this chapter. Among those terms are society, system, and social structure. Define society and modernity as thoroughly as possible. At this point, only use the information contained in Chapters 1 and 2.
- Explain the relationship between the state and society.
- Using Spencer's theory, explain how societies evolve. What problem does society encounter as a result of social evolution?

  > *Helpful hints:* Look under the heading "Concepts and Theory: Social Evolution." (Headings are very helpful for finding things.) There you will see that "one of the basic factors in evolution is structural differentiation." So, you know that social evolution involves structural differentiation. But what makes differentiation happen? Remember, theory explains how something works. What makes structural differentiation work? If you keep reading, you'll see that segmentation and specialization are part of structural differentiation. So, those concepts help define differentiation, but they do not tell us what causes it to happen. Keep reading and you'll find this statement: "the most basic force in back of social evolution is population growth." Anytime you see terms like "force" or "dynamic," it's telling you that this factor causes other things to happen. Thus, population growth makes structures differentiate, which in turn causes societies to evolve (become more complex).

- Theories can be expressed in many ways, and often using different expressions can help us see things we might otherwise miss. Draw a diagram, picture, or figure of Parsons' theory of the unit act.
- Explain Parsons' theory of revolutionary change; use the headings as a map and look for key terms.
- Using Parsons' theory, explain how different subsystems are "nested" within one another.
- Explain the historical changes that have happened with civil society. Why does Alexander use the term *civil sphere*? What is the function of the civil sphere in modern society?
- According to Alexander, how are the political discourses in a democracy structured? Put another way, what causes political conflict and discussion?
- What part does mass media play in a democratic society? Explain how multiculturalism facilitates democracy.

(Continued)

(Continued)

Skill Set 1: Inference and Application

- What can you infer about the importance of culture and religion in modern society from Parsons' cybernetic hierarchy of control?
- What implications does Alexander's idea of multiculturalism have for you? In doing this exercise, keep in mind what we learned in Chapter 1 about the importance of diversity for democracy. On a scale of 1–10, how would you rate yourself on inclusion and diversity? Provide specific examples of *practices* in your life.

Skill Set 2: Interpretation, Analysis, Evaluation, Synthesis

- Use Spencer's societal typology to analyze what is happening in your nation.
  - ➢ *Helpful hints:* The more thoroughly you define an idea or concept, the easier it is to find empirical connections or real-life examples.
- How would Alexander critique Spencer's answer to the problems of coordination and control?
  - ➢ *Helpful hints:* First, clearly define Spencer's answer (in this case, the concentration of power). Then, look for that specific issue in Alexander's theory. But be careful. Don't just find the first place that Alexander talks about power. Sometimes Alexander talks about power in a positive way, and what you're looking for is a possible critique, or negative commentary.
- Analyze the presence of mass media in your life using Alexander's explanation of mass media in the civil sphere. Provide examples from your life to illustrate your point.

3

Self

In one sense, the shift from society to self is a huge leap. We're going from large-scale systems of social structures and institutions down to the face-to-face situation and the individual person. Theorists talk about these two social fields in terms of macro- and micro-level processes. The relationship between these levels—usually referred to as the micro–macro link—is a central tension in sociological theory. In fact, George Ritzer (2008), a well-known contemporary theorist, states that Marx, Weber, Durkheim, and Simmel "were most generally concerned with the micro–macro linkage" (p. 500). However, there's more to this issue than is first apparent.

The deeper issues involved here are precisely those we raised in Chapter 2: What is society? And how does society exist? In response to those questions, we saw that functionalists (and many others like them) define society as a macro-level system of interrelated structures and institutions that by and large determine human action. However, the theorists in this chapter see society differently. The person who first clearly articulated this different perspective is George Herbert Mead. According to Mead (1934), society is made up of institutions that are "nothing but an organization of attitudes which we all carry in us"; they are "organized forms of group or social activity—forms so organized that the individual members of society can act adequately and socially by taking the attitudes of others toward these activities" (pp. 211, 261–262). Notice that while Mead uses the word *institution*, he has a unique way of defining it. For Mead, an institution is *made up of attitudes*—feelings, opinions, and dispositions about acceptable actions. Also notice where society is located for Mead: It is *in the person*.

These ideas were elaborated by a student of Mead's, Herbert Blumer (1900–1987), who coined the term now given to this perspective: **symbolic interaction.** Blumer (1969) argues that there are three assumptions that define symbolic interaction: (1) Human beings *act according to meaning*; (2) meaning is not intrinsic to an object, nor is it a feature of an individual's psychological perception, but rather, *meaning emerges out of social interaction*; and (3) individuals use these emergent meanings to *interpret actions*, their own and others'. As Blumer notes, these three simple assumptions have "profound implications" (p. 5). The most important implications for us come from the first two assumptions and have to do with the nature of society and self.

A simple example of the first two assumptions is a country's flag. There are groups of people that love what a flag stands for, and there are those that hate it. The meaning isn't in the flag itself; it's created in group-specific social interactions. Still using the flag, we can see something more profound: There are those who will kill for what a flag represents, and those who will die for it. Here, we see not only that people act according to meaning, but also that human life isn't inherently meaningful. Here's another example to further illustrate: A number of years ago, Tom Hanks starred in a movie called *Apollo 13*, which portrayed the near-disastrous third manned moon mission. The drama began when Hanks' character, the astronaut Jim Lovell, said, "Houston, we've had a problem." As portrayed in the film, what followed was an intense period of time when Americans sat on the edge of their seats, waiting to see whether the space shuttle crew of three would live or die. Fortunately, they lived. However, during that same period of time, the U.S. military killed hundreds of Vietnamese. This is obviously a dramatic example, but it's important to see that the same principle applies to everything in our lives: The only meaning anything has—including human life—is the meaning we give it.

Because of this quality, meaning can change on a moment-to-moment basis because it emerges out of interactions. To emerge means to rise from or come out into view. In social interactions, different elements such as language, symbols, individuals, values, and goals encounter one another. Out of this caldron of sociability emerge different meanings and actions. These emergent meanings and actions are never certain; they are subject to interpretations and spontaneous behavior. Every social contact thus carries with it the potential for change—people can always decide to act differently and create different versions of society. As Blumer (1969) notes, "The essence of society lies in an ongoing process of action—not in a posited structure of relations" (p. 71). Further, anytime we look to psychological or social structures as the impetus behind human behavior, "The human being becomes a mere medium through which such initiating factors operate to produce given actions" (p. 73). Yet Mead's way of thinking doesn't simply give us a new vision of society; he also crystallized the new idea of the person that was gaining momentum in the beginning years of the twentieth century.

Recall the Enlightenment's idea of the person: the autonomous individual whose core divine essence—the self—is present at birth and unfolds during the person's lifetime; holds inalienable rights; and is capable of self-directed, reasoned decision making. This power of reason would be used to further life, liberty, and the pursuit of happiness. The idea of the autonomous individual emerged out of the social and cultural configurations of the seventeenth and eighteenth centuries. But by the time Mead was writing, society and culture had changed: The abuses of capitalism had come to the fore (such as a 20-year worldwide depression, forced labor, unsafe working conditions, robber barons, and so on), American manifest destiny and genocide had swept the North American continent, the global slave trade had culminated in the American Civil War, and the almost continuous wars during the nineteenth century had battered humanity and claimed countless lives around the globe. Just as important in changing the idea of the person was the cultural impact of two scientific claims: Darwin's theory that the human species evolved from lower primates, and Freud's premise that within humankind lies an unconscious dynamic that is fueled by the primal desires of the *id*.

As a result of these social and cultural changes, the Enlightenment's idea of the intrinsic worth of the autonomous individual began to waver. In its stead, various versions of what Stuart Hall (1996, p. 597) calls the sociological subject were proposed. The principal idea is that there is a necessary and symbiotic relationship between the person and society: Society creates the person through socialization, and people create society. It was Mead who first and most clearly formulated this idea. The sociological subject forms a bridge between the individual and society, making the self intrinsically social rather than autonomous. However, the social nature of the self doesn't do away with reason, responsibility, and the possibilities of democracy. Quite the contrary, Mead (1932) argues that this view of the self is in fact a necessary precondition for democracy: "Democracy, in the sense here relevant, is an attitude which depends upon the type of self which goes with the universal relations of brotherhood" (p. 286). This type of self recognizes that people are universally social—selves are reflections of society; and this in turn implies a "universal society" (p. 287).

According to Mead, self and society are ongoing constructions that emerge out of the ideas and sentiments that people have formed as they contend, moment by moment, with the practical necessities of daily life. Other societies—other sets of attitudes—are simply that: a group's way of supplying its members' physical, mental, and emotional needs. All societies are thus essentially the same; that is, the motivations and the way in which they are formed and continue to exist are identical, though the actual practices and meanings may be different. This pragmatic understanding of society and self opens the door for diverse groups coming together to form new wholes with new sets of attitudes, because all societies and selves are formed in precisely the same way. Thus, no social type or person has claim to natural superiority—an idea that dominated early modernity and empowered Western imperialism and racism. Rather, the sociological subject provides a broadening base of acceptance, away from the early modern assumptions about human nature that ended up being used to discriminate against blacks and women. Or, as Mead (1932) puts it, "The individual maintains himself as a citizen only to the degree that he recognizes the rights of everyone else to belong to the same community" (p. 286).

Creating the Self—George Herbert Mead

George Herbert Mead (1863–1931) was born in South Hadley, Massachusetts, and began his college education at Oberlin College when he was 16 years old. After short stints as a schoolteacher and a surveyor, Mead did his graduate studies in philosophy at Harvard. In 1893, John Dewey asked Mead to join him to form the Department of Philosophy at the

University of Chicago, the site of the first department of sociology in the United States. Mead's major influence on sociologists came through his graduate course in social psychology, which he started teaching in 1900. Those lectures formed the basis for Mead's most famous work, *Mind, Self, and Society*, published posthumously in 1934 by his students. Mead's other major work, *The Philosophy of the Act* (1938), also wasn't published until after his death. Mead's (1934) central theoretical question is this: "How can an individual get outside himself (experientially) in such a way as to become an object to himself? This is the essential psychological problem of selfhood or of self-consciousness" (pp. 136, 138).

Concepts and Theory: Human Action

One of the defining features of being human is the capacity to act rather than react. Reaction is an automated response, like a knee-jerk reflex. **Action,** on the other hand, involves choice. As Mead characterizes it, the uniquely human act contains four distinct elements: impulse, perception, manipulation, and consumption. For most animals, the route from impulse to behavior is rather direct—they react to a stimulus using instincts, or behavioristically imprinted patterns. But for humans, it is a circuitous route. After we feel the initial *impulse to act,* we then perceive our environment. This *perception* entails the recognition of the pertinent symbolic elements—such as individuals and social groups, whether present or not—as well as alternatives to satisfying the impulse. After we symbolically take in our environment, we *manipulate* the different elements in our imagination. This manipulation takes place in the mind and considers the possible ramifications of using different behaviors to satisfy the impulse. We think about how others would judge our behaviors; and we consider other possible future implications. After we manipulate the situation symbolically in our minds, we are then in a position to bring the act to conclusion by acting *(consumption).*

Notice that action is based on people having a **self.** We can obviously see it in the manipulation phase, where we consider how others will judge our behaviors. Such judgments can only have relevance to our self. We can also see the self in that there must be something other than impulse working inside us, some way of taking our self outside the immediacy of the moment. For Mead (1934), there could be no society without individual selves: "Human society as we know it could not exist without minds and selves, since all its most characteristic features presuppose the possession of minds and selves by its individual members" (p. 227). Thus, we don't have a self because there is a psychological drive or need for one; we have a self because society demands it.

To emphasize this point, Mead (1934) says that "the self is not something that exists first and then enters into relationship with others, but it is, so to speak, an eddy in the social current and so still a part of the current" (p. 26). Eddies are currents of air or water that run contrary to the stream. It isn't so much the contrariness that Mead wants us to see, but the fact that an eddy only exists in and because of its surrounding current. The same is true for selves: They only exist in and because of social interaction. The self doesn't have a continuous existence; it isn't something that we carry around inside of us. It's a mechanism that allows conversations and action to happen, whether that conversation occurs in the social situation or within the individual.

Concepts and Theory: Creating a Self

Before getting into this theory, let me again point out Mead's central question: "How can an individual get outside himself (experientially) in such a way as to become an object to himself?" Notice carefully how Mead is defining the self. The **self** is a part of us that actually *stands outside* of our actions, thoughts, and feelings—we are in some degree *not immediately present* in situations or events. Think about how a dog eats. What you see is an animal utterly present in what it is doing. Now, think about when you eat. In some eating situations, you're not really there; you're *watching and evaluating*. Of course, this varies. There are times when we can simply and purely, without thought, enjoy a meal. But there are other times, such as a formal dinner or when you're on a diet, when you're not completely present in the experience. There's a part of you that is watching, evaluating, and controlling.

We take this strange brand of "multiple personality disorder" as ordinary, because it's been there for as long as we can remember. But it hasn't always been there; we aren't born with a self, and some feral (wild) children never develop a self. And while it's ordinary for us, we have to see the oddity and uniqueness of what we humans do. We talk to ourselves about ourselves. While we're doing something, we're also not doing it. We exist concretely in this moment and in this place, yet we likewise exist abstractly outside the bounds of space and time. To top it all off, society is utterly and completely dependent upon us having this strange, amorphous being we call the self. Mead's question is, just how exactly did we create this thing?

Mead's answer is that the self is constructed or achieved over time through four distinct phases of role taking. **Role taking** has a very specific definition, and it is easily confused with role playing. Role playing is when a person plays at being a particular kind of person. It could be done in jest, as part of an illegal scam, or as part of daily life. We role-play almost constantly. For example, when you go to class tomorrow, you'll be playing the role of a student; in fact, you're playing that role right now in reading this book. This kind of role play is the question that concerns Goffman, whom we'll talk about later in the chapter. Role taking, however, is something quite distinct. Role taking is *the process through which we place our self in the position (or role) of another in order to see our own self*. As adults, we role-take all the time. We saw it in our consideration of the act: When we think about how others will judge our actions, we're role taking. We also role-take in preparation for a special event, such as a job interview or first date. On such occasions, we think about how the interviewer or our date will look at us, and we dress and act accordingly.

The reason role taking is so important is because it is the direct answer to Mead's question: How can a person get outside of him- or herself? In role taking, we step outside our self in order to see our self. The first time we were able to role take as a child didn't automatically create a self. Repeated episodes of role taking must build up over time in order to create a symbolic, yet firm space for us to stand and watch ourselves continually. The self, then, is a *perspective* from which to view and assess our own actions. Notice that the perspective of the self is essentially that of other people. This perspective is built up through four phases of role taking—preparatory, play, game, and generalized other—that together form a complete self. As you'll see, each of these phases depends upon the child becoming more oriented toward abstract thinking and symbols.

The *preparatory stage* is the time of language acquisition. When babies are hungry or tired or wet, they can't take care of themselves. Instead, they send out what Mead calls "unconventional gestures"—gestures that do not mean the same to the sender and hearer. In other words, babies cry. The caregivers must figure out what the babies need. When they do, parents tend to vocalize their behaviors ("Oh, did Susie need a ba-ba?"). Babies eventually discover that if they mimic the parents and send out a significant gesture ("ba-ba"), they will get their needs met sooner. This is the beginning of language acquisition; babies begin to understand that their environment is symbolic—the object that satisfies hunger is "ba-ba," and the object that brings it is "da-da" (or "ma-ma"). Eventually, a baby will understand that she has a symbol as well: "Susie." Thus, language acquisition allows the child to symbolize and eventually to symbolically manipulate her environment, including herself and others. The use of reflexive language also allows the child to begin to role-take.

As children, we began role taking in the *play stage*. During this stage, the child can take the role, or assume the perspective, of certain significant others. Mead calls this the play stage because children must literally play at being some significant other in order to see themselves. Children play at being Mommy or being Teacher. The child will hold a doll or stuffed bear and talk to it as if she were the parent. When the child is playing Mommy or Daddy with a teddy bear, who is the bear? The child herself. She is seeing herself from the point of view of the parent, literally. Language is fundamental because the separation of the self from the immediacy of the moment is a symbolic move (Perinbanayagam will help us see some of the ramifications of the self being a linguistic construction, later in this chapter.). But by itself, learning language doesn't create a self. The self begins to form here in the play stage because it is then that the individual divorces his or herself from the immediacy of the moment.

The next level in the development of self is the *game stage*. During this stage, the child can take the perspective of several others and can take into account the rules (sets of responses that different attitudes bring out) of society. But this is still very concrete. At this stage of development, the child will apply rules equally. If lying is wrong, for example, it's always wrong, even if telling the truth means saying Aunt Martha's outfit is ugly; there is no such thing as "white lies" at this stage. The fourth stage, the *generalized other*, refers to sets of attitudes that an individual may take toward him- or herself—it is the general attitude or perspective of a community. The generalized other allows the individual to have a less segmented self, as the perspectives of many others are generalized into a single view. It is through the generalized other that a community influences the conduct of its individual members. Up until this point, the child has only been able to role-take with specific others. As the individual progresses in the ability to use abstract language and concepts, he or she is also able to think about general or abstract others.

The most important thing to take away from this theory is that the self is a *social object*; it's a perspective from which to view your own actions and give them meaning. During the preparatory stage, you learned that the human world is a symbolic one—every need, action, and person exists linguistically. That stage marked the beginning of your withdrawal from the tyranny of the moment. Language allows you to transcend and break the bounds of time and space. Because your world is symbolic, you can take into account the past and consider the future. In the play stage, you began to understand that you (your self) are always viewed from the perspective of others. You began to develop the different voices that form your self-concept and self-esteem. And in the generalized other, you became able to construct different perspectives based on more general attitudes. This is when and how society at large forms your consciousness, your awareness of self.

The Internal Conversation

The self, then, is an active process, not a thing that we carry around inside: *The self is an emergent effect of interaction,* whether that interaction occurs inside the person or with others. Part of what we mean by the self is an internalized conversation, and by necessity interactions require more than one person. Mead thus postulates the existence of two interactive facets of the self: the "I" and the "Me." The **Me** is the self that results from the progressive stages of role taking and is the perspective that we assume to view and analyze our own behaviors. The **I** is that part of the self that is unsocialized and spontaneous: "The self is essentially a social process going on with these two distinguishable phases. If it did not have these two phases, there could not be conscious responsibility and there would be nothing novel in experience" (Mead, 1934, p. 178).

We have all experienced the internal conversation between the I and the Me. I may want to jump for joy or shout in anger or kiss a stranger or run naked. But the Me opposes such behavior and points out the social ramifications of these actions—I may want to, but it wouldn't be good for me. The I presents our impulses and drives; the Me presents to us the perspectives of society, the meanings and repercussions of our actions. The social voice that the Me provides is what enables us to take conscious responsibility for our actions, by providing us with socially approved alternatives to simple impulse. However, it's important to see that actions aren't determined by that part of us; we're not simply social robots acting out the will of generalized others. The I may act spontaneously before the Me can intercede or by disregarding the Me's perspective. Just like the way meaning emerges out of social interaction, our actions emerge out of this internal interaction between these two elements of our self. It's this emergent quality that allows there to be something novel and unpredictable in experience.

Performing the Self—Erving Goffman

Erving Goffman was born on June 11, 1922, in Alberta, Canada. He earned his PhD from the University of Chicago. For his dissertation, he studied daily life on one of the Scottish islands (Unst). The dissertation from this study became his first book, *The Presentation of Self in Everyday Life* (1959), which is now available in 10 different languages. Among his other important works are *Asylums, Encounters, Stigma, Behavior in Public Places, Interaction Rituals,* and *Frame Analysis.* In 1958, Herbert Blumer invited Goffman to teach at the University of California, Berkeley. He stayed there for 10 years, moving to the University of Pennsylvania for the remainder of his career in 1968, where he was the Benjamin Franklin Professor of Anthropology and Sociology. He also served as president of the American Sociological Association in 1981 and 1982. Goffman died of cancer on November 19, 1982.

Goffman's Dramaturgy

While the focus on self and the primacy of the encounter are both qualities that Mead and Goffman share, there are also a couple of differences we should note. Goffman's perspective has become known as dramaturgy. **Dramaturgy** is a way of understanding social encounters using the *analogy of the dramatic stage.* In this perspective, people are seen as performers who are vitally concerned with the presentation of their character (the self) to an audience. The most significant difference, then, is that Mead is centrally concerned with internalization processes—how the self is formed—and Goffman focuses on how the self is presented and perceived outside the individual. Another difference is that for Mead the self is a social object that may or may not become the focus of an interaction. Goffman, however, argues that the self is more basic to the interaction than a topic. The self isn't one of many possible social objects; rather, the self is *the central organizing feature* of all social encounters. For Goffman, it's the presentation of a self that creates and maintains social order. The core, driving force in this social organization is the need to avoid embarrassment, or what Goffman (1967) refers to as saving **face**—the positive social value that a person claims in an interaction: "His aim is to save face; his effect is to save the situation" (p. 39).

The significance of Goffman's work lies in his emphasis on the presentation of self, or what we would today call *image.* Like Mead, Goffman's idea of the self is informed by his historical context. Goffman's work was published from the 1950s through the early 1980s. This period of time is culturally marked by the emergence and then dominance of television. Prior to this period, words, whether written (books and newspapers) or spoken (radio), defined mass media. Words give importance to story, and story emphasizes coherence and meaning. Television, however, shifted the power of mass media from word to image. What became important in news, for example, is not whether the story was complete and meaningful, but rather, whether or not there was film or video to illustrate it. This emphasis on image that television conveyed was bolstered by technical advances in movie and magazine production. Movies became spectacles, and magazines were filled with glossy pictures. These shifts in the cultural context impacted the way people understood themselves. Self-image became increasingly important, and at the same time became less tied to real social groups and more informed by images seen on television and commercials, in movies, and in advertisements. The importance of meaning and coherence gave way to the power of an image to gain attention, to be attractive. What Goffman gives us, then, is a theory that explains how we manage our images and the impression we make on others.

Concepts and Theory: Impression Management

The basic concept Goffman uses to explain the presentation of self is that of a front. A **front** is the expression of a particular self or identity that is formed by the individual and read by others. The front is like a building façade. Merriam-Webster's (2002) first definition of façade is remarkably like Goffman's idea of a front: A façade is "a face (as a flank or rear facing on a street or court) of a building that is given emphasis by special architectural treatment." Like a façade, a front is constructed by emphasizing and deemphasizing certain things that are intended to convey meanings that we want associated with our self-image. In every interaction, we hold things back, things that aren't appropriate for the situation or that we don't want those in the situation to attribute to our self; we accentuate other aspects in order to present a particular kind of self with respect to the social role. A social front is constructed using three main elements: the setting, appearance, and manner.

The idea of the *setting* is taken directly from the theater: It consists of all the physical scenery and props that we use to create the stage and background within which we present our performance. The clearest example for us is probably the classroom. The chalkboard, the room layout with all the desks facing the front, the media equipment, and so on are all used by the professor to make claim to the role of teacher. All this is obvious, but notice that the way the setting is used cues different kinds of professorial performances. I may choose to "de-center" the role of teacher and instead claim the role of facilitator by simply rearranging the desks in a circle and using multiple, mobile chalkboards placed all around the room.

Settings tend to ground roles by making definitions of the situation consistent. For example, it would be more difficult (but not impossible) for me to use the classroom as a setting for the definition of *bar*. This grounding of settings is part of what makes us think that roles, identities, and selves are consistent across time and space. There is a taken-for-grantedness about the *definition of the situation* when we are in a geographic location that becomes more pronounced the more institutionalized the location is. When

I say that a location is *institutionalized,* I mean that the use of a specific place appears restricted: The front of the classroom looks as if students are restricted, yet it is available to many professors; the office of the CEO of Microsoft, on the other hand, is even more institutionalized and restricted. However, there is still a great deal of flexibility and creativity available to those that use the space.

In addition to the physical setting, a front is produced by using appearance and manner. *Appearance* cues consist of clothing, hairstyle, makeup, jewelry, cologne, backpacks, attaché cases, piercings, tattoos, and so on—in short, anything that we can place upon our bodies. While appearance refers to those things that we do *to* our bodies, manner refers to what we do *with* our bodies. *Manner* consists of the way we walk, our posture, our voice inflection, how we use our eyes, what we do with our hands, what we do with our arms, our stride, the way we sit, how we physically respond to stimuli, and so on. Both appearance and manner function to signify the performer's social status and temporary ritual state. What we mean by social status should be fairly clear. Bankers and bikers have different social statuses, and they dress differently. They don't dress differently because they have dissimilar tastes; they do so because different appearance cues are associated with different status positions.

Ritual state refers to at least two things. The most apparent is the ritual state associated with different life phases. We have fewer of these than do traditional societies, but we still mark some life transitions with rituals, like birthdays, graduations, promotions, and retirement. The second idea that the notion of ritual state conveys is our readiness to perform a particular role. Our appearance tells others how serious we are about the role we claim. For example, if you see two people riding bicycles and they are dressed differently, one in normal street clothes and the other in a matching nylon/lycra jersey and shorts along with cycling shoes and helmet, then you can surmise that one is really serious about riding and the other is less so.

As in the theater, fronts are prepared backstage and presented on the front stage. Most of what is implied in these concepts is fairly intuitive. For example, every day before you go to school, you prepare your student-self in the *backstage.* You pick out clothes, shower, do your hair, put on makeup, or whatever it is that corresponds to the self that you want others to see and respond to. Your work in the backstage for school is different from your work in the backstage of a date (unless someone you're dating will see your performance at school). You then present the student-self that you've prepared in the *front stages* of class, the lunchroom, the hallway, and so forth. But the backstage of school extends further back than your morning preparations. All students will study, read, and write to a certain degree in preparation for class. This, too, is part of the backstage for class. Even if you don't read or study, you are preparing to perform as a certain kind of student. As I said, most of this is intuitive. However, we need to realize that there are multiple front and back stages and that they can occur at almost any time and place.

There is another way that we can use the idea of front and back stages. Certain roles and thus encounters are particular to different kinds of stages. For example, the role of company CEO is more on the front stage than the role of line worker. The CEO represents the company as a whole, while the factory worker is rarely involved in representing the company directly. These sorts of front- and backstage differences significantly impact the person. People who play front-stage roles tend to be identified with the role, by both others and the person him- or herself. These roles are sort of like ritual centers—images and practices around which encounters are organized: They are the focus of attention. Front-stage people tend to emotionally connect with and value their performances in these roles, thus creating a consistent and protected face.

Relating to Roles

Every definition of a social situation contains roles that are normal and regularly expected. Goffman considers **roles** as *bundles of activities* that are effectively laced together into a situated activity system. Some of these role-specific activities we will be pleased to perform, and others we perhaps will not. We can thus distance ourselves from a role, or we can fully embrace it. *Role distancing* is a way of enacting the role that simultaneously allows the actor to lay claim to the role and to say that he or she is so much more than the role. Let's take the role of student, for example. There are certain kinds of behaviors that are expected of students: They should read the material through several times before class, they should pay close attention and diligently take notes, they should ask questions in class and consistently make eye contact with the professor, they should systematize and rewrite their notes at least once every week, they should make it a point to introduce themselves to the professor and stop by during office hours to go over the material, and so forth. You already know the list, though you probably haven't taken the time to write it out.

But how many of you actually perform the role in its entirety? Why don't you? It isn't a matter of ignorance or ability; you know and can perform everything we've listed and more. So, why don't you? You don't perform the role to its fullest because you want to express to people—mostly your peers—that there is more to you than simply being a student.

When presenting the role of student, it is difficult to simultaneously perform another role. Thus, in order to convey to others that you might be more than a student, you leave gaps in the presentation. These gaps leave possibilities and questions in the minds of others—who else is this person? Sometimes we fill the gaps with hints of our other selves (like "athletic female" or "sensitive male") that aren't necessarily part of the definition of the situation.

The corollary to role distance is role embracement. In *role embracement,* we adhere to all that the role demands. We effectively become one with the role; the role becomes our self. We see and judge our self mainly through this role. We tend to embrace a role when we are new to a situation or when we feel ourselves to be institutional representatives (like a parent or teacher). When we do embrace a role like this, we *idealize the situation and its roles.* Anytime we present a self or role, we're implicitly asking the audience to recognize it; this is especially so with role distancing (so, for example, I could ask you to recognize me as a "man who doesn't like sports"). However, Goffman (1959) wants us to see that embracing a role actually places an obligation on the audience, precisely because we "incorporate and exemplify the officially accredited values of the society" (p. 35). By embracing a role, we go further than asking to be recognized, and we place claims upon the audience—first, to recognize the self that we are presenting as one that embodies society, and second, to support our performance by aligning their impression management with ours. Roles never exist alone (for example, I can't be a teacher without students). Thus, if I embrace my role and idealize the situation, then I'm placing a claim upon you to idealize your role performance as well, because to reject the idealized role is to question or reject broader social values. The important idea that Goffman wants us to see here is that social encounters become organized around and because of impression management. How you present your self has significant social consequences.

Some of the decision to distance or embrace a role is personal, but most of it is situational. For example, we expect university students to experiment and try out different things. It's a time between highly institutionalized spaces. You are no longer a child, fully under the demands of your parents, nor are you working at a job that fully demands your time, effort, and impression management. However, when you do become a full-fledged, adult participant in the economy, you won't have the time or occasion to experience different situations and the selves they entail. Your daily rounds will be more restricted and managed by others. And you will be expected to more fully embrace the self that work requires. Of course, role distancing is still possible, but you'll have to work harder at it, and it is circumscribed by your situations.

Concepts and Theory: Sacred and Stigmatized Selves

One of the most important things we convey using a front is deference and demeanor. **Deference** refers to the amount of respect, honor, or prestige we give someone, and **demeanor** refers to the way in which we use a front to convey to others how much respect we expect. Respect, honor, and prestige are utterly social feelings: "If the individual could give himself the deference he desired, there might be a tendency for society to disintegrate into islands inhabited by solitary cultish men, each in continuous worship at his own shrine" (Goffman, 1967, p. 58). We all convey various levels of deference and demeanor, depending on the situation, through manner, appearance, setting, and even by simply taking turns in conversations. For example, Zimmerman and West (1975) found that men dominate conversations with women by controlling the turn taking; thus, "men deny equal status to women as conversational partners" (p. 125).

In every situation, then, we make claim to be a certain type of person. These claims constitute the individual's *virtual self* in the situation. Participants compare the virtual self to the *actual self,* the actual role-related behaviors. The differences between the virtual and actual selves—and there are always differences—create the possibility of **stigma**, a word that comes from the Greek and originally meant a brand or tattoo. Today, stigma is used to denote a mark of shame or discredit. There are some well-known and readily apparent stigmas; among the ones that Goffman mentions are disabilities and deformities. People with such apparent stigmas are *discredited* by those that Goffman calls "normals." Having someone with an obvious stigma creates tension in encounters. Normals practice careful "disattention," and the discredited use various devices to manage the tension, such as joking or downplaying.

There are also well-known but not so apparent stigmas. People in this category are *discreditable:* They live daily and in every situation with the potential of being stigmatized. One such category that is common today in the United States is that of homosexuals. Being homosexual in this society is a stigmatized identity—the homosexual is viewed as having failed to live up to the expectations associated with being a sexual person. Many homosexuals practice information management (as compared to tension management); they work to pass as a "normal." *Passing* is a concerted and well-organized effort to appear normal based on the knowledge of possible discrediting; this impression management entails a directedness that isn't usual for normals.

The deeper truth that Goffman wants us to see is that all of us "pass," because we all engage in information management. We know what cues to avoid in order to successfully pull off a performance. Remember when we listed the cues associated with the perfect student? Well, we could just as easily record the signals associated with being a poor student. If we think back to the issue of role distance, we can see that role distancing requires a delicate balance between claiming enough cues to still be considered a student and not claiming so few as to be discredited as a poor student. Since we all pass, we are constantly in danger of being stigmatized: "The issue becomes not whether a person has experience with a stigma of his own, because he has, but rather how many varieties he has had his own experience with" (Goffman, 1963, p. 129).

The reason that stigmas can exist and are an issue is that **identities** belong to and represent society's values and beliefs. The representational, symbolic character of identities and the way in which we interact around those identities indicate that identities and selves are *sacred objects*. Sacred things represent society, are reserved for special use, and are protected from misuse by clear symbolic boundaries. The sacred self, like all sacred objects, has boundaries that are guarded against encroachment. The sacred quality of identities and selves is the source of *shame:* "As sacred objects, men are subject to slights and profanation" (Goffman, 1967, p. 31). The flip side of stigma and shame is equally related to this collective feature of identities: It is a sense of *pride* in the sacred self.

Goffman uses the idea of face to express the dynamics of the sacred self. As noted earlier, face refers to the positive social value that a person claims in an interaction. As we've seen, when we present cues and we lay claim to a social identity, others grant us the identity and attribute to us a host of internal characteristics. Through role distancing, we can negotiate some of these attributions, but in order to make an effective claim on the situated self, we must keep our performance within a given set of parameters—otherwise we could not be identified. Every established identity has positive social values attached to it, and over time we can become emotionally involved with those values. As individuals, we experience these emotions as our *ego identity*. Every time we present an identity, we expose our face, our ego identity, to risk. We risk embarrassment, but the risk is necessary in order to feel pride and a strong sense of self.

The Language and Reality of the Self—R. S. Perinbanayagam

R. S. Perinbanayagam earned his bachelor's degree in Sri Lanka (University of Ceylon) and completed his doctorate in the United States (University of Minnesota). He is currently department head of sociology at Hunter College,

City University of New York. Among his more important works are *The Karmic Theater: Self, Society, and Astrology in Jaffna, Sri Lanka; Signifying Acts: Structure and Meaning in Everyday Life; Discursive Acts;* and *The Presence of Self* (for which he won the Charles Horton Cooley Award). Perinbanayagam was also awarded the George Herbert Mead Award for Lifetime Achievement in 1998. His newest book, *Games and Sport in Everyday Life: Dialogues and Narratives of the Self,* investigates the myth-building narratives that not only create and present the athlete's identity and self, but also promote and sustain some of society's most cherished values.

The Linguistic Turn

Like Goffman, Perinbanayagam moves our understanding of the self and action forward by incorporating more current cultural and social shifts, the most important of which is the **linguistic turn**. Though the roots go further back, the linguistic turn occurred between the 1960s and 1980s and refers to a sea change in philosophy, the humanities, and the social and behavioral sciences that continues to this day. This dramatic shift is a move away from the idea that language could represent reality and toward the conviction that language constitutes reality. One of the founding tenets of the Enlightenment was the belief that people could discover how the physical and social worlds work and then use that knowledge to better the human condition. Behind this belief was the assumption that scientific language could truly and accurately correspond to these worlds: Language thus expresses reality. The linguistic turn assumes just the opposite: Language *is* reality for human beings.

According to this view, there is no relationship between a physical reality and the language (and culture) we use. Rather than being a window through which we can see the universe, language is a kind of mirror that only reflects our own image back to us. In other words, language only refers to itself. An important implication of this idea is that every field or system of knowledge has its own language and is created through the rules of the game. The idea of *language games* is simple but profound: The rules of the game constitute the game. For example, what makes a game "baseball"? Isn't it the rules of baseball that make it what it is? The rules tell us what kinds of objects to use (bases, bats, gloves, and so on), how to relate the objects to one another (like the distance between home plate and first base), what we're supposed to do with the objects (hit the ball), the division of play (innings), and so forth. It's only when we play by the rules that baseball exists. By analogy, the same is true of other fields such as science, religion, nationalism, race, gender, sexuality, and so on.

Let's take a simple example from science. Some facts discovered by early science have been proven incorrect by later discoveries. What makes a fact scientific, then, isn't that it correctly corresponds to physical reality; it's the application of scientific methodology—the rules of the language game—that creates a scientific fact.

The roots of this sea change in thought are many and include such diverse sources as existentialist philosophy, quantum physics, feminism, cultural studies, sociology of knowledge, poststructuralism, and so forth. At this moment, it's not important for you to know the sources or how this shift came about, but I do want you to see that this isn't an obscure idea and that it has changed the way in which we understand the self. Perinbanayagam's work reflects this sea change; his questions are deep. Perinbanayagam asks, what are the implications of seeing the self as a language game? What are the rules of the game that constitute a self? What is its reality? How is it given presence in social interactions? We'll also see effects of this sea change in the chapters concerning power, gender, and race, so keep it in mind.

Concepts and Theory: Dialogic Acts and Agency

Perinbanayagam builds on the idea that language constitutes reality, but gives it a base in pragmatism and Mead's symbolic interaction. Following Mead, Perinbanayagam (2000) argues that anytime we act, we are actually interacting. Remember that human action is always meaningful and nothing has intrinsic meaning; through social interactions, we place meaning on everything. These meanings create relationships and are like symbolic bridges forming a matrix of meaning within which people act and have their being. Because we are situated within this matrix, Perinbanayagam characterizes human behavior as **dialogic acts**. These are simply *actions that are based on conversation,* but the implications of this simple definition are profound. This quality of action is clear when we're talking about actions that are directed toward people—it's plain that we're talking to one another—but it is also true when we act toward things. Remember the internal dialog in Mead's theory of human action. While things may not intentionally speak to us, we understand everything in terms of meaning, and these meanings talk to us, even if the objects are inanimate and can't deliberately speak. The meanings of objects and actions are results of that conversation you have with yourself.

From all this, Perinbanayagam (2003) concludes that "the individual, then, is not so much an agent as an *interactive agent. . . .* Being is always understood concretely in terms of actions and roles, in doings and becomings" (p. 70, emphasis original). Perinbanayagam is saying we exist in interactions. It's kind of like a fish: If you take a fish out of water, it will die. Everything about a fish is determined by its existence in water. The same sort of thing is true about you and me—we only exist in conversations; take us out of conversation and the self no longer exists. The reality of the self is language and dialogue. People, then, are never truly individual, and they don't exist in and of themselves. Because of the matrix of relationships within which every act occurs, there is always an element of other in the self. I exist in "the paradox of being simultaneously an individual and an other" (Perinbanayagam, 2000, p. 10). But this is only a paradox if we don't understand emergence and interaction; self and other mutually constitute one another, and the self is forever in process—it exists in ongoing, never-ending streams of dialogic acts. As the philosopher Heraclitus implied, you can't step twice in the same river. Every dialogic act is new and alive with potential for human beings. As we'll see, there are ethical implications from understanding dialogic acts.

Putting the Self Into Play

Generally speaking, when we communicate either verbally or nonverbally (dialogic acts), we are addressing not only the others present but also our self. And we can respond to our self, such as when we laugh at our own joke or become embarrassed. In addition to the self, there are three different **kinds of others** that may be addressed in the dialogic act, each with its own particular influence. The *interactional other* is immediately present in the interaction and provides situational control through immediate feedback to the self. The *significant other* speaks for the people the individual cares for the most and provides an emotional basis for the act; significant others may be distant from or present in the dialogic act. Finally, the *generalized others* are clusters of attitudes and perspectives and provide the individual with the standards of the community in the dialogic act.

Perinbanayagam (2000) also builds upon Goffman's idea of the presentation of self. As we've seen, Goffman argues that social encounters can't take place without selves being presented. Because of the nature of the self, Perinbanayagam adds that selves can't exist apart from dialogic acts. Thus, in every act, we put the self into play. As an analogy, let's again think of a baseball game. At the beginning of every game, the ball is "put into play." Sometimes it is significant, as when the president or vice president of the United States throws in the first ball of the first game of the season; other times its significance is mundane, as when the umpire throws the ball into play. But in every case, there is a specific method or ritual and meaning that follows how the ball is put into play. The same is true when the different players are put into the game, especially if there is a substitution. There are specific ways in which players are "put into play," and each method conveys meaning.

The conversational or discursive nature of the self implies that people use **rhetorical devices** in interactions to be seen and noticed. *Webster's New Universal Unabridged Dictionary* (1983) defines rhetoric as "the art or science of using words effectively in speaking or writing, so as to influence or persuade" (p. 1555). The use of rhetorical devices with the self, then, implies that people use particular ways of communicating in order to make the self felt, present, known, and in some ways indisputable to others. Perinbanayagam (2000) gives us four rhetorical modes the self uses: the reflexive process, addressive process, answerability process, and referential process. The *reflexive process* is basic to the self and communication in general. Every act of the self is reflexive in that it involves an internalized conversation between the I and the Me. People are also reflexive in the sense that they track the acts of others "as *expressions* and *indices* of the others' attitudes in order to organize one's own self" (Perinbanayagam, 2000, p. 55, emphasis original).

The addressive and answerability processes are the specific ways in which we present a self in the dialogic act. *Addressive processes* are ways of addressing someone, such as Mrs., Mr., Professor, Sam, Samuel, buddy, friend, loser, and so on. These others may be physically present or not, because what matters is the symbolic life we give them. In addressing others, we also address our self. Each form of address denotes a different kind of self and has a dialogue or discourse that goes along with it. For example, I once gave a presentation at another university and in a particular part of that talk, I referred to my wife. But I didn't address or refer to her as "my wife"; I called her "my partner." My wife wasn't at the talk, but because I addressed her, she was a significant other who was present in the act for the other people. After the talk, a lesbian graduate student came up and asked if I was married. I said, "Yes," and she replied, "You called your wife the right thing. I'm impressed." So in addressing my partner, I also addressed myself and created a specific image in the minds of the people listening.

Once addressed, selves may be answered or unanswered. It is impossible to have an interaction without such addressive acts, yet it is a risky endeavor. When we put a particular kind of self or other into play, we risk not being answered as such. Using my talk example, if I had addressed my spouse as "wife" instead of "partner," my self would not have been answered by that specific woman in the audience. How the self is answered or not answered is important. In their study of homeless people, David Snow and Leon Anderson (1992) quite clearly point out the power involved in answered and unanswered selves. Homeless people are constantly putting a self into play that is unanswered. As a result, "To be homeless in America is not only to have fallen to the bottom of the status system; it is also to be confronted with gnawing doubts about self-worth and the meaning of existence" (p. 199).

This point concerning the answered and unanswered selves is, perhaps, even more important than it might seem. Perinbanayagam (2000) says that one of the principal reasons for conversation is that it *"enables the individual to objectify himself or herself as well as enables the other to objectify himself or herself"* (p. 189, emphasis original). Notice carefully what Perinbanayagam says: Conversations give us the ability to objectify the self. As we learned from Mead, the self has only a symbolic existence; it is a perspective, an eddy in social settings, a cluster of meanings that we attribute to our own actions and inner experiences. In other words, the self doesn't objectively exist, yet we're driven to make it seem as if it has a substantial, objective existence. Social interactions provide an opportunity to substantiate the self in just such a way. As Jonathan H. Turner (1988) claims, "The most central . . . [motivation in interaction] is the need to sustain a self-concept" (p. 61). In other words, one of the most important reasons we engage in conversation is because we need to present a self that is answered and thus confirmed by others—it is only in its answerability that the self is experienced as objectively real. In an interesting analysis of a conversation at a book club, Perinbanayagam (2000) notes that "it really didn't matter what novel they talked about, so long as they . . . gathered and discussed something and *gave presence to their selves*" (p. 195, emphasis added).

In addition to addressive processes, the self is involved in *answerability processes*. We've just talked about the answered and unanswered self, but Perinbanayagam (2000) has something else in mind with answerability processes, so be certain to keep them separate. While the concept of the answered and unanswered self involves the response others give to the presented self, answerability processes are part of the way an individual puts a self in play. Answerability refers to *the obligation we have to the self we present.* For example, if I present myself as a professor, I am answerable or obligated to the expectations that go along with such a self. Perinbanayagam's point is that we choose the way in which we present a self—in some modes of self-presentation the answerability is clear, but in others it is not. A good example of the lack of clarity in answerability is when people dress androgynously and don't make a clear claim to a gender identity. This ambiguous answerability can make others uncomfortable because they don't know how to "answer" that person's gender. Because of this reciprocal link between selves that are put into play, Perinbanayagam concludes that making a self clearly answerable "confers a 'gift' on the other, making it an act of grace; the other can thereby understand what has been put forward and resolve—however tentatively—the mystery of the other, appreciate it, and answer it" (p. 67).

Concepts and Theory: Language of Identity

Up to this point of Perinbanayagam's theory, we have a picture of a self that is only present in conversations (both internal and external), emerges out of the interaction process, and is dependent upon the reaction of others for its objective existence. This position is indeed where interactionism leaves us. However, Perinbanayagam includes a structural component to his theory with the idea of identity. The self uses signs and words to make itself present. Those signs, words, and language constitute **identity**.

Situations and interactions are negotiated and emergent. They may or may not happen, and they may proceed in almost any direction. Situations are also insular—that is, they are not naturally connected to one another. Your day is filled with isolated dialogic acts with people at school, home, work, the grocery store, gift shop, and so on. What connects all these acts? Well, you do, but as we've seen, the self is situational, not trans-situational (it doesn't span situations). There is, however, something intrinsic to dialogic acts that *is* trans-situational and structured: language. In order to carry on a conversation, we must use language, and the particular language that is relevant to the self is the discourse or language of identity. While the self is emergent, we can think of identity as "a *regulated way* of 'speaking' about persons" (Barker, 2008, p. 224, emphasis added). In fact, the word *identity* comes from the Latin root *idem*, which implies "sameness and continuity" (Marshall, 1998, p. 293).

We've already noted that people use rhetorical devices in the act to be seen and noticed. The way in which this occurs is through the linguistic structures of identity. There are three ideas that accompany this way of seeing identity. First, identities differ by range and depth. *Range* speaks of the number of people who can claim an identity, and *depth* captures the complexity of an identity. For example, the depth of the Christian identity is far more profound than the identity of student. If we picture depth as a web of identity, the Christian is situated in a many-stranded web of mythic and linguistic structures that span all of time and creation, and the strands of this web reach into every facet of the Christian's life. The identity of student, as important as it might be, does not have nearly the same sort of depth: The myths and stories associated with the student identity are far fewer in number and lower in complexity, and the strands of the identity web only connect to certain portions of the student's life.

The second effect of the linguistic structure of identity *provides continuity* among people and situations. As we've noted, in and of themselves, situations are insular. But the language of identity links them together. Yesterday, as I put myself into play at work, I claimed the identity and was answered as professor; tomorrow, I will do the same thing. Though both days and situations are separated by many hours and many other interactions, the language of "professor" remains relatively unchanged. Thus, when I claimed and will again claim the identity of professor, the language and discourse used in such claims and their addressive and answerability processes link those emergent selves and their situations together. Further, the language of identity—in this case, professor—links the claimed identity to the interactional, significant, and generalized others. That is, the word *professor* is part of an entire way of talking that includes other terms such as student; dean; chancellor; full, associate, and assistant professor; and so on.

In contrast, the third idea that follows from the notion that language is the basis of identity is *differentiation*. Linguistically, identities work like categories, and the basic function of categories is to include and exclude. The strongest kind of categorical distinction is dichotomous, as with gender: To be male simultaneously means to not be female. This kind of bifurcation indicates a powerful element of social control around gender that is structured into our language. Other identities aren't as strongly differentiated but are nonetheless always formed over and against another: "Differentiation of identity, with whatever cultural vocabulary that is available, is not something that a functioning human consciousness can avoid; rather it is an ontological condition of the beingness of itself and of the others it encounters" (Perinbanayagam, 2000, p. 107).

Artful Ethics

We've seen that there are various tensions or paradoxes at work in formulating a self. On the one hand, you have a self that is an emergent property of interactions; on the other, you claim and use identities that are structured by language and push toward sameness and continuity. You are also individual and other at the same time, and you are simultaneously a being and a performance. These tensions imply that "human agents bring both *artistry* (the intentional use of form and shape, order, and discipline) and *artfulness* (connecting method to purpose) to their performances" (Perinbanayagam, 2003, p. 78, emphasis original). As Goffman noted, we manage the impressions we give to others. This is because we are principally oriented toward meaning. And because meaning isn't intrinsic, we have the freedom to paint the canvas of life and reality any way we choose. Yet that absolute freedom of agency is tempered by the demands of dialogue and sensibility. Our art must make sense to those who view it; it must communicate to and enter into a dialogue with others. The way in which we do that becomes our style, our individuated self. "For one's life to become a work of art, for it to develop 'style,' an individual must be able to take control and fashion a self that conforms to the exacting demands of an artistry and an aesthetic" (Perinbanayagam, 2000, p. 33).

Yet the purpose of this expression isn't simply individualistic. Symbols, language, and dialogic acts are ways through which we persuade others to cooperate with our expression of self in the world. The art of selfhood thus inevitably asks others, both people and physical things, to bend to and support our expression in the world. Because of these intrinsic connections, a dialogic act is "capable of inducing an ethical dimension into it" (Perinbanayagam, 2000, p. 5). When we act, when we make our self present, we invariably insert our values and realities into the social and physical worlds around us. Because of the time period in which we live, this ethical dimension of action falls more squarely upon us as individuals than ever before. In traditional societies, and even early modern societies, there were fewer choices and fewer realities from which to choose. There were more and clearer guidelines, and people knew less of the consequences of choice. The politics of choice is more real today than ever before. The question Perinbanayagam leaves us with, then, is what kind of artists will we be? To what type of values and realities will we ask the world to conform?

The Craft of Citizenship   Self

The Basics: Comprehension and Explanation

- What are the central questions that each of our theorists attempts to answer? How are these questions similar and how are they different?
- There are two sociological perspectives presented in this chapter. Go back to Chapter 1 and review the section on perspectives. Using that information, define symbolic interaction and dramaturgy.
- Define the following terms theoretically: emergence, society, sociological subject, pragmatism, action, self, role taking, I and Me, front, roles, deference and demeanor, linguistic turn, dialogic acts, kinds of others, rhetorical devices.

  > *Helpful hints:* As you know, I've put the main terms in bold and the supportive ones in italics. But I want you to notice two things. First, some main terms have a good number of explanatory ones. For example, go back and look at the explanation for **front**. The supporting terms go from setting through front and back stages. Second, some of the explanatory terms come before the main concept as well as after, such as with **stigma**. One of the skills being built here is your ability to discern main concepts and supporting ideas on your own. You need to be able to relate defining ideas to their main concept no matter where they are found in a chapter.

- Explain how the self is formed as a social object (from the discussion of Mead).
- Explain Goffman's theory of the presentation of self.
- According to Perinbanayagam, precisely how is the self put into play?
- What are identities, and how are they structured?

Skill Set 1: Inference and Application

- What is the sociological subject, and how is it related to democracy? Is this idea of the person more or less well suited for democracy compared to the Enlightenment's idea?
- Explain how the historical context influenced each of the theorists in this chapter. What does this imply about social theory in general?
- Take one of your identities and explain how you "pass." What does Perinbanayagam's theory of identity add to your understanding of this process?
- What are the implications of Perinbanayagam's idea of artful ethics for your personal involvement in democracy?
- In what situations do you role distance and why?

Skill Set 2: Interpretation, Analysis, Evaluation, Synthesis

- Mead's theory of interaction seems to indicate that there is a great deal of freedom in the way the self emerges out of interactions. Evaluate this idea using Goffman's (stigma) and Perinbanayagam's theory of identities and artful ethics.
- Compare, contrast, and evaluate Mead's notion of institutions with that of Parsons (Chapter 2). Which do you think gives a more powerful explanation? Explain/justify your answer.
- Both Goffman and Perinbanayagam are concerned with how we present or manage a self in social encounters. Compare and contrast their theories. How could these theories be brought together to give us a fuller understanding of the self in interactions?
- Analyze and evaluate the ideas of society that are presented in Chapters 2 and 3. What assumptions are at work? How do those assumptions inform what each theorist sees? Which set of assumptions do you think is most relevant for today? Why?

4

Religion

rior to modernity, religion occupied a central position in society as a whole and in government specifically. This dominance of religion dates back to 140 BCE in the East, with Emperor Xiao Wu and Confucianism, and 313 CE in the West, with Constantine and Christianity. Yet since the dawn of modernity, there has not been a more troubled institutional relationship than that between the state and religion. Some of this is intentional, with the democratic state seeming to separate itself from religion; and some of the tension is simply the result of general trends toward secularization, developing most notably out of science, bureaucratic organization, and capitalism. Yet despite the troubles and all the doubt concerning the place of religion in modern times, God isn't dead and religion hasn't gone away. It's clear from the founding documents of most modern nations, and even clearer from the printed works of the social thinkers engaged in the founding of modernity, that religion, or at least the religious orientation, was to have an intricate part in the social project of modernity. But given the push–pull relationship between the state and religion, what is the role of religion in modernity?

To answer that, we start with the work of Émile Durkheim. Durkheim is a functionalist and, like Spencer and Parsons, he sees society as a macro-level entity. He talks in the same structural, institutional terms that they do, and he considers society to be a social fact, an objective entity that has its own processes that can be discovered through scientific methodology. However, Durkheim also focuses on the consciousness of the individual, similar to Perinbanayagam. For Durkheim, society and religion can't be separated because both are built out of the same material—that is, the experience of transcendence, the sense of something greater than ourselves. Our second theorist, Robert Bellah, picks up Durkheim's point and explicitly shows how this connection between religion and society works itself out in modern democracies. Far from being antireligious, modern nation-states are religious-like institutions, and they succeed only in so far as they provide a religious experience. But at the same time, religion poses one of the greatest threats to democracy, one that is often expressed as terrorism. In our discussion of war and religion, later in this chapter, I'll be drawing on the work of Mark Juergensmeyer in his book *Terror in the Mind of God* (2000), as well as using other theoretical ideas.

The Religious Basis of Society—Émile Durkheim

Émile Durkheim (1858–1917) was born in Epinal, France. His father was a rabbi, descended from generations of rabbis. Durkheim did well in high school and attended the prestigious École Normale Supérieure in Paris, the training ground for the new French intellectual elite. In 1887, Durkheim was appointed as Chargé d'un Cours de Science Sociale et de Pédagogie at the University of Bordeaux, and thus became the first teacher of sociology in the French system. In 1902, Durkheim took a post at the Sorbonne and by 1906 was appointed Professor of the Science of Education, a title later changed to

Professor of Science of Education and Sociology. In this position, Durkheim served as chief advisor to the Ministry of Education. Durkheim was a central figure in establishing sociology as a social science, especially with the publication of *The Rules of Sociological Method* and *Suicide*. Other important works include *The Division of Labor* and *The Elementary Forms of the Religious Life*. Durkheim also founded the journal *L'Année Sociologique*, which became the leading journal of social thought in France. Along with Spencer, Durkheim is considered a founding thinker in functionalism. Durkheim died of a stroke at the age of 59, on November 15, 1971.

The main question that concerns Durkheim has to do with modern society and social integration: How can modern society integrate in the face of increasing diversity? His basic argument is built around the idea that society is fundamentally an experience. He doesn't disagree with Spencer or Parsons; he understands society as a functional system of interrelated parts, and he is primarily concerned with social integration, just like Spencer and Parsons. However, Durkheim is more concerned with the impact that society has on a person. Durkheim assumes that, apart from society, humans are individualistic and self-seeking. So his main question is, how does society control the actions of the individual? His answer is that society is more than structures and institutions. Society exists as a collective consciousness: shared ideas, representations, beliefs, and feelings. In Durkheim's way of thinking, then, society exists as the collective consciousness forms our minds and our awareness of the world. The question of what constitutes society thus becomes, what could have such a profound influence on human beings? For Durkheim, there's only one answer: religion.

Concepts and Theory: The Collective Consciousness

Apart from human ordering, the physical world and the stream of life are unremarkable. What I mean by that is that everything flows together. Where one thing or experience ends and another begins isn't clear. Let me ask you this: Where does the ocean end and land begin? Precisely what is the shade of skin color that indicates one race and not another? When does Monday begin? Where does one nation begin and another end? Those boundaries don't exist in the natural, physical, temporal worlds, nor do they exist in immediate experience. The boundaries exist in the mental categories we use to slice up the world into discrete but ordered chunks, which then give meaning to our actual free-flow experience. The scalpel that we use is a social scalpel. "It is society that underlies the way we generate meaningful mental entities" (Zerubavel, 1991, p. 61).

To understand how this scalpel comes to be and how it is used, Durkheim conceptualizes the **collective consciousness** as having two parts, cognitive and emotional. The *cognitive elements* are found in linguistic categories. Yet Durkheim argues that the real core of society and consciousness is emotion. One reason for this comes out of his concept of **human nature**: Humans "are by nature boundless and insatiable" (Durkheim, 1957/1992, p. 11). Because of our nature, the human world is an open-ended one. In other words, there aren't any natural stopping places. We didn't stop when we discovered fire; we didn't stop when we invented trains; we didn't stop when we landed on the moon; we didn't stop when we created the Internet; and on and on and on. We can't stop because our nature is defined through an ongoing world-building project. Humans by nature, then, are never satisfied.

Durkheim argues that these human characteristics cannot be managed by rational thought alone. Because our entire being is involved, we need to be emotionally bound to the collective consciousness. We have to have an *emotional sense* of something greater than ourselves, something that lies outside our individual, subjective humanness. Social emotions or sentiments "dominate us, they possess, so to speak, something superhuman about them. At the same time they bind us to objects that lie outside our existence in time" (Durkheim, 1893/1984, p. 56). It is this specific kind of emotional attachment to the collective consciousness that is able to transcend the boundless and insatiable qualities of the human spirit, to guide our behaviors in such a way as to give us satisfaction, and provide meaning to the open-endedness of human existence. The collective consciousness, then, transcends the individual, provides us with primary categories of thought, and thus creates a sensible cultural reality. That is, it guides our behaviors and provides motivations for action; it creates a whole out of individuals; and it renders the innate openness of human existence meaningful. What is the basis for such a thing? To begin to answer that question, we need to understand that for Durkheim, **society** *is fundamentally an experience*.

Creating Society

Durkheim's explanation for where society, and thus, the collective consciousness, originated is religion. As I emphasize in this book, definitions of concepts are of great consequence. And the way Durkheim defines **religion** is significant to understanding his argument. For Durkheim (1912/1995),

> A religion is a unified system of beliefs and practices relative to sacred things, that is to say, things set apart and forbidden—beliefs and practices which unite into one single moral community called a Church, all those who adhere to them. (p. 44)

Note carefully what is missing from Durkheim's definition: There is no mention of the supernatural or God. Durkheim argues (1912/1995) that before humans could think about the *supernatural,* they first had to have a clear idea about what was natural. The term supernatural assumes the division of the universe into two categories: things that can be rationally explained and those that can't. This division is recent. It took quite a bit of human history for us to stop believing that there are spirits in back of everything. The concept of nature—those elements of life that occur apart from spiritual influence—didn't fully exist until the advent of science. So the idea of supernatural can't be included in a definition of religion, since there has never been society without religion. Durkheim also argues that we cannot include the idea of *God* in the definition of religion. His logic here concerns the fact that there are many belief systems that are generally considered religion that do not require a god. Though he includes other religions such as Jainism, his principal example is Buddhism. The focus of Buddhist faith is the Four Noble Truths, and "salvation" occurs apart from any divine intervention. There are deities acknowledged by Buddhism, such as Indra, Agni, and Varuna, but the entire Buddhist faith can be practiced apart from them. The practicing Buddhist needs no god to thank or worship, yet Buddhism is considered a religion.

Thus, three things constitute religion in its most basic form: the presence of the *sacred, beliefs and practices,* and a *moral community.* The important thing to notice about Durkheim's definition is the centrality of the notion of the sacred. Every element of the definition revolves around it. The beliefs and practices are relative to sacred things, and the moral community exists because of the beliefs and practices, which of course brings us back to sacred things. So at the heart of religion is this idea of the sacred, and it is the experience of the sacred that forms the basis of society.

Creating the Sacred

How many different things throughout human history have we made sacred? The list is almost endless. Humans have used crosses, stones, kangaroos, snakes, birds, water, swastikas, flags, and yellow ribbons—almost anything—as sacred objects. It's obvious, then, that sacredness isn't something that is intrinsic to the object; objects themselves aren't sacred. We could argue that sacredness comes through association, and that's true at least in part. We think the cross is sacred because of its association with Jesus. But what makes all other symbols sacred? If it's association, then all the entities in back of all the sacred symbols that humanity has ever used are in fact sacred. On the other hand, we could say it's belief that makes symbols sacred. But that just begs the question, what is it that makes us believe one thing and not another? Durkheim finds the source of sacredness in social rituals.

Durkheim's basic argument is that when human beings gather together in specific kinds of interactions—**rituals**—we are able to create very high levels of emotional energy, much more than we could ever generate individually. We've all felt something like what Durkheim is talking about at concerts or political rallies or sporting events. Randall Collins (1988), a contemporary theorist, has captured Durkheim's theory in abstract terms. Generally speaking, there are three principal elements to the kind of interactions that Durkheim is describing: *co-presence,* which describes the degree of physical closeness in space (we can be closer or further away from one another); *common emotional mood,* the degree to which we share the same feeling about the event; and *common focus of attention,* the degree to which participants are attending to the same object, symbol, or idea at the same time (pp. 192–197).

When humans gather together in intense interactions—with high levels of co-presence, common emotional mood, and common focus of attention—they produce high levels of *emotional energy,* or what Durkheim calls "effervescence." People feel caught up in something greater than the individual and thus have a tendency to symbolize the emotional energy, which produces a *sacred symbol,* and to create rituals: These rituals are *patterned behaviors designed to replicate the three interaction elements.* The symbols allow people to focus their attention and recall the emotion, and they also ground the emotions created by the collective: "Without symbols, moreover, social feelings could have only an unstable existence" (Durkheim, 1912/1995, p. 232).

Emotion and Collective Life

Durkheim's theory not only explains the origin of sacred symbols, but also explains the emotional component in the collective consciousness, which includes ideas, categories, social connections, morals, motivations, values, beliefs, identities, and so on. For Durkheim, then, every aspect of human individual and collective life is based upon and has an emotional component. Recent advances in neuroscience and theory confirm the importance that Durkheim places on emotion. Specifically important is the work demonstrating that human beings evolved a unique kind of brain structure, one that privileges emotion over language (and thus cognition) for creating social connections, community, and a sense of belonging to a specific physical place (Turner, 2000). Also critical are Damasio's (1999, 2003) and LeDoux's (1996) work on the effects of emotions on the brain, especially their importance for producing consciousness, identity, memory, and decision making.

Emotion, then, is essential for human existence, and Durkheim's theory provides an explanation for how our most powerful emotions are created. It's important to note that all of the elements in the collective consciousness vary by their level of invested emotion and significance. Some guidelines for behavior are like folkways, generally accepted ways of doing things, like the way we position ourselves in an elevator. Others, however, are more powerful moralistic guides and constraints, all of which vary by the level of invested emotional energy. For humans, reality isn't simply cognitive; it's emotional. Realities and behavior guides are more or less sacred based on the degree of ritual performance.

There are three other effects of Durkheimian rituals that we need to consider. The first is the issue of social solidarity. There are three components to solidarity: the *subjective sense* of individuals that they are part of the whole, the actual *constraint* of individual desires for the good of the collective, and the *coordination* of individuals and social units. Each of these elements varies by ritual performance. So if the level of ritual performance is high in a group, individuals will have a very strong sense of belonging, the guides for behavior will tend to be moralistic, and different social actors (individuals, organizations, and so forth) will be well integrated.

The other two effects of ritual performance I want us to consider are transcendence and immanence. To transcend something is to rise above or go beyond it. In this case, the something that we rise above is our experience as an individual; it's the emotional sense of something greater than ourselves—society. That experience is based upon the level of collective emotion that we are able to produce through rituals. These collective emotions are also related to immanence. Immanence and transcendence are in fact opposites. Something is immanent if it stays within the limits of possible experience. The Latin root of the word means to stay in place. Yet it is actually the combination of immanence and transcendence that allows us to see the power of the collective consciousness. For Durkheim (1912/1995), the collective consciousness is a "form of moral power that, while immanent in us, also represents something in us that is other than ourselves" (p. 213). In other words, the consciousness that we have within us is intrinsically linked to the collective consciousness. This, then, is our link to society; it is how society comes into existence and exists within us.

Concepts and Theory: The Problem of Modernity

Durkheim says that there are two "great currents" in society: similarity and difference. In early societies, similarity ruled, as there were very few personal differences, and there was little competition and high egalitarianism. Ritual performance was high, the collective consciousness thus permeated and dominated individual consciousness, and these groups experienced what

Durkheim calls **mechanical solidarity**. Gradually, the other current, difference, became stronger and similarity receded. Dissimilar social units are held together through mutual need and abstract ideas and sentiments. Durkheim refers to this as **organic solidarity**. While organic solidarity and difference tend to dominate modern society, similarity and mechanical solidarity never completely disappear—there can be groups with mechanical solidarity within a larger collective that is based on organic solidarity, and, more importantly, a modern society can quickly produce high levels of social solidarity in response to things such as threat.

Remember from Chapter 2 that modern social systems are characterized by high levels of *structural differentiation,* which in turn create problems of coordination and control. To this idea we need to add **social differentiation**. Social differentiation simply refers to the *degree that people are different* from one another. Most of us assume that we are naturally different from one another, and to some degree that's true, but the greater influences on difference come from social factors. Due to structural differentiation, new and different spheres of interaction are created. Because the tasks and orientations of these spheres are different, new values, ideas, sentiments, norms, and so on are created as well. In other words, a group-specific consciousness is fashioned. As people interact and perform rituals related to this *particularized culture,* it becomes increasingly important (sacred) and has greater impact on the formation of the people within the group. With particularized culture, the level of the collective consciousness tends to decrease in modern society. Durkheim also links this decrease to the division of labor. The *division of labor* refers to a stable organization of tasks and roles that coordinate the behavior of individuals or groups that carry out different but related duties. Increasing the division of labor (the number and complexity of jobs) in society has the same type of cultural effect as structural differentiation. It tends to decrease the collective consciousness as people become increasingly different from one another.

In terms of the general collective consciousness, greater levels of the division of labor and structural differentiation, both characteristics of modern society, will decrease the level of the **collective consciousness**, which varies by the degree to which it is *shared;* the amount of *power* it has to guide and shape an individual's thoughts, feelings, and actions; and the degree of *clarity* the prescriptions and prohibitions have. If people share different rather than similar cultures, the way they think and feel about the world will be different, and the norms, ethics, and morals they hold will be different as well. The Durkheimian question of modernity, then, is how low can the collective consciousness go without destroying society?

The Real Problem

Durkheim's response is similar to what we saw in Chapter 2. First, as structures and other social units separate, they come to need one another (structural interdependency). Second, these interdependent relations need to be regulated. Structural and social differentiation then creates pressures for society to generate laws and political power to manage interstructural relations. Durkheim adds that these laws have a rational rather than moral basis; Durkheim calls these **restitutive laws**, in comparison to restrictive or moral law. Now, from Durkheim's position, what's the problem with restitutive law? Think back to the most important element of the collective consciousness. By definition, restitutive law is not based in emotion; it is rational rather than moral. While restitutive law and centralized political power will help guide interstructural and interpersonal relations, they simply aren't sufficient. Humans still need the emotional component. Here is where the third solution to the problem of modernity comes in: **culture generalization.** In order for culture to embrace increasing diversity, it must become more general. We considered this with Parsons. In fact, Parsons got this idea from Durkheim. But Parsons missed Durkheim's most important point. For Durkheim, ideas aren't simply cognitive things, especially as they relate to the collective consciousness. Ideas have emotion; and the more important ideas, such as the kind that unite people, need to have and elicit high levels of emotional energy. In other words, in order for a generalized collective consciousness to truly be effective, it must be emotionally infused through repeated performances of Durkheimian rituals. In plainer words, the culture that binds together a diverse population must be religious in nature but modern in form.

In order to talk about modern religion, Durkheim emphasizes two **religious functions.** The first is to provide a *cosmology.* Every religion has given its own version of the origin and purpose of the universe. These cosmologies not only provide explanations for all that exists, but also place humankind in the grand scheme of things. In modernity, however, science has taken over this function. The second function of religion, what Durkheim (1912/1995) calls the "true function," is

> not to make us think, enrich our knowledge, or add representations of a different sort and source to whose we owe to science. Its true function is to make us act and to help us live. The believer who has communed with his god is not simply a man who sees new truths that the unbeliever knows not; he is a man who is *stronger.* (p. 419)

This is the realm of transcendence and immanence. This is where those ideas that have ethical and moral power originate. It is these ideas that can live in my soul and simultaneously in yours, without the uncertainty that can come with cognitive thought. These are the ideas that can transcend our individual lives and thus impel us forward for the common good.

To avoid the mire of uncertainty, insignificance, and apathy that can come with pure rational thought and unguided action, humanity needs the religious. We need to be driven forward by a vision that inspires us and provides meaning beyond our individual existence. We need to be better; we need to be stronger. "A faith above all is warmth, life, enthusiasm. . . . Except by reaching outside himself, how could the individual add to the energies he possesses? How could he transcend himself by his own power?" (Durkheim, 1912/1995, p. 427). Yet if humanity still needs religion and "the former gods are growing old or dying" (Durkheim, 1912/1995, p. 427), from where will this faith spring? Durkheim didn't know. After he says that old gods are dying, he adds, "others have not been born." He characterizes much of modernity as being in a "state of uncertainty and confused anxiety." But, he says, this condition cannot last. "A day will come when our societies once again will know hours of creative effervescence during which new ideals will again spring forth and new formulas emerge to guide humanity for a time" (p. 429).

Modern Religion—Robert Bellah

Robert N. Bellah (1927–) was born in Altus, Oklahoma. He was a student of Talcott Parsons and graduated from Harvard in 1955 with his PhD in Sociology and Far Eastern Languages. Bellah taught at Harvard from 1957 to 1967, at which time he moved to the University of California, Berkeley. There he served as the Ford Professor of Sociology (1967–1997) and chaired the Center for Japanese and Korean Studies (1969–1974). Among his most important works are *The Broken Covenant: American Civil Religion in Time of Trial* (winner, Sorokin Award, American Sociological Association), *Beyond Belief: Essays on Religion in a Post-Traditional World, Habits of the Heart* (winner, *The Los Angeles Times* Book Prize), *Varieties of Civil Religion,* and *The Good Society.* In 2000, Bellah received the United States National Humanities Medal, from President Bill Clinton. In talking about his own works, Bellah (1970) says that "they are attempts to find patterns of meaning in a world where all the great overarching systems of belief, conservative and radical, have lost their viability" (p. xxi).

Robert Bellah gives an answer to Durkheim's hope in the rise of new gods. Remember Durkheim's definition of religion: It focuses on the sacred but doesn't include God or the supernatural. This definition allows for the possibility that other institutions could fulfill the functions of religion. That is exactly what Bellah is proposing in his idea of **civil religion**, a cultural sphere most closely associated with nationalism. To get us to see how this works, Bellah explains more fully what Durkheim meant when he talked about the function of religion being to make us stronger—the strength religion gives is specific to identities, motivation, and legitimacy. Yet, like Durkheim, Bellah also sees dangers for modern religion. He talks about these dangers in terms of a continuum from private religion to exclusionary groups.

Concepts and Theory: The Evolution of Religion

Bellah argues that religion has two main functions in society: These are to solve the problems of identity and legitimacy. *Identities* form bridges between the individual and society as a whole. They are created as part of an institutional setting, like "father" and "daughter" in a family. As part of an institution, identities motivate and guide our behavior and connect us to others. Yet identities are also personal—they are an intrinsic part of defining who we are as individuals. We experience our self as a student or professor; as a man or a woman; as heterosexual, bisexual, or homosexual; and so on. Because identities are culturally and socially created, they must be institutionally embedded to make them stable. In the previous chapter, we saw that identities are structured in language; Bellah finds that function in religion. Religion permits individuals to feel an ultimate sense of rightness about their identities. If all the behaviors and feelings that come with our social position are only social constructions, then our sense of rightness will always be tainted with doubt: Am I being a good father? Should I have told Cynthia about what I saw? Should I have given that street person money? The scrutiny of our behaviors and feelings can be endless, unless there is a firm base upon which to stand. And there is no base firmer than religion, at least for those who believe. The second problem that religion solves is legitimacy. *Legitimacy* acts to give a moral basis to power, especially political power. Bellah draws this idea from Max Weber (1922/1968), who argued that religion provides guidance and solidarity: "There is no concerted action . . . without its special god. Indeed, if an association is to be permanently guaranteed, it must have such a god" (p. 411).

Weber (1922/1993) also gives us a theory explaining the evolution of religion. He argues that religion evolved as the needs of governance changed, together with improvements in technology and professionalization. Technology was particularly important in the move from magic to religion. As people began to be able to control the natural environment, it became, in Weber's words, "demystified." Improvements in technology also made it possible for people to begin specializing in their work—this freedom *professionalized* religious service. More important for legitimation, religion and gods changed as more diverse peoples started coming together to form a single society. Each group brought its own god, but the needs of governance meant that these gods were placed in a hierarchical order so that the ruling god was the deity of the ruling group. This god became the god of gods, and through continuing improvements in technology, further professionalization, and the broadening of governance, this god became the only God. Notice that this process is what Durkheim means when he talks about culture generalization. Further, as the ruling elite became interested in controlling people's behavior for the common good, religious doctrine legitimated only certain types of behaviors, while assigning the rest to outer darkness. Keep this brief sketch in mind as we review Bellah's theory.

Religious Symbols

In defining **religion**, Bellah (1970) focuses on one primary aspect of Durkheim's definition—symbols: "[R]eligion [is] a set of symbolic forms and acts that relate man to the ultimate conditions of his existence" (p. 21). The reason for this specific definition is that Bellah wants to talk about the evolution of religion in a specific way. He makes the case that *symbolic systems* evolve, not the ultimate conditions of human existence. The other issue Bellah wants to point out is that the religious person is fully religious at any given point in time. In other words, the modern religious person isn't any more or less religious than the person in primitive religion. People can only respond to the available system of religious symbols. So Bellah wants to assure us that in talking about the evolution of religion, he isn't calling into question the ultimate conditions of life (or God) or our potential to be religious at any specific time. The only thing that has evolved is the system of religious symbols.

It's important to keep in mind that as religion evolves, prior forms don't necessarily die out. Historic religions can exist in a society with modern forms. But Bellah is also arguing that there is an interdependent relationship between the historical forms of society and religion: Religious forms more in keeping with society as a whole will tend to function better than past religion types. Bellah asserts (1970) that there are five distinct stages in religious evolution: primitive, archaic, historic, early modern, and modern. For Bellah, the key issue in religious evolution revolves around symbols becoming more abstract and symbolic. In *primitive religion,* there was a high correlation between the mythical world and the physical world in which humans lived. In other words, the spiritual and physical worlds were the same. For example, the physical entity of water and its spirit were one and the same. *Archaic* religions were characterized by the organization of gods into hierarchies with complex systems of priests and rites. Here we begin to see the beginning separation of the physical from the spiritual.

With *historic religions,* like Judaism and early Christianity, we begin to see religion become entirely separated from this world and thus completely abstract and symbolic. The notion of monotheism (one God) collapses the pantheon of archaic religion and places God outside of space and time. Here, for the first time, it became possible to begin to think about the individual in a relationship to his or her God, rather than as a part of a clan or tribe. In other words, because religion (and God) was separated from any physical location or time, religion could embrace more diverse kinds of people. We see this clearly as Elohim became the God of Jews and Gentiles alike in early Christianity.

Early modern religion began with the Protestant Reformation. While Catholicism still maintained sacred hierarchies, Protestantism collapsed them. Rather than a system of saints and priests between the individual and God, Protestantism sees a direct relationship between the individual and transcendent reality. In an inversion of primitive religion, the individual's behaviors became symbolic of the spiritual world that exists outside of time and space. We see this most clearly in Luther's idea of a *calling:* Rather than a calling being the exclusive domain of priests, every individual is called to service unto God. That service may take the form of laying brick or giving to the poor, but all work done in this physical world is symbolically related to eternity. Rather than symbolic behavior being restricted to the activities of the priests within the confines of the church, Protestantism made it possible that every word, deed, and thought could be symbolically related to spiritual existence.

Modern religion takes this symbolism further by collapsing the sacred–profane "dualism that was so crucial to all the historic religions" (Bellah, 1970, p. 40). Where early modern religion made the distinction between the sacred and profane most clear, modern religion breaks that barrier down. Rather than being focused on the essential differences between the spiritual and physical worlds, honoring one and decrying the other, modern religion sees earthly life as essentially spiritual. For modern religion, the Kingdom of God is here and now, rather than simply in the afterlife, and it exists specifically in the search for ethical social justice. Ethics is concerned with right and wrong, but it isn't necessarily based on something that exists spiritually or outside of the human condition, as in early modern religion. Rather than religion based in a dichotomy of sacred and profane, modern religion is found in an "infinitely multiplex" world, and life, in terms of religion, has become filled with infinite possibilities (Bellah, 1970, p. 40).

Modern Civil Religion

Bellah (1970) argues that this diverse field of possibilities calls into existence a specific form of religion, civil religion, which is well suited for this democratic field. **Civil religion** is a "public religious dimension . . . expressed in a set of beliefs, symbols, and rituals" that is separate from institutional religion and separate from the state as well, though many of the beliefs concern the state and governing in general (p. 171). There are three elements to civil religion: representative characters, historical moments, and public rituals. *Representative characters* are historical figures that take on mythic proportions, which in turn help to legitimate the system and to provide ideals for identity construction. In the United States, examples include such people as Abraham Lincoln, Helen Keller, Eleanor Roosevelt, John Kennedy, Rosa Parks, and Martin Luther King Jr. Today, we might also add such media figures as Oprah Winfrey and sports heroes like Lance Armstrong. Each of these is capable of being the focus of stories that legitimate and build identities around the culture of democracy in the United States.

Historical moments, such as the American Revolution or landing the first person on the moon, especially when they are associated with *public rituals,* such as the Fourth of July in America or the coronation in Great Britain, also provide vehicles for social solidarity and grand narratives. A narrative is a story, and a **grand narrative** is a story that works as a myth that gathers together diverse groups of people into a common belief system. Modern nation-states have a particular need for such narratives, because they are the form of government that uniquely seeks to create solidarity out of diverse groups. The grand narratives of civil religion provide clear, generalized identities ("American") that motivate people to sacrifice ("give one's life for his or her country") in the service of a transcendent ethical or moral value ("freedom"). One reason it's important to note the place of grand narratives for nation-states is that previously such mythical stories were the domain of religion. Organized pantheons and monotheism did the same thing as grand narratives: They linked together different clans, tribes, and families under a single story.

Before we look at the qualities Bellah says this civil religion ought to have, it's important to understand that Bellah is not arguing that religion per se is diminishing or unimportant for the public life of a democracy, nor is he arguing that religion is a private affair and ought to be kept away from politics. His stand on both these issues is quite the opposite. In the United States especially, understanding the historical place of religion is paramount to understanding democracy: "To leave it out is to empty the story of an utterly central dimension of its truth, of its being, of that which makes us citizens" (Bellah, 1985). Further, religion must retain its public voice in a democracy, not only because of its historical place, but also due to its essential character. Religious loyalty transcends national patriotism, thus "religious groups have frequently voiced disruptive demands that polarized society and led to severe conflict" (Bellah, Madsen, Sullivan, Swidler, & Tipton, 1992, p. 181)—and diversity, tension, and conflict are necessary for democracy.

Concepts and Theory: Civil Religion in Action

In sociology, community has generally been used to designate a group of people who have shared values and goals. Bellah's (1995) definition intends this sense of shared values but with one major qualification: "My idea of community is one in which there is argument, even conflict, about the meaning of the shared values and goals, and certainly about how they will be actualized in everyday life." This addition to the idea of community is significant because of what it says about culture. For those who study culture from a Durkheimian tradition, as does Bellah, culture is generally understood in terms of how it works to create social solidarity through consensus and how it presents itself as *sedimented.*

Picture a glass bottle filled with water and sand. If you shake the bottle up, the sand and water mix; you can't really point to where the sand is because it is everywhere yet nowhere in particular. If you set the bottle down, eventually the sand will settle at the bottom. Where the sand is located is now clear; you can point to it. That sand at the bottom is sediment. When we speak of culture being sedimented, we mean that culture is able to function to provide consistent meaning because it is established—it's settled. For example, today, we all pretty much agree on the meaning of equality. However, when modern countries were in the process of being created, the meaning of equality was hotly debated. Like the sand in water, the meaning wasn't specified—it wasn't in one place. Now, we can all agree on the meaning of equality because its meaning has been established. It's generally argued that these settled meanings create social solidarity.

Bellah says no—culture that is settled in this way is dead; it's out of the public discourse and simply taken for granted. In a way, Bellah agrees with Durkheim that culture and real interactions are related. But unlike Durkheim, Bellah argues that living culture must be the subject of almost constant debate, as does Alexander (see Chapter 2). For Bellah (1995), civil religion isn't based upon unthinking acceptance of the way things are, nor, obviously, is community established simply because of geographic concentration, like a neighborhood. Community "is a form of intelligent, reflective life, in which there is indeed consensus, but where the consensus can be challenged and changes, often gradually, sometimes radically over time."

There are two significant things to note about Bellah's concept of community. First, community is always a *moral or ethical process.* This process is particularly important now: In modernity, many of the institutions "are not working as they were intended" and others have "alarming and unintended consequences that affect not only people but the natural environment" (Bellah et al., 1992, p. 4)—thus, modern community and civil religion aren't settled. Take what was said earlier about freedom. If you believed what I said about it being settled, then that part of culture is dead for you and not part of community. If, on the other hand, you see freedom as incomplete, as an ongoing project, then you are a potential member of community. Issues such as freedom, social justice, and equality are precisely what Bellah has in mind in his idea of community.

The second thing to notice about Bellah's concept of community is that it intrinsically *involves the person*. Community, because it is unsettled and unsettling, requires a specific type of individual. Now notice the connection here with the idea of institution. Institutions provide us with persons, or typified identities. They are ways of understanding who and what we are. They provide us with meaning and methods of assessing our actions, thoughts, and feelings. So there is a specific type of person involved in community and civil religion: He or she is someone who has a set of values informed by the ideas of democracy, *who doesn't hold those values dogmatically* and is able to articulate them in an open debate.

The italicized words above are very important. Bellah sees the role of religion in modern society as maintaining a balance between loosely and tightly bounded culture. The distinction here is very similar to Durkheim's notion of mechanical and organic solidarity, but Bellah is specifically concerned with identity construction. **Identities** are constructed through boundaries, as they mark what is included and excluded from a group. For example, the identity of "Jewish" can only exist if there are others who are "not Jewish." Thus, drawing boundaries and creating identities are inevitable, but how those boundaries are drawn is not. We can think about boundaries in terms of a tight–loose continuum. *Tightly bounded cultures* create almost impenetrable walls. The rules of inclusion and exclusion are strictly enforced, and people within a tightly bounded group feel their identity is absolutely right. The danger with tightly bounded cultures is that they are a "source of intergroup hostility and conflict" (Bellah, 1987, p. 220).

At the other end of the spectrum are *loosely bounded cultures*. These cultures create extremely weak boundaries and identities, with very few if any compelling norms or values. The danger with such cultures is that they don't provide the fodder for "a genuine argument to take place" (Bellah, 1987, p. 222). Since there aren't any directing norms or values, issues and situations are subject to continual renegotiation, which is "an endless, exhausting, and finally impossible task" (p. 222). However, our choices aren't limited to creating absolute boundaries or dissolving them altogether. A balance between strong commitment to one's own group and simultaneously recognizing that all communities are ultimately included in the human race is the bedrock upon which modern democracy must be built.

Bellah does see a threat to democracy, but it isn't found in tightly bounded groups, despite their tendency to hostility. The threat comes from loosely bounded culture. Loosely bounded culture devolves into flaccid individualism and the complete privatization of religion. Privatized religion is entirely personal, with no collective connection or expression, thus producing antidemocratic energies. "Should loose-boundedness triumph completely, the ground will be prepared for administrative despotism, since only the state will be left to control the atomized individuals" (Bellah, 1987, p. 229). While Bellah doesn't address it, there is a danger from religious groups that have tightly bounded culture as well. When Bellah was writing, this danger wasn't as apparent as it is today. The danger with tightly bounded religious cultures is the potential for terrorism.

The God of War

The danger on the tightly bounded side isn't the threat of meaninglessness, as it is with loosely bounded cultures, but rather, it's the threat of meaning that has become too strong—meanings worth fighting and killing for. As we've seen, the categories and ideas that provide meaning for humans are by and large social constructions; the power of categories to create order is based on the strength of their boundaries. Let's take race as an example. The boundary that produces race is a symbolic one that has for many years been sacred. (Note that sacred things aren't always what we might think of as "good.") One of the qualities of the sacred–profane dichotomy is that the categories are mutually exclusive, and generally any association with the profane will defile the sacred. With race in the United States, that quality is seen in the "one drop rule," or hypodescent: In a mixed marriage of black and white, the children are still considered black. The bigotry that has surrounded the race issue is an example of a boundary that is too meaningful, an element of a tightly bounded culture. This is the type of boundary that religion, more than any other institution, is capable of creating.

Concepts and Theory: Religion and Violence

Almost all historic religions contain violence and killing, whether it's the Old Testament God of wrath, the Muslim jihad, the Christian Crusades, or the casting of souls into a lake of fire. But why is there this association? What is it about religion that leads to violence? Let's explore two fundamental reasons, one that involves the functions of religion and the other the intrinsic nature of human existence. As we think about these issues, keep in mind that we are referring to tightly bounded religions, not religion generally.

Historically, religion has been used for **social control**. As Durkheim points out, human beings order the world around them. We impose the ordering of days, weeks, months, and years; we impose the social order of race, gender, and sexual identities; we impose the order of nations and states on geographic space; and so on. The purpose of all of the ordering is control. We need to control time, physical space, and social relationships. However, because our reality is socially constructed, all of this human order is subject to question—which is why humans need and use legitimation. Religion provides the strongest type of legitimation because it takes responsibility completely out of our hands—society has used religion to justify racial and gender oppression, and many segments of society are currently using religion to control sexual identities. In this sense, religion is used as a social control mechanism, giving privileges to some and not to others, which, of course, intrinsically creates conflict.

Equating human and divine order divides the world into two camps of people, the sacred and the profane—those adhering to God's order (righteous) and those who are not (evil). This kind of dichotomous ordering invariably produces the greatest amount of conflict and war. When there are only two groups or realities, beliefs and people are automatically pitted against one another. Enemies are clearly seen, and the purpose of conflict is viewed as holy. Out-group members are "satanized" (Juergensmeyer, 2000, p. 183). They are seen as the incarnation of evil, just as in-group members are seen as holy. The fate of the unbeliever is clear, and it is an easy step, then, to justify any type of oppressive behavior, from belittling scorn, to killing, to eternal damnation.

Implied in the issue of control is another way in which tightly bounded religion is used: Religion has been utilized to create high levels of motivation. People are of course motivated to action by such basic needs as food and sex, but most of the actions we engage in are meaningful or symbolic in nature. These actions require a motivation that is constructed, which is precisely why Durkheim argues that the emotional component of collective consciousness is so important. We can see this in the idea of the religious warrior. War requires the highest level of sacrifice and motivation, in terms of both willingness to kill and willingness to die. Motivation and legitimation come together and help explain why wars are often viewed in religious terms.

In addition to these uses or functions of religion, there is another reason, more intrinsic to human nature, for the association between religion and violence: **existential angst.** While existential philosophy can be difficult to understand, we can get a handle on this idea fairly easy. Simply put, existential angst is a sense of worry or questions concerning human existence. There are two sources for the worry. The first source is impending death. As far as we know, humans are the only species that knows its life is limited. Death is the great certainty of our life, and it is the certain knowledge of death that makes us anguish over life, that makes us ask, what is the purpose of life?

The other source of existential angst is the fundamental *uncertainty of meaning*. Meaning and order are socially created, and, as humans, we are principally oriented toward meaning. We don't care about things that have no meaning, and apart from meaning, we are confused and don't know how to act. Yet meaning is always imposed; meaning is forever something other than the thing-in-itself. On an unconscious level, we know this, and this knowledge creates a diffuse sense of angst about the social world. In general, this anxiety impels us to find a way to trust in meaning and order, which religion provides. But this anxiety also motivates us to search out experiences that have a sense of ultimate reality, and these experiences tend to involve issues of life and death—in other words, war.

When war and religion come together, they provide experiences of absolute certainty and fundamental reality:

> The enduring attraction of war is this: Even with its destruction and carnage it can give us what we long for in life. It can give us purpose, meaning, a reason for living. . . . And war is an enticing elixir. It gives us resolve, a cause. It allows us to be noble. (Hedges, 2002, p. 3)

As General George S. Patton is reputed to have said, "Compared to war, all other forms of human endeavor shrink to insignificant. God, I do love it so."

The combination of war and religion gives us a sense of rightness and morality about meaning, life, and identity, which is undoubtedly why war takes on symbolic value in religion. This struggle, this war, is seen as a struggle for order against chaos, for light against darkness. Even when there isn't person-to-person violence, the struggle for order continues. The believer is expected to be as diligent as a warrior:

> For our struggle is not against flesh and blood, but against the rulers, against the authorities, against the powers of this dark world and against the spiritual forces of evil in the heavenly realms. Therefore put on the full armor of God. (Ephesians 6:12–13, *New International Version*)

Concepts and Theory: Religious Terrorism

Although there is this general association between religion and violence, people in the United States today are more concerned with the association between religion and terrorism. According to Juergensmeyer, this specific association with terrorism exists for most of the same reasons that religion is generally related to violence. Juergensmeyer (2000) sees religious terror- ism as forms of **ritual performance**, rather than political strategy, and argues that "religion is crucial for these acts, since it gives moral justifications for killing and provides images of cosmic war that allow activists to believe that they are waging spiritual scenarios" (p. xi).

We can understand ritual performance in three ways. First is the way we've been talking about it in this chapter. *Durkheimian rituals* create high levels of emotional energy, which in turn create sacred symbols and group-specific identities and morals. Generally speaking, this type of ritual performance varies by *social network density,* with high network density producing high levels of ritual performance and its effects. Social networks are simply a way of talking about a person's circle of friends and acquaintances and how he or she interacts with them. If a person tends to interact with the same people in the same circumstances over long periods of time, we would say that he or she has high network density with that group of friends. It's really important that you notice something here. The kind of social network a person has actu- ally structures how often he or she will be involved in ritual performance, which, as Durkheim tells us, will influence the kinds of morals, beliefs, group symbols, and so on that the person will have. This kind of network creates a tightly bounded culture, which in turn enables group members to see things in terms of absolute right and wrong, have fundamentally real identities, and have the necessary motivation (emotional energy) to protect their reality and impose it on others. This type of ritual performance is necessary for a terror- ist group to act, whether it's Al Qaeda, the Christian Identity movement, or Reconstruction Theology. Acts of terrorism, in turn, provide further symbols for ritual performance.

The second way that acts of religious terrorism are ritual performances is symbolic. Rituals do more than create high levels of emotional energy. Rituals are also in every case deeply symbolic; they are a form of *dramatic enactment.* Rituals dramatize and remind us of important events, experi- ences, and values. The fireworks at Fourth of July celebrations in the United States, for example, dramatize the "bombs bursting in air." (It's not inci- dental that the full lyrics of "The Star Spangled Banner" end with "Then conquer we must, when our cause it is just, / And this be our motto: 'In God is our trust.'") The September 11 attacks on the World Trade Center, then, were not intended as a beginning invasion of the United States. Their intent was to play out a drama on the world stage. The deaths, including the suicides of the religious warriors, gave the ritual deep meaning. Such a dramatic enactment gives voice to the voiceless.

Rituals can also be *performative*. The difference between performance and performity is that in addition to symbolic value, performity calls something into existence. A clear example is a marriage ceremony. There is quite a bit of symbolism in a wedding, but it also creates something that didn't exist previously (a family). Religious terrorism does the same thing—it's directed toward calling into existence the Kingdom of God, however that might be understood, and modern democracies and states are at odds with the Kingdom. This is important: Modern states intentionally decenter religion, in order to bring equality to more diverse populations. As Juergensmeyer (2000) puts it, "One of the reasons government is easily labeled the enemy of religion is that to some degree it is" (p. 224).

Current religious terrorism is also a response to other influences of **modernization**, specifically cultural and economic ones. *Modern culture* is overwhelmingly popular culture that is commodified and transmitted through mass media. Because its intention is to sell commodities rather than establish, guide, and reinforce social ties, modern culture is egoistically centered on the individual, oriented toward stimulation rather than communication, and is overwhelmingly sexual as it uses sex as a vehicle for advertising. That previous sentence carries a lot in it, but the points it makes are easy to see. Just watch television, see a movie, or look through a magazine. What you'll find are images that are designed to stimulate you, and these images must become more spectacular or bizarre to do so. (Just compare the original *Frankenstein* film to the latest installment in the *Saw* series.) You'll also find advertisements and product placement everywhere, and you'll see that sexual images permeate the media. This entire media barrage is directed at you as an individual, because you are the one who must be enticed to buy. A member of modern culture is thus diametrically opposed to the religiously informed traditional cultures of terrorist groups. They rightly see this culture as a threat to their morals, values, and way of life.

These religious groups also see the *capitalist economy* as intrinsically exploitive. Most of the "developing" nations that are being brought into the world economy are at the bottom of the food chain. The products they are given to produce are the ones that have the lowest profit margin. As new products are created for the fully modernized nations to produce, such as computer technologies and pharmaceuticals, the older products that are no longer protected under patent laws are given to these fledgling economies. In addition, these modernizing economies do not have the worker protection and environmental laws that restrict capitalist profit in more developed countries.

Juergensmeyer (2000) gives us three factors that indicate **religious terrorism** is likely to explode (pp. 162–162). Two are related to the symbolic value of the conflict. First, if the conflict is defined in terms of *transcendent rather than rational goals,* the tension is likely to be seen as cosmic war. Holy wars are not fought for gain in *this* world, which is why, when the United States goes to war, it is characterized in terms of freedom and democracy rather than economic ends. These kinds of issues are related to basic identity and dignity. Second, if *losing the struggle is unthinkable,* then there is further impetus to see the conflict in cosmic or holy terms. One reason why fundamentalist religions create transcendent goals and unthinkable loss comes back to Durkheimian rituals. Remember, rituals are possible because they evoke a single focus of attention, and that's what we see in these first two factors. The presence of rational rather than transcendent goals opens the possibility of negotiation, of pursuing different means to achieve similar goals, rather than a single focus. Goals that are based in otherworldly concerns, on the other hand, don't allow the possibility of negotiation. This is one reason why the loss of such a struggle is unthinkable.

The third factor in cosmic war is in some ways the most important. If *resolving the conflict seems hopeless* for the group, the likelihood of terrorism increases. Generally speaking, historic religions have met the first two criteria. Such religious forms are unquestionably founded on transcendent goals that are non-negotiable. One of the primary differences between the terrorism of Al Qaeda today and the 200 years of the Crusades waged by the European Christian Church is that the Christian Church was a powerful political entity capable of achieving its goals in real time, and Al Qaeda is not. It is perhaps this factor more than any other that defines terrorist acts as symbolic performances.

The Craft of Citizenship   Religion

The Basics: Comprehension and Explanation

- What are Durkheim's questions? What questions is Bellah asking? How are Bellah's questions related to Durkheim's? In the section "The God of War," I don't provide you with a specific question. If you were to phrase the subject in that section as a question, what would it be? How does that question relate to Durkheim's and Bellah's concerns?

- List and define the most important terms for each theorist. There are a good number of terms that are in bold—which of those do you think are absolutely necessary to understand the theories? Don't feel as if you need to include all terms, but know why you include some and exclude others.

  ➤ *Helpful hints:* The most important terms are the ones that you absolutely need in order to answer the theorists' questions.

- According to Durkheim, what is the problem of modernity? How did it come about, and how can it be solved?
- Explain Durkheim's theory of ritual.
- How does Durkheim's assumption of human nature inform his theorizing?
- Explain Bellah's theory of civil religion and how it answers the problem that Durkheim left us: What form of religion can take up where the "old gods" left off and provide a belief system for modernity?
- Explain how religion evolved into its present form.

  ➤ *Helpful hints:* This is a more general question than my asking you to explain Bellah's theory of religious evolution. So you'll have to draw from our discussions of both Weber and Bellah to answer this question.

- Under what conditions do democratic tensions devolve into religious terrorism?
- Explain why religion is generally associated with violence.

Skill Set 1: Inference and Application

- What does the idea of culture generalization imply about religion in modernity?
- Using Durkheim's ideas of mechanical and organic solidarity, explain why democracy is specifically fitting for modernity.
- What are the implications of your religious practices and beliefs for a democratic society? In other words, how do your religious practices and beliefs hinder or further democratic energies?

  ➤ *Helpful hints:* This is not an easy task, but it is a necessary one given the demands of democracy and critical thinking. The issue here isn't whether your religion is right or wrong. For this task, that isn't important. Here, you want to understand how your religion impacts society.

  ➤ *Helpful hints:* You aren't off the hook if you claim to have no religious beliefs and practices. Given what the theorists in this chapter as well as Chapter 2 have to say, what are the implications for democracy and society if you have no religious practices and beliefs?

(Continued)

(Continued)

- Define ritual using all the elements presented in this chapter. Come up with at least two examples of each type of ritual that you see in your life.

Skill Set 2: Interpretation, Analysis, Evaluation, Synthesis

- Using Durkheim, Bellah, and the material in "The God of War" section, construct a comprehensive definition of religion.
- What does Durkheim add to your understanding of society (what it is and how it works)?
- Explain Bellah's ideas of tightly and loosely bounded cultures using Durkheim's theory of ritual performance.
- In addition to civil religion, Bellah also tells us that religion itself is necessary for democracy. Yet religion can also generate antidemocratic energies that result in terrorism. What kind of religion can generate democratic tension and discourse without becoming militant?
- How does Durkheim's theory of the collective consciousness in modernity elaborate Alexander's ideas of tension, diversity, and universal commitment to diversity?
- Compare and contrast Alexander's and Bellah's arguments concerning the source of cultural tension necessary for democracy.
- Compare and contrast Perinbanayagam's theory of identity with that of Bellah in terms of their explanatory power (the limits of what they explain). How can these two theories be brought together to form a single, more powerful understanding of identity?

5

Capitalism

Adam Smith is often considered the founder of free market capitalism, the person who more than any other before him explained that modern governments should not interfere with capitalist enterprise. Smith (1776/1937) articulated that capitalism is the result of social evolution, a superior economic system that would preserve the natural rights of humanity:

> The obvious and simple system of natural liberty establishes itself of its own accord. Every man . . . is left perfectly free to pursue his own interest his own way, and to bring both his industry and capital into competition with those of any other man, or order of men. (p. 247)

The reason that capitalism shouldn't be regulated is because it, like biological evolution, contains a type of natural selection dynamic that Smith called "the invisible hand." Unfettered competition would weed out weaker businesses, regulate prices, and result in the best product for the least cost. In this free market capitalism, which Smith termed "economic individualism," the differences in wealth or social standing among people would be the result of their own actions and effort.

That was the hope and the ideal. While capitalism did achieve some of its goals, the reality, especially in the early stages of development, in the opening decades of the 1800s, was quite different from the ideal. Child labor was common, with children as young as four being forced to work in factories and mines, and many lost their lives or were maimed. (Child labor is a continuing issue in developing nations.) There were no safety regulations, there was no minimum wage, no limit on hours worked, no health insurance, and so on. Rather than producing an even playing field, if left to itself, capitalism produces monopolies and insurmountable gaps between the rich and poor. Thus, instead of uplifting the dignity of humankind, capitalism will push exploitation to its furthest limits. My purpose here isn't to rehash the litany of early abuses of capitalism. Rather, I want you to see the ideal of capitalism in modernity on the one hand, and on the other, the unanticipated consequences of that system. This world of early capitalism is the one that Karl Marx spoke to. He was among the first to see that capitalism contained intrinsic elements that would create conditions antithetical to its goals and that would in the long run destroy it. He also argued that capitalism produces **ideology**, false beliefs that keep people from truly seeing the damaging effects of capitalism.

Jürgen Habermas argues that ideology is actually a bigger problem than Marx first thought. It's diffused throughout the entire social system, affecting both owners and workers alike, and it ends up destroying democracy. Habermas works in a theoretical discipline called critical theory, or the Frankfurt School, formed in the early 1920s. Though there were many reasons why the school and its critical theory approach came into existence, a primary one was a response to the rise of Nazism in Germany. The propaganda machine in back of Nazism and the subsequent atrocities left the world stunned at the human capacity for inhumanity. It was clear that what happened in Germany was rooted in culture and enforced by propaganda. The sociological attempt at understanding this horror demanded that culture be studied as an independent entity, something Marx didn't want to do. Ideology thus became seen as something different, something more insidious, than perhaps Marx had first suspected.

Yet Marx was specifically concerned with the way in which class is structured. You'll remember that sociologists use the idea of structure to explain how things are patterned over time. So one of the paramount questions about capitalism is why there is so little social mobility: How are class inequalities structured across time and generations? Later in the chapter, Pierre Bourdieu gives a unique and insightful answer to that Marxian question. Rather than ideology and false consciousness (defined further below), Bourdieu argues that class is structured in our bodies—by our bodily habits, ways of speaking, tastes, and so forth. Furthermore, the competition for scarce resources is played out in symbolic markets.

The Contradictions of Capitalism—Karl Marx

Karl Marx (1818–1883) was born in Trier, Germany. His parents were Jewish, and he came from a long line of rabbis on both sides of the family. In fact, Marx's father was the first to have a secular education: He was a lawyer who was baptized Protestant in an attempt to avoid anti-Semitism. Marx studied law at the University of Bonn and philosophy at the University of Berlin. He finished his studies at the University of Jena with a dissertation on the philosophies of Democritus and Epicurus. One of his mentors, Bruno Bauer, had recently been dismissed from the university for holding politically incorrect views. Reading the writing on the wall, Marx turned his attention to writing and editing rather than university work, though he continually battled government censorship. Marx moved from Germany to Brussels, Paris, and eventually London. His writings were instrumental in founding one of the first labor unions, the First International. The movement, and Marx's involvement, continued to gain strength worldwide until the Paris Commune of 1871, when the working people took over Paris, which ended in the massacre of thousands of workers. Other than the three-volume *Das Kapital* (Capital), most of Marx's significant writings are shorter works; a good compilation may be found in *The Marx–Engels Reader* (1848/1978), edited by Robert C. Tucker.

Concepts and Theory: The Structure of Capitalism

Marx argues that human history began with the first economic act, and that history moves, or society changes, as economic production changes. By itself, this isn't such a radical idea. We say something similar when we talk about agrarian and industrial societies. Though Marx would accept what we've said so far, he is also saying something a bit more profound. The existence of every animal is tied up with the way it survives. Marx argues that the principal way humans survive is through the economy, and so there is a natural connection between the worker and the product. Thus, different economic forms impact human nature differently. Moreover, not only will different forms impact human nature, the degree to which an economic form is in harmony with true human nature has implications for the economy as well.

In humanity's purest economic form, people produced what they needed through collective cooperation, what Marx calls "primitive communism." It began small, but eventually we started using economic systems that were contrary to the social nature of humans. In these economies, the structures have contradictions that will eventually destroy it because the system is out of sync with the social, collective nature of people. Marx talks about these economic antagonisms or contradictions as **dialectical materialism**. The *material* in his use of materialism isn't the physical universe as it is with most philosophers; it's the world of material goods that people create. The word *dialectic* looks very much like dialogue; in fact, the two words are related. In this case, the dialogue is among the contradictions present in every economic form except communism.

Marx is saying that every economic system, other than one that is socially and collectively based, contains contradictions. These structural contradictions create tensions within the economy that push it toward change by resolving the contradictions in some way. In capitalism, for example, there are things that capitalists must do (such as expanding markets) that naturally create pressures within capitalism (such as **overproduction**) that will eventually lead to its downfall. Notice that the contradictions, while detrimental, are necessary for the economic system. These economic contradictions are what produce history—the contradictions are the energy that pushes for social change. According to Marx, the economic system with the most powerful contradictions—the one most out of touch with human nature—is capitalism. We'll come across the idea of dialecticism again, but for now, keep these features in mind: (1) A dialectic contains different elements that are necessarily locked together in some kind of tension, (2) a dialectic thus implies a dynamic process, and (3) a dialectic inevitably brings change that comes out of and is related to the initial tensions.

Private Property

Without **private property,** capitalism couldn't exist. It's the idea that allows others to own the means of production as well as the products. We need to also understand that the idea we have of private property is distinctly modern. During the founding of modernity, private property was hotly debated. One issue was based on the assumption that God had given the earth to humanity as a whole. Eventually, of course, these rights to property were assured in such documents as the Constitution of the United States (the Fifth and the Fourteenth Amendments). My point is that the modern idea of private property was an achievement and was seen as something that needed explaining and legitimation. For Marx, the idea of private property couldn't exist without a more primary factor, **alienation.** Marx uses the term in four ways: separation from the product, separation from the work process, separation from others, and separation from one's human nature. For now I want us to focus on separation from the product. To truly understand Marx's theory, we have to always keep in mind his idea of human nature, and the connection between the producer and the product. Every product by nature belongs to its producer. This implies that in order for private property to exist—in order for someone else besides the worker to own the product—the worker must first be separated from the work of his or her own hands. In the idea of private property, then, the humanity of the product is denied; it is based on alienated labor.

Creating Class

As we've seen, economic **class** was intended to set free the natural potential within each woman and man. What resulted was the furthest thing from that goal. The reason is that class distinctions are based on alienation. Here we want to think about the second and third kinds of alienation—separation from the work process and alienation from others. These two forms of alienation are linked to Marx's main concerns with capitalism, which are the means and relations of production. For Marx, the **means of production** include the capitalist system and industrialization—those are the means through which production is accomplished. By definition, the capitalist system alienates the worker from the work process; the use of machinery to augment the production process further separates the worker. The **relations of production** include our relationship to our self and to others.

The reason the means of production can impact our psychological, personal, and social relations is that human nature is defined through production. Marx is saying that as a result of private property and capitalist ownership of the means of production, we are cut off from true human, social relations. Imagine a world in which everything you owned reflected the people you know and your relationships with them. That world of social connectivity would be utterly different from the world we live in today, where our only connection to the things we have is money. If our relationships with other people aren't true social relationships, what are they? They are class relationships, and class relationships in capitalism are based on money and exploitation. Capitalism "has left remaining no other nexus between man and man than naked self-interest, than callous 'cash payment'" (Marx & Engels, 1848/1978, p. 475).

Contained within the means and relations of production is the **division of labor**. This idea concerns the way in which work is divided in any economy. For Marx, there are fundamental differences between a voluntary and a forced division of labor. Under voluntary labor, people are allowed to work at those jobs that are an expression of their natural talents and skills. In capitalism, however, people are forced to work at jobs or die, and most often these jobs are alienating. Under a severe division of labor, as in assembly lines, an individual's relationship to the means of production is piecemeal, without any complete sense of his or her relationship to the world of production. Under these conditions, the humanness of our relationships with the self and others is alienated. As Marx (1932/1995) says,

> We arrive at the result that man (the worker) feels himself to be freely active only in his animal functions—eating, drinking, and procreating, or at most also in his dwelling and in personal adornment—while in his human functions he is reduced to an animal. The animal becomes human and the human becomes animal. (p. 99)

By definition, class relations in capitalism are based on exploitation. **Exploitation** is the appropriation of another's labor for profit and is a measurable entity. It's the difference between what you get paid and what you actually earn or produce. Capitalists must pay workers less than they earn, and they will always gravitate to the lowest possible wage. The lowest amount is set by two things: bare sustenance plus any social amenities deemed necessary. Marx calls this necessary labor, and the difference between what a worker gets paid (necessary labor) and what he or she earns is surplus labor, or exploitation. The level of exploitation is increased through extending the work day (absolute surplus labor) and through **industrialization** and technology (relative surplus labor). Thus, part of the reason that capitalism failed to produce a level playing field is that by its nature capitalism is built upon alienation and exploitation. The beginning premises are at odds with the social project of modernity. The way capitalism structures class is also at odds with equality and freedom. Further, exploitation itself implies a contradiction: It is the power through which the capitalist controls the worker, and at the same time, it is the leverage that workers can use to improve their condition in life, through such things as unions and worker strikes.

Capitalism's Primary Contradiction: Overproduction

One of the defining features of modern capitalism is the endless pursuit of **accumulation.** People have always sold products to make money. The difference is that in modern capitalism, people sell commodities to make money in order to invest it. Thus, modern capitalism is characterized by the endless accumulation of capital to create more capital. As we've seen, there is a relationship between **industrialization** and profit. There is also a relationship among markets, commodification, and profit. In fact, industrialization, markets, and commodification work together to increase profit margins and thus accumulation.

The idea of **commodification** is about the process of creating commodities, things to buy and sell. Part of that is obviously wrapped up in production. But underlying both commodification and production is another, more profound idea: Human beings can create new or *relative* needs (felt needs above simple sustenance). Organically, our basic needs include food, shelter, and clothing. But that isn't where our needs stop. In contrast to other animals, we are actually able to create new needs. For example, one of the main reasons that you likely own an iPod is that the market for cassette tape players and compact discs bottomed out. Most people who were going to buy a CD player had already done so, and the only time another would be purchased is for replacement, or an improvement in that technology. Both of these motivations for purchase are limited, so capitalists invented something new for you to buy in order for their profit margin to increase. So far, the theoretical relationships we have described look something like this: Drive for profit → accumulation of capital for investment → increases in commodification and industrialization → expansion of existing and creation of new needs and markets → profit → investment → commodification and industrialization → market expansion, and so on.

Together, this continuous expansion of commodification and production inevitably leads to overproduction—too much production for the current demand. Capitalists will continue to create new and produce existing commodities until the market will no longer bear it. When this happens, production is cut back, workers are laid off, and the economy slumps. Small businesses collapse and capital is concentrated in fewer hands; capital is thus accumulated, and the failures of small businesses increase the size of the working class. With the renewed accumulation of capital, the market picks back up and the cycle starts again. Each economic cycle is larger and deeper than the previous, and the working class becomes larger and larger. Over time, then, class is structured around two polar opposites, the bourgeoisie (owners) and proletariat (workers). In the end, accumulation, overproduction, and the bipolarization of classes will lead to the collapse of capitalism. Yet before the collapse takes place, there must be a change in people's awareness of the issues.

Concepts and Theory: Class Consciousness

As we've seen, Marx argues that all animals are defined by the way in which they survive or adapt to their environment. In other words, the reason birds and lions are different is that they adapt differently to the natural environment. Everything that makes a bird a bird—wings, feathers, beak, and so on—is there because it enables birds to live. Similarly, everything that defines human beings is determined by economic production. But note this: Rather than living in harmony with their environment, as do other animals, humans create their own environment. Wherever you are, look around. What do you see? You may see a desk, chair, walls, lights, house, streets, and so on, but if you took it all together, what one thing would you see? You see human production; you see human nature. Seeing our product, and seeing ourselves in the product, is what makes us conscious of the unique features of humankind. Marx refers to this idea of human nature as **species-being** (or species existence). Marx (1932/1978a) argues that human consciousness comes out of economic production: "The production of ideas, of conceptions, of consciousness, is at first directly interwoven with the material activity and the material intercourse of men, *the language of real life*" (p. 154, emphasis added). Notice the emphasized section: The language of real life is the language of material, economic activity. In species-being, production acts like a mirror—we see human nature reflected in the world that we produce and we thus create consciousness, shared ideas and sentiments. Again, imagine a world where every product that you use brings a sense of awareness of the people who made it, your social connections to them, and a sense of the humanness and humanity of the social world.

Commodification of Consciousness

But that's not our world. Rather, our world is a world of commodities. Commodification translates all human activity and relations into objects that can be bought or sold. In this process, value is determined not by any intrinsic feature of the activity or social relations, but by the impersonal forces of markets and the drive for profit, over which individuals have no control. In commodification, the objects and social relations that will truly gratify human needs are hidden, and the commodified object is internalized and accepted as reality. Thus, our consciousness—our fundamental awareness of the world—is a **false consciousness**.

As a result, we become obsessed with commodities. We intrinsically know that our nature is tied up with creative production—we know that we should see our nature and self in products—and we try to fill that need by purchasing. Marx calls this drive and resulting emptiness **commodity fetishism**. We buy commodities and then more commodities in a mindless search for substance, reality, and fulfillment. But each time we are left with emptiness, because the commodity itself is empty. The insidious thing about this fetish is that it is never-ending—first, because the humanity has been leached out of the product and our efforts at fulfillment through purchase are doomed to fail, and second, because commodification has no limits, based as it is upon the creation of relative or nonessential needs.

Further, in commodity fetishism, we **misrecognize** the social relations in the product. Rather than human relations, it contains relations of exploitation. That is, rather than our judging the worth of a product based upon the labor it took to make it and thus its human merit, we see only the value as measured in dollars.

> Money is the *pimp* between man's need and the object, between his life and his means of life. But that which mediates *my* life for me, also *mediates* the existence of other people *for me*. For me it is the *other* person. (Marx, 1932/1978b, p. 102, emphasis original)

Ideology and Reification

In consciousness that has become commodified, we believe in ideologies. For Marx (1932/1978a), **ideology** originates with the elite: "The ideas of the ruling class are in every epoch the ruling ideas" (p. 172). So, ideology originates from the people who benefit most from the economic system, and it functions to legitimate the system. This notion that ideology is created by the elite to suppress the lower classes became known as the *dominant ideology thesis*. This is a top-down approach to understanding ideology, and it portrays ideology as a cohesive whole: a collection of ideas that work together to protect the interests of the ruling class.

There's something important to note here: The elite ideology can legitimate a system of inequality because the ideas are universalized. That is, ideology appears to be based on high morals or beliefs. For example, the feudal system was legitimated through the idea of "the divine right of kings to rule," and the ancient caste system in India was legitimated through belief in reincarnation. People misrecognize what's going on— their awareness of the world is false—and in such a condition, people participate in their own oppression. Marx argues that all true ideas must have a connection to the real world, the world of material production and the social relations that emerge. These ideas are historically specific, because they are related to social production that changes with time. Ideological beliefs, on the other hand, are seen as timeless.

Of course, the most timeless beliefs are those associated with religion. For Marx, **religion** is the archetypal form of ideology. It is based on an abstract idea, like God, rather than the firm reality of human production. Religion is seen as the way through which humans can come to know their true nature. So, for example, in the evangelical Christian faith, believers are exhorted to repent from not only their sinful ways, but also their sinful nature, and to be born again with a new nature—the true nature of humankind. Christians are encouraged to become Christ-like, because they have been created in the image of God. Religion thus takes an abstract (God), treats it as if it is materially real (**reification**), and then replaces real, materially based human nature (species-being) with non-materially based ideas of spirituality (alienation).

Religion, like the commodity fetish, erroneously attributes reality and causation. Just as with commodities, we pour ourselves out, this time into a religious idea, and we misrecognize our own nature as that of a god or devil. As Marx (1932/1978b) says,

> It is clear that the more the worker spends himself . . . the poorer he himself— his inner world—becomes, the less belongs to him as his own. It is the same with religion. The more man puts into God, the less he retains in himself. (p. 72)

The Production of Class Consciousness

Marx's solution to ideology and false consciousness is the creation of **class consciousness**. Marx notes that classes exist objectively, whether we are aware of them or not. He refers to this as a "class in itself," that is, an aggregate of people who have a common relationship to the means of production. But classes can also exist subjectively, as a "class *for* itself." Class consciousness refers to the latter. Class consciousness has two parts: The first is the subjective awareness that experiences of deprivation are determined by structured class relations and not individual talent and effort, and the second is the group identity that comes from such awareness. Part of what helps create this political sense of class are alienation and exploitation. We talked about their structural qualities in the previous chapter, but Marx also calls attention to our feelings of alienation and **exploitation**. According to Marx, we are alienated, exploited, and financially oppressed in capitalism, but **ideology** blinds us to our condition. The question then becomes, how can people who have false consciousness and believe an ideology come to have a truer consciousness, a critical consciousness that sees the reality of class?

For Marx, this shift in consciousness is initially brought about because of certain structural conditions. The structural factors aren't enough—the creation of a critical consciousness still takes work on our part—but the structures open up the possibility of class consciousness. Structurally, class consciousness is dependent upon increasing levels of **industrialization**, worker education, geographic concentration (urbanization), and increasing levels of communication and transportation technologies. All of these structural factors are set in place by the intrinsic nature of capitalism. In order to increase profits, capitalists industrialize and create large factories and urban centers. The close proximity of workers, not only at the factory but also in neighborhoods, makes it easier for workers to communicate; and increasing education, demanded by higher technologies, makes the workers better able to communicate and to be critical of their situation. As we've seen, capitalism motivates people to increase the size of markets, which also pushes for increases in transportation and communication technologies. These, in turn, facilitate worker communication across geographic locations.

The issues that we're talking about—ideology and false consciousness— are broadly understood as questions of culture, but Marx is a structuralist. He sees the economic structure as the most important social factor in creating and changing society, including such cultural issues as ideology and false consciousness. Thinking like this ties structure and culture together in a way that makes culture dependent upon structure. Culture may reinforce class inequalities, but culture doesn't work independently from structure. However, many contemporary theorists see these as distinct domains. In other words, the things that influence consciousness may lie outside the structure of the economy. This approach is the one Habermas takes, and it originated in the Frankfurt School.

Colonization of Democracy—Jürgen Habermas

Jürgen Habermas (1929–) was born in Düsseldorf, Germany. His teen years were spent under Nazi rule, which undoubtedly gave Habermas his drive for freedom and democracy. His educational background is primarily in philosophy, but also includes German literature, history, and psychology. In 1956, Habermas took a position as Theodor Adorno's assistant at the Institute of Social Research in Frankfurt, which began his formal association with the Frankfurt School of critical thought. In 1961, Habermas took a professorship at the University of Heidelberg, but returned to Frankfurt in 1964 as a professor of philosophy and sociology. From 1971 to 1981, Habermas worked as the director of the Max Planck Institute, where he began to formalize his theory of communicative action. In 1982, Habermas returned to Frankfurt, where he stayed until his retirement in 1994. Among his most important works are *The Theory of Communicative Action* (vols. 1 & 2), *The Structural Transformation or the Public Sphere: An Inquiry Into a Category of Bourgeois Society, The Philosophical Discourse of Modernity: Twelve Lectures,* and *On the Logic of the Social Sciences.* Habermas is centrally concerned with how knowledge and ideology are produced in advanced capitalist countries.

Ways of Knowing: A Critique of Positivism

As mentioned, Habermas' roots are deep in the Frankfurt School. In general, the Frankfurt School took ideas from Karl Marx, Max Weber, and Sigmund Freud. Marx gave the school the central concepts of ideology and false consciousness; and Weber gave these early critical theorists a conceptual path to understand culture as an independent social factor. The inclusion of Freud was especially significant because of the way he conceptualized the psyche: The ego and superego come into existence as the id encounters the culture as well as the structures of society. The Frankfurt School thus focused on the social production of knowledge and its relationship to human consciousness. Like Marx, the Frankfurt School focuses on ideology, but unlike Marx, its critical theory sees ideological production as linked to culture and knowledge rather than class and the material relations of production.

Specifically, Habermas argues that there are three kinds of **knowledge** and interests: empirical, analytic knowledge that is interested in the technical control of the environment (science); hermeneutic or interpretive knowledge that is interested in human understanding and cooperation; and critical knowledge that is interested in emancipation. Because scientific knowledge seeks to explain the dynamic processes found within a given phenomenon, social science is historically bound. That is, it only sees things as they currently exist. That being the case, scientific knowledge of human institutions and behaviors can only describe and thus reinforce existing political arrangements (since society is taken "as is").

Further, positivistic social science is blind to its own conditions of knowledge: It uncritically places itself fully within the political and economic framework of modernity and then claims to express objective truth or knowledge. The main problem is that the social science model has bought into the wrong part of the discourse of modernity. Remember the first assumption of science: The universe is empirical and objective. It's out there, and we can observe it objectively and discover how it works. But human beings aren't simply objective; they are subjectively oriented toward meaning. Society is not "out there" in the same way the moon is. We can study the moon objectively because it truly exists apart from us; if human beings had never existed, the moon would still be exactly what and where it is. But this can't be said about society. Human beings make up society; it exists only because of us. Therefore, according to critical theory, we can't stand outside of it to create objective knowledge.

Critical theory, on the other hand, purposefully stands within the social world where the dramas of oppression and social justice are played out. Rather than aligning itself with the assumption of objectivity, as social science has done, critical knowledge embraces the democratic project as its foundation. Its values, then, are known, questioned, and at the center of the production of critical knowledge, rather than hidden and denied as in social science. The intent of critical knowledge is to further the democratic project and social justice by exposing the distortions, misrepresentations, and political values found in our knowledge and speech. Generally speaking, there are five characteristics of critical theory: (1) a critique of positivism and the idea that knowledge can be value free, (2) an emphasis on the relationship between history and society on the one hand and social position and knowledge on the other, (3) the need for *praxis* or emancipatory practices, (4) a desire for participatory democracy, and (5) a sense (and consensus) of where society ought to be heading.

Concepts and Theory: Liberal Capitalism and the Public Sphere

The combination of the ideals of the Enlightenment, the transformation of government from feudalism to nation-state democracy, and the rise of capitalism created something that had never before existed. Habermas calls this new space the **public sphere**. (Be very careful here with terminology; this is the same early modern arena that Alexander calls civil society.) The public sphere is a space for democratic, public debate. The ideals of the Enlightenment indicated that this citizenry would be informed and completely engaged in the democratic process, and the public sphere is where this strong democracy could take place. Habermas sees the public sphere as existing between a set of cultural institutions and practices on one side and state power on the other. The function of the public sphere is to mediate the concerns of private citizens and state interests. There are two principles of this public sphere: access to unlimited information and equal participation. The public sphere thus consists of cultural organizations such as journals and newspapers that distribute information to the people, and it contains both political and commercial organizations where public discussion can take place, such as public assemblies, coffee shops, pubs, political clubs, and so forth. The goal of this public sphere is pragmatic consensus.

The public sphere was able to exist in part because of the institutional space that liberal capitalism provided. **Liberal capitalism** occurred during the time when modernity was beginning, before the abuses that concerned Marx. During liberal capitalism, the relationship between the state and capitalism could best be characterized as *laissez-faire,* which is French for "allow to do." The assumption undergirding this policy was that the individual will contribute most successfully to the good of the whole if left to his or her own aspirations. The place of government, then, should be as far away from capitalism as possible. In this way of thinking, capitalism represents the mechanism of equality, the place where the best people are defined through successful competition rather than by family ties. Thus, during liberal capitalism, it was felt that the marketplace of capitalism had to be completely free from any interference so that the most successful could rise to the top.

Organized Capitalism

However, two demons intrinsic to capitalism raised their heads to put an end to liberal capitalism and, thus, the public sphere: monopolies and economic fluctuations, both of which Marx had predicted. Despite the promise of capitalism, free markets in practice tend to create monopolies, rather than producing equal competitors on an even playing field. Thus, by the end of the nineteenth and beginning of the twentieth century, the U.S. economy was essentially run by an elite group of businessmen. Perhaps the attitude of these capitalists is best captured by the phrase attributed to William H. Vanderbilt, a railroad tycoon: "The public be damned." The response of the U.S. government to widespread monopolization was to enact antitrust laws, beginning with the Sherman Antitrust Act of 1890.

The second problem with capitalism's promise is the fact that it is susceptible to economic fluctuations. As Marx had indicated, capitalist economies are subject to periodic oscillations, with downturns becoming harsher over time. By the end of the 1920s, the capitalist economic system had gone into severe decline, creating worldwide depression in the decade of the thirties. What had come to be called "classic economics" fell out of favor, and myriad competing theories clamored to take its place. Eventually, the ideas of John Maynard Keynes took hold and were explicated in his 1936 book, *The General Theory of Employment, Interest and Money*. His main idea was simple, and reminiscent of Marx: Capitalism tends toward overproduction—the capacity of the system to produce and transport products is greater than the demand. Keynes' theory countered the then-popular belief in the invisible hand of the market and argued that active government spending and management of the economy would reduce the power and magnitude of the business cycle.

Keynes' ideas initially influenced Franklin D. Roosevelt's belief that insufficient demand produced the Depression; and after World War II, Keynes' ideas were generally accepted. Governments began to keep statistics about the economy, expanded their control of capitalism, and increased spending in order to keep demand up. This new approach continued through the 1950s and 1960s. While the economic problems of the 1970s cast doubt upon Keynesian economics, new economic policies continued to include some level of government spending and economic manipulation. Thus, due to the tendency of completely free markets to produce monopolies and periodic fluctuations, the state became progressively much more involved in the control of the economy. **Organized capitalism**, then, is a kind of capitalism where economic practices are controlled, governed, or organized by the state. Under organized capitalism, the state intrudes upon the domain of the economy. In many ways, this is obviously a good thing—otherwise the market would be ruled by monopolies, and the economy would be cycling ever deeper through crises. At the same time, the state's regulatory impact on people's lives increases as well. The state and government's primary medium—power— becomes increasingly important in the lifeworld.

Colonization of the Lifeworld and Public Sphere

The idea of the **lifeworld** comes into sociology through the work of Alfred Schutz. It refers to the world as an individual experiences it; it is the commonsense world of everyday reality. There are a few important things to see about this concept. First, the lifeworld has limits; it doesn't refer to all social existence. The limits of the lifeworld are the limits of your experiences. Second, it's a world of everyday meanings. Here, meanings emerge through interactions and encounters with others and through a person's sets of assumptions, beliefs, and meanings against which the individual judges and interprets everyday experiences. Third, the idea focuses analysis upon the actual experience of the person. The analysis of race, for example, would shift away from an emphasis on structure and be concerned with the experience of being black. And, finally, the function or purpose of the lifeworld is communication that produces consensus.

By definition, then, the lifeworld is the primary place of friends, family, and real communication. It's the place where we come face-to-face with others, the place of mutual understanding, socialization, and integration. Habermas (1981/1984, 1981/1987) claims that this lifeworld has been colonized. The meaning of *colony* is important. According to Merriam-Webster (2002), a colony is "a body of people settled in a new territory, foreign and often distant, retaining ties with their motherland or parent state . . . as a means of facilitating established occupation and [governance] by the parent state." Colonizing is thus a method of controlling by placing elements of the original system within the colony.

According to Habermas (1981/1984, 1981/1987), the **colonization of the lifeworld** has involved both the economy and the state. This means that in organized capitalism, certain elements of the state and economy have become too important and highly valued in the lifeworld. The lifeworld values under liberal capitalism and the public sphere involved beliefs in progress, communicative action, and consensus. These values, however, have been put aside. We now tend to value power and money over any of these democratic values. The state protects the worker through laws governing minimum wages, safety, health care, social security, and so forth. In doing so, the state also creates specific types of people and cultures. Under organized capitalism, we become clients and consumers. Our lifeworld is now a world of entitlement and power.

Money and power have a certain logic or rationality to them. Habermas uses Max Weber's forms of rationality to talk about their influence. Weber talked about four distinct forms of rationality, two of which are pertinent here: instrumental and value rationality. *Value rationality* is governed by ethical principles. This kind of behavior is engaged in because the person believes in the intrinsic worth of the ethic. *Instrumental rationality,* on the other hand, is action that is strategic and motivated by means-and-ends calculation.

Value rationality is specifically tied to the lifeworld and instrumental rationality to the state and economy. Thus, what happens when the lifeworld is colonized by the ever-increasing intrusion of instrumental rationality and the emptying of value rationality from the social system is that "systemic mechanisms—for example, money—steer a social intercourse that has been largely disconnected from norms and values. . . . [N]orm-conformative attitudes and identity-forming social memberships are neither necessary nor possible" (Habermas, 1981/1987, p. 154). In turn, people in this kind of modern social system come to value money and power, which are seen as the principal means of success and happiness. The high value we place on money and power is the antithesis of open communication and consensus building, the cornerstones of democracy. A lifeworld colonized by money and power cannot build consensus through reasoning and communication, and people in this kind of lifeworld lose their sense of responsibility to the democratic ideals of the Enlightenment. In short, *clients and consumers are not citizens.*

In addition to an unencumbered lifeworld, the kind of free speech that democracy requires is based on free and accurate information. That's one of the reasons for freedom of the press—democratic citizens require all possible information in order to become engaged in public discussions over pertinent issues. The social space where that kind of information is supposed to be available is the **public sphere**. However, in organized capitalism, the public sphere has been colonized as well. The public sphere, rather than a social space dominated by independent news sources and active places of public debate, has become the place of public opinion and news entertainment.

Public opinion is something that is manufactured through social science. It's a statistic, not a public forum or debate that results in consensus. It is constructed through opinion polls taking snapshots of individualized views on items selected for people and companies who purchase the information. Public opinions aren't the result of vibrant lifeworld discussions where the ideas that matter emerge. Rather, the people who decide which issues are placed on the polls are companies who want to use poll results in some capitalist venture, or politicians looking for the right spin to get them elected. Rather than a public sphere motivated by the search for information in an age of reason, most of the venues through which we obtain our news and information today are motivated by profit. In other words, news media aren't primarily concerned with creating a democratic citizenry or with making available information that is socially significant. As such, information that is given out is packaged as entertainment most of the time. In a society like the United States, the consumers of mass media are more infatuated with "wicked weather" than they are concerned about the state of the homeless.

Further, the information these polls produce is itself antidemocratic. These polls are carried out through social science methodologies. By assuming that the universe is empirical, science objectifies nature and thus makes it something that can be used—controlled—without remorse. This insight is even truer when we're talking about human beings. When the scientific approach is used to study people, it automatically objectifies them and implicitly seeks to predict and control behaviors. Even if the researcher claims that he or she is only studying society as it exists, for no other purpose than explaining how it works, the way society works is through the unequal distribution of scarce resources, and simply studying it leaves it unchallenged and merely replicates it.

Concepts and Theory: Rebuilding Democracy

However, there is a way out of the ideological colonization of the lifeworld and public sphere. Unlike Marx, who focused on the structural conditions of praxis, Habermas sees the potential of overcoming ideology in every act of speech. Praxis for Habermas is centered in communication and the creation of ideal speech communities. Here, communication is a skill, one that as democratic citizens we need to cultivate in order to participate in the civil society. As we consider these points of the **ideal speech community**, notice how many of them have to do more with listening than with speaking. In an ideal speech situation,

- Every person who is competent to speak and act is allowed to partake in the conversation—full equality is granted, and each person is seen as an equal source of legitimate or valid statements.
- There is no sense of coercion; consensus is not forced; and there is no falling back on objective standings such as status, money, or power.
- Anyone can introduce any topic, anyone can disagree with or question any topic, and everyone is allowed to express opinions and feelings about all topics.
- Each person strives to keep his or her speech free from ideology. (Habermas, 1992/1996)

Let me point out that this is an ideal against which all speech acts can be compared, and toward which all democratic communication must strive. The closer a community's speech comes to this ideal, the greater is the possibility of consensus and reasoned action.

Ideal speech communities are based upon and give rise to civil society. **Civil society** for Habermas is made up of voluntary associations, organizations, and social movements that are in touch with issues that evolve out of communicative action in the public sphere. In principle, civil society is independent of any social system, such as the state, the market, capitalism in general, family, or religion. Civil society will obviously be concerned with and draw information from such arenas, but it will be colonized by none. The elements of civil society provide a way through which the concerns developed in a robust speech community get expressed to society at large. One of the more important things civil society does is continually challenge political and cultural organizations in order to keep intact the freedoms of speech, assembly, and the press. Examples of elements of civil society include professional organizations, unions, charities, women's organizations, advocacy groups, and so on.

Habermas (1992/1996) gives us several conditions that must be met for a robust civil society to evolve and exist:

- It must develop within the context of liberal political culture, one that emphasizes equality for all, and an active and integrated lifeworld.
- Within the boundaries of the public sphere, men and women may obtain influence based on persuasion but cannot obtain political power.
- A civil society can exist only within a social system where the state's power is limited. The state in no way occupies the position of the social actor designed to bring all society under control. The state's power must be limited, and political steering must be indirect and leave intact the internal operations of the institution or subsystem.

Bourdieu has a number of the same concerns as Marx and Habermas. Class and capitalism are seen as roadways to equality, a social space where people could compete freely for position. But as Marx points out, class became a structure that stood in the way of free competition and in fact patterned class inequalities over time. The structure of class and the effects of capitalism are insidious. They are unseen, doing their work unnoticed or misrecognized through ideology and the colonization of the lifeworld and public sphere. Bourdieu shares these concerns. He is critical of the idea that capitalism is an instrument of equality; and he argues that class becomes an unseen structure that patterns the unequal distribution of scarce resources across time. Bourdieu, however, locates this structure and its non-conscious work in an entirely difference place than either Marx or Habermas—Bourdieu argues that class is structured in the human body.

Capitalism and the Body—Pierre Bourdieu

Pierre Bourdieu (1930–2002) was born in Denguin, in southern France. He studied philosophy under Louis Althusser at the École Normale Supérieure in Paris. After his studies, he taught for 3 years, 1955–1958, at the university in Moulins. From 1958 to 1960, Bourdieu did empirical research in Algeria that laid the groundwork for his sociology. In his career, he published over 25 books, one of which, *Distinction: A Social Critique of the Judgment of Taste*, was named one of the twentieth century's 10 most important works of sociology by the International Sociological Association. He was the founder and director of the Centre for European Sociology, and he held the French senior chair in sociology at Collège de France (the same chair that had been held by sociologist and anthropologist, Marcel Mauss, Durkheim's nephew). Craig Calhoun (2003) writes that Bourdieu was "the most influential and original French sociologist since Durkheim" (p. 274). In addition to *Distinction*, Bourdieu's important works include *Language and Symbolic Power, An Invitation to Reflexive Sociology, Acts of Resistance: Against the Tyranny of the Market,* and *Weight of the World: Social Suffering in Contemporary Society.* Bourdieu died of cancer on January 23, 2002.

Concepts and Theory: The Distribution of Capitals

As Marx noted, capitalism is defined by the accumulation of capital for investment. In addition to money, capital resources are typically understood as buildings, equipment, inventories, land, and labor. Bourdieu, however, sees that the reproduction of class inequalities is based on more than this classic definition of capital. To get at this complexity, he defines four forms of capital—economic, social, symbolic, and cultural—all of which are invested and used in the production of class. Keep this in mind: Each of these capitals can be used to gain or increase the levels of the others. Economic capital can be used to gain social, symbolic, and cultural capital, and in the same way, cultural capital can be used to gain social, symbolic, and economic capital. The closest or perhaps most direct relationship is between economic and cultural capital.

Bourdieu uses economic capital in its usual sense. It is generally determined by one's wealth and income. As with Marx, Bourdieu sees economic capital as fundamental. However, unlike Marx, Bourdieu argues that the importance of economic capital is that it strongly influences an individual's initial level of the other capitals, which in turn have their own independent effects. Social capital refers to the kind of social network an individual is set within. The idea of social capital can be captured in the saying, "It isn't what you know but who you know that counts." Symbolic capital is unique to Bourdieu and is important in understanding his theory of class. The definition of symbolic capital is the capacity to use symbols to create or solidify physical and social realities. Bourdieu (1991) tells us that objective categories and structures, such as class, race, and gender, are given existence through the use of symbolic capital: "Symbolic power is a power of constructing reality" (p. 166); it is the power of "world-making . . . the power to make groups. . . . The power to impose and to inculcate a vision of divisions, that is, the power to make visible and explicit social divisions that are implicit, is political power par excellence" (Bourdieu, 1989, p. 23).

This power of world-making is based on two elements. First, and most obviously, there must be an underlying reality. There must be something objectively present to then be symbolically constituted. But objective reality isn't enough; human beings relate primarily to meaning, and meaning is created through symbolic culture. The second element, then, is that the group, event, behaviors, and so on must be symbolically recognized, named, and defined by a person or group that is officially recognized as having the ability to create identity. In our society, such people include scientists, legislators, and academics. Thus, because legitimated existence is dependent upon symbolic capacity, an extremely important conflict in society is the struggle over symbols and classifications. Here are a few examples: the heated debate over race classification in the U.S. 2000 census, debates concerning what clusters of behaviors or symptoms will be officially recognized in the *Diagnostic and Statistical Manual of Mental Disorders,* and the debates leading up to laws being passed against spousal rape. While I framed these in terms of debate, note that what is at issue is the power to name and thus bring into existence.

There is a clear relationship between symbolic and cultural capital. The use of symbolic capital creates the symbolic field wherein cultural capital exists. Cultural capital is defined as cultural competences and markers that a person accumulates as a result of his or her social position and experiences. More specifically, cultural capital refers to the informal social skills, habits, linguistic styles, and tastes that a person garners as a result of his or her economic resources. Bourdieu (1979/1984) identifies three different kinds of cultural capital: objectified, institutionalized, and embodied. *Objectified cultural capital* refers to the material goods (such as books, computers, and paintings) that are associated with cultural capital. *Institutionalized cultural capital* alludes to the certifications (like degrees and diplomas) that give official acknowledgment to the possession of knowledge and abilities. *Embodied cultural capital* is the most important in Bourdieu's theory of class structure. It is part of what makes up an individual's habitus (defined below), and it refers to the cultural capital that lives in and is expressed through the body. This function of cultural capital manifests itself as taste.

Structuring Class: Habitus

Taste refers to an individual preference or fondness for something, such as "she has developed a taste for expensive wine." What Bourdieu is telling us is that our tastes aren't entirely individual; they are strongly influenced by our social class—our tastes are embodied cultural capital. Here, a particular taste is legitimated, exhibited, and recognized by only those who have the proper cultural code, which is class specific. Thus, when we express a preference for something or classify an object in a particular way, we simultaneously classify ourselves. For example, you may not like classical music, but it's less an individual preference than a preference of your social class, status, or group. In other words, if you were born into an upper class or you were older (status), the chances are better that you'd like classical music. Taste also involves the ability to classify. So, for example, you may not be able to tell the difference between classical and baroque music, but you may be able to classify a song in an instant as gangsta rap versus crunk music. Taste may appear as an innocent and natural phenomenon, but it is an insidious revealer of position. As Bourdieu (1979/1984) says, "Taste classifies, and it classifies the classifier" (p. 6). The issue of taste is "one of the most vital stakes in the struggles fought in the field of the dominant class and the field of cultural production" (p. 11).

Bourdieu uses the term **habitus** to refer to embodied cultural capital and taste. Class isn't simply an economic classification or social group; class is inscribed in our bodies. Habitus is the durable organization of one's body and its deployment in the world. It is found in our posture, and our way of walking, speaking, eating, and laughing; it is found in every way we use our body. Habitus is both a system whereby people organize their own behavior and a system through which people perceive and appreciate the behavior of others. Pay close attention: This system of organization and appreciation is *felt in our bodies* and works

> beyond the reach of introspective scrutiny or control by the will . . . in the most automatic gestures or the apparently most insignificant techniques of the body . . . [it engages] the most fundamental principles of construction and evaluation of the social world, those which most directly express the division of labour . . . or the division of the work of domination. (Bourdieu, 1979/1984, p. 466)

There are two factors important in the production of habitus: distance from necessity, and education. In **distance from necessity**, necessity speaks of sustenance—the things necessary for biological existence. Distance from the necessities of life enables the upper classes to experience a world that is free from urgency. In contrast, the poor must always worry about their daily existence. As humans move away from that essential existence, they are relieved of constant worry and are freed to practice activities that are valued for their intrinsic enjoyment rather than what they can bring. For example, a laborer looks at a meal in terms of what it can do: It can stop the hunger and give energy for work. An upper-class person, however, enjoys a meal for its aesthetic value—what it is, rather than what it does. The person will relate to a meal in terms of the way it looks and is presented, its inviting scents and complex flavors, and so on. Another part of cultural capital at work here is that the upper-class person will have the language to describe and analyze food in this way.

The second way habitus and cultural capital vary is through **education.** One obvious difference between the education of the elite and that of the working classes is the kind of social position in which education places us. The education system channels individuals toward prestigious or devalued positions. Another important difference is the kind of education we receive—simple knowing and recognizing of facts versus more sophisticated knowledge. This factor varies by number of years of education, which in turn varies by class position. Education also influences the kind of language we use to think and through which we see the world. The more education we receive, the more complex our language will be. Moreover, because we don't just think *with* language, we think *in* language, the complexity of our language affects the complexity of our thinking, and our thinking influences the way we see the world. These language issues not only affect our thinking, but also influence who we want to hang out with. For instance, I had a previous student come by my office the other day. One of the things she said was that a graduate education in sociology should come with a warning label: "If you really think about this stuff, it will change who you are." She explained that she doesn't like to hang out with her family or friends anymore because they don't talk about the things she's now interested in, and they don't think past the surface meaning of things. She's heartbroken about this because she doesn't fit in with her people anymore. I didn't say this to her, but this is exactly Bourdieu's point with habitus and linguistic markets.

Enacting Class: Linguistic Markets and Symbolic Violence

The **linguistic market** is like any other market: It's a place of exchange and a place to seek profit. Linguistic markets occur every time you interact with other people. When you interact with friends, you're in a market where everybody is fairly equal, in terms of cultural capital. It's comfortable and non-threatening. It's also a situation where you can't make good returns on your investment. If you all have equal levels of cultural capital, you can't gain more cultural capital from the interaction. However, when you interact with someone from a different social class or status, the market is no longer even, and you could possibly increase your level of cultural capital. The problem, of course, is that like my graduate student, most of us shy away from interaction with people who have different cultural capital.

Linguistic markets are structured through formal language. Every society has formalized its language as a result of the unification of modernization and the state, economy, and culture. The education system is used to impose restrictions on popular modes of speech and to propagate standard language. We all remember times in grammar school when teachers would correct our speech ("There is no such word as *ain't*."). Universities are actually becoming more focused on training and thus are sanctioning correct written and spoken language. My own university, for instance, has intensive writing and speaking requirements to complete any degree on campus. Every student must take three courses that are writing intensive and three that are speaking intensive.

Linguistic markets are also structured through various configurations of the capitals. For example, the linguistic market of sociology is heavily based on cultural and symbolic capital. In order to do well in that market, you would have to know a fair amount about Karl Marx, Émile Durkheim, Michel Foucault, Pierre Bourdieu, Dorothy Smith, and so forth. Further, you would have to be able to apply these theorists to social research, a prime source and expression of symbolic capital. In another situation, say at a dinner hosted by IBM, you would have to have a high level of cultural capital in relation to economic capital. These two different examples illustrate an extremely important point in Bourdieu's theory: Individuals in a given market recognize their position, have a sense of how their habitus relates to the present market, and anticipate differing profits of distinction. For me, those two examples represent two very different linguistic markets. In the academic market, I can hold my own and am able to gather more cultural, social, and symbolic capitals, which I can then parlay into economic capital. However, if I was at an event hosted by IBM, I would know that I have little to no cultural capital in that field.

The result is that in the academic linguistic market, I would anticipate high rewards and would invest my cultural capital. But in the economic linguistic market, I'd keep my mouth shut. Bourdieu calls this self-sanctioning **symbolic violence**: the exercise of violence and oppression that is not recognized as such. More specifically, "Symbolic power is that invisible power which can be exercised only with the complicity of those who do not want to know that they are subject to it or even that they themselves exercise it" (Bourdieu, 1991, p. 164). By sanctioning ourselves in markets where we are outclassed, the very markets where we could gain cultural capital, we enact and reproduce our class standing. Class, then, is structured and replicated through habitus, linguistic markets, and symbolic violence.

Concepts and Theory: The Symbolic Struggle

Given the way in which habitus works, how can a person or group become upwardly mobile? Bourdieu's theory is more concerned about how class is patterned, but he does give us some hints about how it can change. First, understanding the complexity of the four capitals, what they are and how they work, may enable a person to intentionally work at improving them. The configuration certainly lets us know that there is more than one path to economic success. We've known something of this for some time with the idea of *nouveau riche*: "a person of newly acquired wealth but limited education or culture" (Merriam-Webster, 2002). What the concept of nouveau riche didn't tell us was that there is something other than cultural capital involved, and that the capitals are linked and can mutually affect one another.

For example, a person from a lower economic class or a disenfranchised group can use education to get ahead. The key in this approach is to see that getting a degree isn't sufficient. Earning a degree is obviously part of institutionalized cultural capital, but that isn't what gets played out in linguistic markets. Rather, a college or university education must impact the person. A person must *become educated*—his or her habitus must change. The ways of seeing and understanding the world, the vocabulary and linguistic styles, and the aesthetic tastes of the educated elite must be embodied. Opportunities to accrue social capital must be exploited, and likewise with understanding and properly using symbolic capital. Furthermore, understanding the way symbolic violence within linguistic markets works can be employed by intentionally seeking out, rather than avoiding, situations of differing cultural capitals and strategically using the capital that is available to obtain more.

This kind of **symbolic struggle** can bring some incremental, individual change. Yet there are also hints about how more dynamic change can occur. Bourdieu allows that there are two ways symbolic struggle may be carried out: objectively and subjectively. In both cases, symbolic disruption is the key. Objectively, individuals or groups may act in such a way as to display certain counter-realities. Bourdieu's example of this method is group demonstrations held to manifest the size, strength, and cohesiveness of political groups; the peace marches of the 1960s and the February 15, 2003 global demonstrations against the U.S. invasion of Iraq are good illustrations. This type of symbolic action disrupts the taken-for-grantedness that all systems of oppression must work within—it offers an objective case that things are not what they seem.

Subjectively, individuals or groups may work to transform the categories constructed by symbolic capital through which the social world is perceived. On the individual level, this may be accomplished through insults, rumors, questions, and the like. A good example of this approach is found in bell hooks' book *Talking Back* (1989): "It is that act of speech, of 'talking back,' that is no mere gesture of empty words, that is the expression of moving from object to subject—the liberated voice" (p. 9). Groups may also operate in this way by employing more political strategies. The most typical of these strategies is the redefinition of history—that is, "retrospectively reconstructing a past fitted to the needs of the present" (Bourdieu, 1989, p. 21). But notice that with each of these kinds of struggle, a response from those with symbolic capital would be required. These disruptions could bring attention to the cause, but symbolic power would be necessary to give it life and substance, first within the symbolic field and then within the objective field of class.

The Craft of Citizenship   Capitalism

The Basics

- Identify the central questions driving Marx, Habermas, and Bourdieu. Can you restate their individual questions in a general question or concern that expresses their questions as one? In other words, about what are all three centrally concerned?
- Identify and theoretically define the important concepts of each theorist.

  ➢ *Helpful hints:* In previous chapters, I've been putting supporting concepts in italics and central concepts in bold. In this chapter, I've left out the italics. But I've also repeatedly put in bold the central concepts every time there's a significant discussion. So, look for all the times "ideology" is in bold, for example, and draw the defining characteristics from those sections. In your reading, you may think I have failed to note some important concepts. Good; put them on the list, too.

- For each theorist, identify and explain the important relationships among and between concepts. In other words, explain the theories of Marx, Habermas, and Bourdieu. Remember to focus your explanation on the central issue that each is concerned with. More specifically, what are the three theorists' explanations of how capitalism works and influences people and democracy?

Skill Set 1: Inference and Application

- What does Habermas' theory of the colonization of the lifeworld and public sphere imply about democracy? What implications do Habermas' ideas have for your own practices of democracy?
- Drawing from Marx, Habermas, and Bourdieu, explain the factors that hinder equality and democracy under capitalism. What must happen to remove those factors? What applications do you see for your own life and practices of citizenship?
- What does Habermas' critique of knowledge imply about the social sciences? Should the social sciences be thrown out entirely, or do you see ways in which they can be used?
- What implications does Bourdieu's theory of habitus have for the importance you place on education? In what ways can you use education and symbolic markets to facilitate your own upward mobility?

Skill Set 2: Interpretation, Analysis, Evaluation, Synthesis

- Compare/contrast and evaluate ideas of civil society (from Alexander) and the public sphere (from Habermas). Now do the same with Alexander's theory of the civil sphere and Habermas' theory of civil society. Here's another way to approach this: Use elements from Alexander and Habermas to explain how democracy is threatened in a nation such as the United States; then, explain how democracy can be revitalized.
- Analyze and evaluate the theories presented in this chapter. Which do you think presents the most important or cohesive explanation of capitalism and class? Explain your answer.
- Evaluate the place of capitalism in the social project of modernity.
  - ➤ *Helpful hints:* You'll have to use the notion of capitalism found in Chapter 1 and evaluate it using a synthesized critique based on the theories in this chapter.

6

Power

Social power is for many people an uncomfortable idea, at least in democratic settings. We like to think that democracy is more refined, more oriented toward persuasion than control. As we've seen in Alexander's and Habermas' work, persuasion and consensus building are keys to participatory democracy. Power seems just the opposite: Power, according to Max Weber (1922/1968), is "the chance of a man or a number of men to realize their own will in a social action even against the resistance of others" (p. 926). The truth of it is that power is a complex issue in society. On the one hand, it's necessary for social order. As a small example, think about norms. Norms are guidelines for behavior with positive and negative sanctions, and, as Durkheim and Parsons argued, we need them. Yet the ability to reward or punish behavior is based on power. On the other hand, it's equally clear that power and control are the opposite of freedom, an intrinsic right of human nature. So, in addition to learning about how power works in society, in our reading we need to examine these theories in terms of the social project of modernity.

Our discussion of power will center on the work of Max Weber. Weber is certainly the most notable of the classic theorists to deal directly with power. His theory of power is specifically housed in his ideas concerning authority, class, status, and party. But Weber's work has overall implications for considering power beyond just these four issues. Thus, Weber will be used throughout this chapter to frame and expand the work of the other two theorists. Ralf Dahrendorf's work explains and expands Weber's ideas, especially in relation to the organization of conflict groups and the legitimated exercise of power in bureaucracies. Weber is very clear about the place of knowledge in bureaucracies: They are basically systems that run on expert knowledge. However, Weber didn't fully grasp the significance of the relationship between power and knowledge in modernity. For that, we'll be drawing on the work of Michel Foucault.

The Fundamental Contours of Power—Max Weber

Max Weber (1865–1920) was born in Erfurt, Germany (Prussia). In 1882, Weber entered the University of Heidelberg where he studied law. After a year's military service in 1883, Weber returned to school at the University of Berlin, and in 1893, Weber married Marianne Schnitger (who became an early feminist thinker). Weber began teaching at Heidelberg in 1896 as a professor of economics. While at Heidelberg, Max and Marianne's home became a meeting place for the city's intellectual community. Marianne was active in these meetings, which at times became significant discussions of gender and women's rights.

In 1897, Weber suffered a complete emotional and mental breakdown and was unable to write again until 1903; he left the university and didn't teach again for almost 20 years. During his convalescence, Weber read the works of the philosophers Wilhelm Dilthey and Heinrich Rickert. After his breakdown, Weber wrote the majority of the works for which he is best known. His methodological writings date from this period (now found in *The Methodology of the Social Sciences*), as well as *The Protestant Ethic and the Spirit of Capitalism, The Sociology of Religion, The Religion of China, The Religion of India,* and *Ancient Judaism.* (Several of these weren't finished until later, but were begun during this time.) In 1918, Weber accepted a position at the University of Vienna, where he once again began to teach. He started working on *Economy and Society,* which was to be the definitive outline of interpretive sociology. His *General Economic History* was written based on lectures given during this time. On June 14, 1920, Max Weber died of pneumonia.

Concepts and Theory: The Distribution of Power

Weber defines power as the ability to get others to do what you want, even if they don't want to. But what are the sources of power, and how is it exercised? Obviously, if I have a gun, I can get you to do what I want, even if you don't want to. But coercive situations like that aren't where social power is put into effect. Persuasion isn't specifically what Weber has in mind either. Both persuasion and coercion are based more or less on individual personalities. Persuasion works subtly as we are drawn in by the personal magnetism or interaction skills of the other person. The willingness to use brute coercion is based on individual characteristics as well. In contrast, Weber thinks about power as an element of social structure—specifically, class, status, and party. In other words, there are three arenas of power or three ways in which power is obtained and exercised.

The Unequal Distribution of Class

Weber (1922/1968) defines class as the

> typical probability of (1) procuring goods (2) gaining a position in life and (3) finding inner satisfaction, a probability which derives from the relative control over goods and skills and from their income-producing uses within a given economic order. (p. 302)

Class is thus based on one's ability to buy or sell goods or services that will bring the person inner satisfaction and increase his or her life chances (how long and healthy an individual will live). For Weber, class varies by two types of control: property ownership and market position (commercial class), each with positively privileged, negatively privileged, and middle class positions.

Positive and negative positions are the poles of power: positively privileged people have a good deal of power over property and position, while the negatively privileged have none. The middle class is obviously a place of some power and powerlessness as well.

Control over property can be exercised through production—which is the kind Marx is concerned with—or investment. For Weber, income that results from investment in property is usually in the form of rent. The commercial class, on the other hand, is determined by the ability to trade or manage a market position. Those positively related to commercial position are typically entrepreneurs who can monopolize and safeguard their market situation. Negatively privileged commercial classes are typically laborers. They are dependent on the whim of the labor market. The in-between or middle classes that are influenced by labor market positions are those such as self-employed farmers, craftspeople, or low-level professionals who have a viable market position yet are not able to monopolize or control it in any way.

Weber's idea of the commercial class is extremely important for us today. Commercial classes are able to dominate market positions around skills and knowledge, and this kind of class becomes increasingly significant in what are sometimes called "service" or "postindustrial" economies, such as the United States. Power here is based on the ability to control access to knowledge and specialized skills. Not only is this arena of power becoming increasingly prominent, but it is also the site of ambiguity and conflict. The legal question of "intellectual property" is one that hasn't yet been resolved. Yet the legal order, here and with property as well, only "enhances the chance to hold power or honor; it can not always secure them" (Weber, 1922/1968, p. 927).

Class is thus based upon power over property, skills, and knowledge, and it obviously results in social power as well. Some of this power comes from monopolizing the purchase of certain goods and services; we'll talk more about this when we discuss status. In addition, some power accrues simply from the naked power of money. Whether or not control over purchasing power is monopolized, money simply equates to social power—the ability to realize your own will against that of others. This power is captured in the saying, "Everybody has their price." Having said that, it's important to keep in mind that "'Economically conditioned' power is not . . . identical with 'power' as such" (Weber, 1922/1968, p. 926).

There is one other way that **power** is exercised through class, and that is through class as a social group. Unless and until people develop a similar identity that focuses on their class differences, they remain a statistical aggregate. In other words, the census bureau may know you are in the middle class, but you may not have a group identity around your class position. This kind of class-based social group is most likely to be organized against the most immediate economic class, when the contrasts or gaps between class positions are obvious, when the connection between causes and conse-quences are clear, and when certain cultural conditions are met (like the for-mation of a group-specific culture or ideology). This issue of class and power is what Marx was thinking about with class consciousness, the organization of the working class against the capitalist. Weber opens this idea up by see-ing that *any class position* can become organized and thus exert power as a class, even the elite. In truth, this kind of social group organization is much easier for the ruling class than others, because the three conditions of class organization can be controlled more easily by the elite.

The Unequal Distribution of Status

Just as Weber's idea of the commercial class is important for our time, so is his thinking about status. Basically, **status** is a claim to more or less social honor or esteem that is based on distance and exclusiveness. Where class is based on real, structural conditions, status is a cultural issue: "All stylization of life either originates in status groups or is at least conserved by them" (Weber, 1922/1968, p. 936). It has to do with the meaning attached to a social position. A good example is the clergy. In many parts of society, some-one who is a pastor or priest is held in high regard; the person is given due respect. Most priests and pastors don't have a high class position; the real-ity of their lives in terms of food, shelter, clothing, medical care, and so on isn't any better than the middle class or below. They are, however, given respect and deference. High-status positions exercise power because we will yield to their judgment or preference out of respect for the position.

Status and its **power** may be based on and guarded by one or more of three things: a distinct lifestyle, a formal education, or differences in hered-itary or occupational prestige. For example, being a music fan may entail a distinct lifestyle—people who listen to jazz are culturally different from those who listen to rock—and there are positive and negative privileges involved as well: You can get a degree in jazz at my university, but not in rock. Those who are homosexual can also be seen in terms of lifestyle sta-tus groups; being heterosexual is generally more respected. One's education level can also provide the basis of status. Being a senior at the university is better, status wise, than being a freshman, and you have greater privileges as a senior as well. Professors are a more general example of prestige based on education. They usually rate high on occupational prestige tables but low in class and power. Race and gender are also examples of status founded on perceived heredity.

Status groups maintain their boundaries through particular practices and symbols. Boundary maintenance is uniquely important for status groups because the borders are more symbolic than actual. The differences between jazz and rock, in terms of people's musical tastes and preferences, are in the ear of the listener. Generally speaking, Weber argues, we maintain the boundaries around personal status through marriage and eating restrictions, monopolizing specific modes of acquisition, and different traditions. The norm of marriage restriction is fairly intuitive; we can think of religious and ethnic groups who practice "endogamy" (marriage within a specific group as required by custom or law). But eating restrictions may seem counterintuitive. It may help us to realize that many religious groups have special dietary restrictions and practice ritual feasting. Feasts are always restricted to group members and are usually seen as actively uniting the group as one (the traditional Jewish Yom Kippur being a good example).

We also maintain the symbolic boundaries around status groups through monopolizing or abhorring certain kinds and modes of acquisition, and by having certain cultural practices or traditions. The kinds of things we buy obviously set our status group apart. For example, a BMW is a status symbol that represents wealth. Status groups also try and guard the modes of acquisition. Guilds, trade unions, and professional groups can function in this capacity. Finally, different status groups have different practices and traditions. Stepdancing, pride marches, Fourth of July, Kwanzaa, Cinco de Mayo, and so on are all examples of status-specific traditions and cultural practices.

The Unequal Distribution of Power

Party is most directly related to power, but as with class and status, it isn't power itself. **Party** refers to a group that is focused on the acquisition of power and may represent interests based on class or status position. As Weber (1922/1968) puts it, a party organizes "in order to attain ideal or material advantages for its active members" (p. 284). The social groups that Weber would consider parties are those whose practices are oriented toward controlling an organization and its administrative staff. The Democratic and Republican Parties in the United States are obvious examples of what Weber intends. Other examples include student unions or special interest groups like the tobacco lobby, if they are oriented toward controlling and exercising power.

As I said, Weber lays out the initial sociological framework to think about power. Though he doesn't state this clearly, Weber is arguing that in seeking class and status, people are finding ways to exercise power. In this sense, **power** is a basic trait of not only social organization, but also human behavior. Power is certainly the way that self-seeking actors would be able to achieve their individual goals. This search for power results in different class and status (cultural) positions that then enable power to be exercised. Parties are the most blatant expression of this quest: "Their action is oriented toward the acquisition of social power, that is to say, toward influencing social action no matter what its content may be" (Weber, 1922/1968, p. 938).

Weber also gives us another important idea in thinking about power groups in society: People don't simply occupy one position of power. Every individual sits at a unique configuration of class, status, and party. I have a class position, but I also have a variety of status positions and political issues that concern me. Patricia Hill Collins (2000), a contemporary theorist, refers to this as "intersectionality and the matrix of domination." **Intersectionality** refers to the structured position of people living at the crossroads of two or more systems of inequality, such as race and gender. The different intersectionalities of a society influence the overall organization of power—what Collins calls the *matrix of domination.* These matrices are historically and socially specific, yet they are organized around four general domains of power: structural (the interrelationships of social structures), disciplinary (bureaucratic organization and protocol), hegemonic (cultural legitimations), and interpersonal (personal relationships).

One of the things that the issue of crosscutting interests implies is difficulty in creating party groups. Marx rightly argues that overt conflict is dependent upon bipolarization. The closer issues of conflict get to having only two defined sides, the more likely is the conflict to become overt and violent. The formation of the Allied and Axis powers in World War II is a good example. But Weber gives us an understanding of stratification that shows the difficulty in achieving bipolarization. Polarized conflict is most easily organized around single issues or issues that are seen as being very similar. Identifying such issues becomes increasingly difficult in a society where crosscutting interests create complex political issues and identities.

Concepts and Theory: Authority—Making Power Work

Weber argues that in order for a system of power and domination to work, people must believe in it. Human belief is always based on **legitimation**— stories we tell one another that provide an ethical or moral basis for practices of power. The beliefs and practices that are specific to legitimating stories constitute **authority**, that is, the belief in the right to require and receive submission. If people don't believe in a power structure, then those with power will have to constantly monitor others and use coercive force to bring compliance. Authority, on the other hand, implies the ability to require performance, based upon the performer's belief in the rightness of the system. Because authority is related to socialization, the internalization of cultural norms and values, authority requires low levels of external social control. We can thus say that any structure of domination can exist in the long run if and only if there is a corresponding legitimating culture of authority. There is a way, then, that people participate in their own domination—it's their belief in authority that enables the system to work.

Weber identifies three ideal types of authority: charismatic, traditional, and rational-legal. Each has a different basis of belief. *Charismatic authority* is based on the belief in the intrinsic or supernatural gifts of a specific individual. *Traditional authority* rests on time—the belief that long-established customs are superior. Finally, *rational-legal authority* is belief in rationally established objective procedures and positions found in bureaucracies. Both traditional and rational-legal authorities maintain the status quo—whether by custom or law, systems of domination remain stable. Only charismatic authority can "effect a subjective or internal reorientation born out of suffering, conflicts, or enthusiasm . . . with a completely new orientation of all attitudes toward the different problems of the 'world'" (Weber, 1922/1968, p. 245). Notice Weber's emphasis on the inner, subjective experiences and beliefs of the individual, for both maintaining and changing systems of domination and power.

Weber thus has given us two distinct ways to think about power. The first is to see power embedded in and expressed through certain kinds of social structure, most notably class and status. Parties are political organizations specifically oriented toward obtaining either material or cultural goods for groups. The key for parties is to obtain control over the administrative staff of an organization. This key reveals one of the most important sites for power: organizations. In contemporary social theory, Ralf Dahrendorf explores the idea of organizational power further and adds an interesting element from Marx: dialectical processes.

Organizing Power—Ralf Dahrendorf

Ralf Dahrendorf (1929–2009) was born in Hamburg, Germany. His father, a Social Democratic politician, was briefly arrested by the Nazis in 1933 and then released, after which the family moved to Berlin. During the war (in 1944), his father was sent to prison and Ralf was sent to a labor camp for his anti-Nazi activities. After the war, the family moved to England. Dahrendorf later returned to Germany to study at the University of Hamburg where he

Marx - class = everything

received his first PhD, in philosophy; he earned his second PhD, in sociology, at the London School of Economics. After teaching in Germany from 1957 through 1969, Dahrendorf turned to politics and became a member of the German Parliament. In 1970, he was appointed a commissioner in the European Commission in Brussels. From 1974 to 1984, Dahrendorf was the director of the London School of Economics. In 1988, Dahrendorf became a British citizen, and in 1993 he was given a life peerage and was named Baron Dahrendorf of Clare Market in the City of Westminster by Queen Elizabeth II. From then until his death in June 2009, Sir Dahrendorf was a member of the House of Lords. Among his most important works available in English are *Class and Class Conflict in Industrial Society, Essays in the Theory of Society,* and *The Modern Social Conflict: The Politics of Liberty.* Dahrendorf (quoted in Kreisler, 1989) explains that his work is motivated by

> my firm belief that the regulation of conflict is the secret of liberty in liberal democracy. . . . [We must] devise institutions in which it is possible for people to express . . . differences, which is what democracy, in my view, is about. Democracy, in other words, is not about the emergence of some unified view from "the people," but it's about organizing conflict and living with conflict.

Concepts and Theory:
Associations of Power and Conflict

According to Dahrendorf (1957/1959), **power** is "always associated with social positions or roles" (p. 166). In other words, the legitimated use of power is found in the status positions, roles, and norms of organizations. Obvious examples are your professors, the police, your boss at work, and so on. Because of its organizational embeddedness, Dahrendorf refers to authoritative social relations as **imperatively coordinated associations** (ICAs). If something is imperative, it is binding and compulsory; you must do it. So the term simply says that social relations are managed through legitimated power (authority). It is also important to note that Dahrendorf sees class as more related to power than to money or occupation. Both of those might be important, but their importance is that they contribute to an individual's power within an ICA. Thus, for Dahrendorf, classes "are social conflict groups the determinant . . . of which can be found in the participation in or exclusion from the exercise of authority within any imperatively coordinated association" (p. 138).

ICAs are universal in modern society—they are the chief way that we organize social behavior. What this means is that most people are sandwiched in between power relations. That is, they exercise power over some and are themselves subject to the authority of those above them. People are thus embedded in dichotomous sets of power interests. For example, let's say you're the president of the local chapter of STAND (the student-led division of Genocide Intervention Network) and a student in my class. In the ICA of STAND, you hold power and I don't; in my class, I hold power and you don't. We each belong to several different ICAs that have their own distribution of power. Together, the multitude of ICAs and positions form the warp and woof (the underlying structure) of society.

In modern society, ICAs are generally embedded in bureaucracy. **Bureaucracies** tend to rationalize and routinize all tasks and interactions. Tasks and interactions are rationalized in terms of means–ends efficiency, and they are routinized in the sense that they may be carried out without thought or planning or dependency on individual talents. According to Weber, bureaucracies have six important features that rationalize and routinize human organization: (1) an explicit division of labor with delineated lines of authority, (2) the presence of an office hierarchy, (3) written rules and communication, (4) accredited training and technical competence, (5) management by rules that is emotionally neutral, and (6) ownership of both the career ladder and position by the organization rather than the individual. Each of these characteristics is a variable, and organizations will thus be more or less bureaucratized.

There is a modern irony here as well. One of the reasons that bureaucracy became the organizing principle par excellence in modernity is the rise of mass democracy. Democracy for the masses created demands for equal treatment before the law, regardless of one's level of power or prestige. This expansion implies that rules and laws should be blind to group or individual differences. Yet bureaucratization tends to limit emancipatory change for at least two reasons. First, bureaucracies are quite good at co-optation. To *co-opt,* in this context, means to take something in and make it part of the group, which on the surface might sound like a good thing. But because bureaucracies are value- and emotion-free, there is a tendency to downplay differences and render them impotent. For example, one of the things that our society has done with race and gender movements is to give them official status in the university. One can now get a degree in race or gender relations. Inequality is something we now study, rather than the focus of social movements.

The second reason is perhaps more insidious. Bureaucracies have a propensity to produce a **bureaucratic personality**: psychological predispositions to think, feel, act, and perceive the world in ways that are in keeping with bureaucratic organization. Let me quickly note that people aren't born with these dispositions; they are formed by interfacing with bureaucratic organization on a continual basis. There are at least four characteristics of this kind of temperament: First, individuals tend to live more rationally due to the presence of bureaucracy, and not just at work. People generally become less and less spontaneous and less emotionally connected to others in their lives. They understand goals, the use of time and space, and even relationships through rational criteria. Second, people who work in bureaucracies also tend to identify with the goals of the organization. Workers at levels that are less bureaucratized tend to complain about the organization; on the other hand, people in management who exist at more bureaucratized levels tend to support and believe in the organization. Again, this isn't something that we just put on at work—*we become bureaucratic ourselves.*

Third, because bureaucracies are based on technical knowledge, people in bureaucratic societies tend to depend on expert systems for knowledge and advice. In traditionally based societies, people would trust the advice of those they loved, or those who had extensive experience, or those who stood in a long lineage of oral discipleship. Conversely, in societies like the United States, we look to those who have credentials to help us. Fourth and finally, bureaucracies lead to sequestration of experience. By that I mean that different life experiences are separated from one another, such as dying from living. In traditional society, life was experienced holistically. People would see birth, sickness (emotional, mental, and physical), and death as part of their normal lives. Children were conceived and grandparents died in the same home. Today, most of those experiences are put away from us and occur in bureaucratic settings where we don't see them as part of our normal and daily life; such settings include hospitals, rest homes, asylums, and so on. The world has thus become tidy, clean, and rational—and our bureaucratic personalities like it that way.

Yet the organization of interest groups is still possible. Dahrendorf (1957/1959) makes a distinction between quasi-groups and interest groups (Weber's concept of party). **Quasi-groups** "consist of incumbents of roles endowed with like expectations of interests" and represent "'recruiting fields'" for the formation of real interest groups. Interest groups, Dahrendorf tells us, "are the real agents of group conflict" (p. 180). Unequally distributed power intrinsically implies that society is rife with potential conflict, even in highly bureaucratized settings. The questions, then, are these: What are the social factors that move an aggregate from a quasi-group to an interest group? What are the conditions under which latent conflict becomes manifest?

Conditions of Group Conflict

Dahrendorf gives us three sets of conditions that must be met for a quasi-group to become an **interest group** active in conflict: technical, political, and social conditions. The technical conditions are those things without which a group simply can't function. They are what actually define a social group as compared to an aggregate. The technical conditions include members, ideas or ideologies (what Dahrendorf calls a "charter"), and norms. Members are people who actively identify with group members around a social position of power interests. To function as a group, members also need culture, specifically an ideology and norms. The political conditions refer specifically to the ability to meet and organize. This is fairly obvious but is nonetheless important and can be difficult. As an illustration, let's say that your university raised tuition and students started grumbling about it. In order to become an active protest group, students would have to have places to meet. But at the university, who controls the physical buildings? As you can see, meeting the technical conditions isn't always easy. In fact, most quasi-groups that would want to form interest groups—those with the least amount of power—are the very ones who have the fewest resources to meet the political conditions.

Social conditions of organization must also be met. There are two elements here: communication and structural patterns of recruitment. Obviously, the more quasi-groups are able to communicate, the more likely they will form an interest group. With the abundance of cell phones and availability of the Internet, this condition is almost a given in late modern societies. The social connections that people make must also be structurally predictable. In previous forms of society, this was severely limited by geographic space and the rounds of daily life. However, some recent communication technologies have created different and more accessible ways of structuring patterns of recruitment. When email and the Internet first began, there were few mechanisms that established a pattern for how people got in touch with one another. People would email their friends or business acquaintances, and in that sense computer technologies only enhanced already established social connections. But with the advent of search engines and community sites such as Second Life, Facebook, MySpace, and so on, there are now structural features of the Internet that can more predictably bring people together.

Overt Conflict and Social Change

Once a quasi-group forms as an interest group, conflict becomes manifest, with the degree of conflict varying by its level of intensity and violence. **Conflict intensity** is measured in terms of cost and involvement. The cost of conflict is rather intuitive; it refers to the money, life, material, infrastructure, culture, and emotion that are expended. Involvement refers to the level of importance the people in the conflict attach to the group and its issues. We can think of this involvement as varying on a continuum from the level that a game of checkers requires to that of a front-line soldier. For Dahrendorf, *conflict violence* refers to how conflict is manifested and is basically measured by the kinds of weapons used. Peaceful demonstrations are conflictual but exhibit an extremely low level of violence, while riots are far more violent.

Within a society, conflict violence is related to three distinct groups of social factors: (1) the technical, political, and social conditions of organization; (2) the effective regulation of conflict within a society; and (3) the level of relative deprivation. Violence is negatively related to the three conditions of organization. In other words, the more a group has met the technical, political, and social conditions of organization, the less likely it is that the conflict will be violent and the more likely it is that the group will have rational goals and seek reasonable means to achieve those goals. The violence of a conflict is also negatively related to the presence of legitimate ways of regulating conflict. In other words, the greater the level of formal or informal norms regulating conflict, the greater the probability that both parties will use the norms or judicial paths to resolve the conflict. However, this factor is influenced by two others. In order for the two interested parties to use legitimate roads of conflict resolution, they must both recognize the fundamental justice of the cause involved (even if they don't agree on the outcome), and both parties need to be well organized.

In addition, the possibility of violent conflict is positively related to a sense of relative deprivation. *Absolute deprivation* refers to the condition of being destitute, living well below the poverty line where life is dictated by uncertainty over the essentials of life (food, shelter, and clothing). People in such a condition have neither the resources nor the willpower to become involved in conflict and social change. *Relative deprivation,* however, refers to a sense of being underprivileged relative to some other person or group. The basics of life aren't in question here; it's simply the sense that others are doing better and that we are losing out on something. But it isn't relative deprivation itself that motivates people; it is the shift from absolute to relative deprivation that may spark a powder keg of revolt. People who are upwardly mobile in this way have the available resources, and they may experience a sense of loss or deprivation if the structural changes can't keep pace with their rising expectations.

Within a social system, the level of **conflict intensity** is related to the technical, political, and social conditions of organization; the level of social mobility; and the way in which power and other scarce resources are distributed in society. Notice that both violence and intensity are related to group organization, and the relationship in both cases is negative. The violence and intensity of conflict will tend to go down as groups are better organized—again, for the same reason: Better organization means more rational action. As we've seen, systems of domination work in the long run through legitimated authority. The implication is that social change requires people to question the legitimacy of the distribution of scarce resources. The relationship here is positive: The more legitimated authority in society is questioned, the greater will be the intensity of the conflict. In this case, the interest groups will see the goals of conflict as more significant and worth more involvement and cost. Finally, the intensity of a conflict is negatively related to social mobility. If an ICA sees its ability to acquire society's highly valued goods and positions systematically hampered (social mobility is down), then chances are good the group members will see the conflict as worth investing more of themselves in and possibly sustaining greater costs.

Concepts and Theory: Dialectic Conflict and Democracy

Regardless of how fast or how dramatically societies change, the changes must be institutionalized, as Weber and Parsons note. For Dahrendorf (1957/1959), **institutionalization** occurs within structural changes "involving the personnel of positions of domination in imperatively coordinated associations" (p. 231). What you should notice about this statement is that social change in modernity by and large involves changing personnel in ICAs. Generally speaking, the organizations themselves aren't destroyed, especially in the case of modern bureaucracy. It's also important to note that power and social change are a **dialectic**. You'll remember from Marx that a dialectic contains different elements that are naturally antagonistic or in tension with one another—this antagonism is what energizes and brings change. Dialectics are also cyclical in nature, with each new cycle bringing a different and generally unpredictable resolve. The resolve, or new set of social relations, contains its own antagonistic elements, and the cycle continues. The energy in Dahrendorf's model is the tension over power: Power is necessary for social order, but at the same time, power sets up quasi-groups with intrinsic conflicts of interest. Once the tension erupts in some form of conflict, power is distributed differently through ICAs, which in turn creates new latent antagonisms over power, and the cycle starts all over again.

Thus, conflict is the unavoidable outcome of human society. But more than that, Dahrendorf argues, conflict is necessary and desirable because of democracy. As we've seen, democracy came about to fulfill the social project of modernity, the creation of a good and just society. Dahrendorf argues that both science and democracy are founded on a principle of uncertainty. His argument is philosophical, and I can't do it justice here, but here's a taste of it. Scientific progress and discovery are based on the firm belief that we don't know all there is to know about the universe. It's the uncertainty of scientific knowledge that pushes the boundaries further and further. "The starting point of our reflections in the realm of politics is not uncertainty about truth, but uncertainty about goodness, or (to give goodness in the social sphere its traditional name) about justice" (Dahrendorf, 1968, p. 247). History teaches us that we can't know with certainty what the "good" society is; the definition of "good" and "just" have changed too often and too radically. The uncertainty about what is right implies the necessity of conflict. As Dahrendorf says, "The contest between divergent concepts of the just society is itself the motor that moves the real world closer to that unattainable goal" (p. 251). Notice the dialectical "motor" in Dahrendorf's statement. Continual conflict over the distribution of power in a democratic society is the only way to keep society moving toward the goal of a good and just society: "The ethics of uncertainty are the ethics of liberty, and the ethics of liberty are the ethics of conflict, of antagonism generated and institutionalized" (p. 253).

The Practices of Power—Michel Foucault

Michel Foucault (1926–1984) was born in Poitiers, France. Foucault studied at the École Normale Supérieure and the Institut de Psychologie of Paris. In 1960, returning to France from teaching posts in Sweden, Poland, and Germany, Foucault published *Madness and Civilization,* for which he received France's highest academic degree, le doctorat d'état. In 1966, Foucault published *The Order of Things,* which became a best-selling book in France. In 1970, Foucault received a permanent appointment at the Collège de France (France's most prestigious school) as chair of History of Systems of Thought. Foucault published *Discipline and Punishment* in 1975. That same year, he took his first trip to California, which came to hold an important place in Foucault's life, especially San Francisco. In 1976, Foucault published the first volume of his last major work, *The History of Sexuality,* and the two other volumes of this history, *The Use of Pleasure* and *The Care of the Self,* were published shortly before his death. In Foucault's (1984/1990b) own words,

> As for what motivated me. . . . [i]t was curiosity—the only kind of curiosity, in any case, that is worth acting upon with a degree of obstinacy: not the curiosity that seeks to assimilate what it is proper for one to know, but that which enables one *to get free of oneself.* (p. 8, emphasis added)

Concepts and Theory: Knowledge as Power

Though Foucault doesn't approach it in this way, I think Weber's idea of disenchantment can set the stage for an easier understanding of knowledge and power. Weber talks about **rationalization** as a process through which the universe is disenchanted, emptied of magic and spirituality, and made to seem as if it works like a machine, according to the laws of science. Before the modern age, the world was to one degree or another mystical and awe inspiring. It was enchanted. How and why it worked was seen in spiritual or magical terms rather than rational and causal ones. Moreover, the world was seen as an intrinsic whole. Rationalization, however, breaks the whole down to understand the mechanics of a thing.

Ironically, modern rationalization began in religion: Historically, religion was a major force in secularization, a necessary component of demystification and rationalization. People generally assume that science and capitalism have been the major sources of secularization, and in terms of recent history, that's true. But secularization goes back much further to the dawn of religion. Secularization is "the process by which sectors of society and culture are removed from the domination of religious institutions and symbols" (Berger, 1967, p. 107). The world for humans was initially filled with multiple layers of energies, spirits, demons, and gods. The gods were present everywhere, such as in fertility rites and war—they didn't simply go along with the troops or bless one side over another, as some believe today, but rather, gods were embodied in war itself.

The evolution of religion systematically removed gods and spirits from this world. This removal is in fact a primary distinction between magic and religion. *Magic* is the direct manipulation of forces to achieve a desired end. Thus, to ensure a good harvest, a magician might perform a fertility ritual, because the realities of seeds and fertility are virtually the same. *Religion,* on the other hand, is symbolic. In religion, the gods do not dwell in nature, nor do they live in human activity. In ethical monotheism, for example, God lives outside of time (eternal) and space (infinite). Through the move to symbolic religions, the universe was thus emptied of a unifying soul. God could obviously act within the universe, but those actions by definition are now supernatural, existing outside the boundaries of time and space. This emptying of the universe—the process of secularization—left it open to purely empirical, technical explanations. Science, of course, filled the gap and gave us explanations based on dissecting entities down to their constituent parts, such as quarks and strands of DNA.

Rationalization is an ongoing process. In the beginning of modernity, rationality was comparatively limited. But as the processes of modernity took hold and began to influence different areas of life, rationalization became an almost unstoppable force. For example, education in the United States is becoming more rationalized, with greater emphasis on "outcome-based schooling." Your own life is becoming increasingly rationalized. Most of you use daily planners that render the days, weeks, months, and years into usable pieces that together will bring you to your life goals. Further, when your parents were your age, nobody had even heard of a carbon footprint, let alone set out to measure and be accountable to one. Yet as of 2002, you can not only measure your carbon footprint; you can also measure your water footprint. That isn't simply a measure of the water you use; it's the total volume of freshwater that is used to produce all the goods and services that you consume. Every part of life that can be dissected and rationalized is or will be. Foucault's concern is about how this sort of modern knowledge is used to control our lives.

Ordering Knowledge

Order is an interesting idea. We order our days and lives; we order our homes and offices; we order our files and our bank accounts; we order our yards and shopping centers; we order land and sea—in short, humans order everything. But *how* do we order things? We considered one important answer to that question with Durkheim: Humans order the world based on categories. But a deeper and more fundamental question can be asked: How do we order the *order* of things? In other words, what scheme or system underlies and creates our categorical schemes?

To introduce us to this question, Foucault (1966/1994) tells a delightful story of reading a book that contains a Chinese categorical system that divides animals into the following groups:

(a) belonging to the Emperor, (b) embalmed, (c) tame, (d) sucking pigs, (e) sirens, (f) fabulous, (g) stray dogs, (h) included in the present classification, (i) frenzied, (j) innumerable, (k) drawn with a very fine camelhair brush, (l) et cetera, (m) having just broken the water pitcher, (n) that from a long way off look like flies. (p. xv)

The thing that struck Foucault about this system of categories was the limitation of his own thinking—"the stark impossibility of thinking *that*" (p. xv). In response, Foucault asks an important set of questions: What sets the boundaries of what is possible and impossible to think? Where do these boundaries originate? What is the price of these impossibilities, what is gained and what is lost?

Foucault argues that there is a fundamental code to culture, a code that orders language, perception, values, practices, and all that gives order to the world around us. He calls these fundamental codes epistemological fields or the episteme of knowledge in any age. **Episteme** refers to the mode of a thought's existence, or the way in which thought organizes itself in any historical moment. An episteme is the necessary precondition of thought. It is what exists before thought and that which makes thought possible. Epistemes give birth to and contain discourses. The concept of **discourse** refers to languages, positions, and practices that are specific to a social issue—discourses are intrinsically political, and they structure relations of power. As an illustration, think of the phrase "third world nations." Many people use the phrase without a second thought. However, if there are third world nations, there must be first and second world nations. Most Americans assume that the United States is the first world, but what's the second? This way of talking about the world is actually specific to the Cold War. First world nations were the United States and its allies; second world nations referred to the USSR and its allies; and third world nations were unaligned. So, there really aren't any third world nations anymore. That position is gone. But we have another way of talking about nations. This discourse contains developed, developing, and undeveloped countries. Notice that the names and relationships have changed, yet this is still a discourse that is based on political and economic values and that seeks to control others. Developing and undeveloped countries exist only because of the perceived supremacy of developed nations.

Also notice that discourses work to create **subjects**. In order to participate in the world order of development, nations must take on the positions within the discourse. The import of this might be easier to see using a discourse that situates people. "I'm a man" is such a statement. The discourse of gender sets the conditions of my existence as "a man." For me to be a man, I must meet the conditions of existence that are set down in the discourse of gender, not only for you to accept me as a man, but for me to as well, because the discourse sets out the conditions of subjectivity, how we think and feel about our self. Subjects, and the accompanying inner thoughts and feelings, are specific conditions within the discourse. As we locate ourselves within a discourse, we become subject to it and thus subjectively answer ourselves through discourse.

Concepts and Theory: Modern Power and Control

Two important institutional practices strongly inform the relationship between knowledge and power in modernity. The first is one we've already mentioned: The modern way of knowing is distinctively objectifying. A good portion of the episteme of the modern age is bound up within scientism—the adaptation of the methods, mental attitudes, and modes of expression typical of scientists, which results in universal technologies that allow humans to regularize and routinize their control of the world. None of this is new for us;

we've been talking about it as the technical project of modernity. However, we now need to begin to think about the implications of the wholesale move to, and legitimation of, scientific knowledge. As a result of scientism, modern discourses are intrinsically demystifying, rationalizing, and objectifying.

The second set of practices belongs to the **state**. Prior to modernity, most societies were organized, diverse ethnic groupings with relatively fluid political and physical boundaries. Power and control under such systems as a monarchy were obviously at stake, but the span of control was comparatively narrow and intermittent. Modernity, however, brought with it a unique form of government: the nation-state with different kinds of interests. Weber (1922/1968) defines the state in terms of three factors: an identifiable and defendable territory, the availability of physical force, and a governing unit distinct from economic pursuits. These issues give nations rigid territorial boundaries to protect, a separate economic sphere to protect and provide for, and a standing army to support. Foucault furthers Weber's definition by arguing that the state finds its method of control in the modern episteme found in scientism, specifically the social and behavioral sciences.

To understand the form of modern governmental control, Foucault (1975/1995) uses the analogy of the panopticon. The word **panopticon** is a combination of two Greek words, which together mean "all seeing." The kind of panopticon that Foucault is interested in was developed in the late 1700s by a man named Jeremy Bentham, who developed a new kind of prison building. Bentham's panopticon was a round building with an observation tower in the middle that optimized surveillance. The building was divided into cells for individual prisoners that extended from the inner core to the outer wall. Each cell had inner and outer windows; each prisoner, then, was backlit by the outer window, allowing for easy viewing. "They are like so many cages, so many small theatres, in which each actor is alone, perfectly individualized and constantly visible" (Foucault, 1975/1995, p. 200). The tower itself was fitted with Venetian blinds, hallways that zigzag, and screens placed among the observation rooms in the tower. Together, these made the tower guards invisible to the prisoners who were being observed. The purpose of the panopticon was to allow the observers to see without being seen. Here, "inspection functions ceaselessly. The gaze is alert everywhere" (p. 195). Because prisoners could never be sure if they were being observed or not, they had to act as if they were under surveillance 24/7. The prisoners thus became their own guards.

Foucault isn't really interested in the panopticon as such. He sees the idea of the panopticon as illustrative of a shift in the fundamental way people thought and the way in which power is practiced. In terms of crime, it involved a shift from the spectacle of torture (which fit well with monarchical power) to regulation in prison (which fits well with the nation-state);

from seeing crime as an act against authority to an act against society; from being focused on guilt (did she or he do it?) to cause (what social or psychological factors influenced the person); and, most importantly, from punishment to discipline—more specifically, to the self-discipline imposed by the ever-present but unseen surveillance of the panopticon. Foucault (quoted in Davidson, 1994) talks about this form of ruling as **governmentality**: "The government of the self by the self in its articulation with relations to others" (p. 119).

In a play on words, Foucault argues that the discipline associated with panopticon surveillance of the entire population comes from the "disciplines," in particular the human sciences. The modern episteme created the possibility of the human sciences, such as psychiatry, psychology, and sociology. The human has been the subject of thought and modes of control for quite some time, but in every case the person was seen holistically, as part of the universal scheme of things. In the modern episteme, however, humankind becomes the object of study, not as part of an aesthetic whole, but as a thing in-and-of-itself, a singular object to be governed. Almost everything that we think, feel, and do is scrutinized by a human science, and we are provided with the knowledge gained so that we too can understand our own life and bring it under the dominion of modern governmentality.

The Governmentality of Sex

The bulk of Foucault's work is a series of **counter-histories**. When most of us think of history, we think of a factual telling of events from our past. We are aware, of course, that sometimes telling can be politicized, which is one reason we have Black History Month here in the United States—we are trying to make up for having left people of color out. But most of us also think that the memory model is still intact; it's just getting a few tweaks. Foucault wants us to free history from the model of memory. He doesn't say anything directly about whether any history is more or less true; that's not an issue for him because *history in all its forms is part of and generated by discourse*. Thus, Foucault's concern is how the idea of true history is used. What Foucault wants to produce is a counter-history—a history told from a different point of view from the progressive, linear, memory model. The purpose of these counter-histories "is to discover that truth or being does not lie at the root of what we know and what we are, but the exteriority of accidents" (Foucault, 1984, p. 81). He is particularly interested in demonstrating that the modern episteme and discourses are not necessarily the products of a steady progress toward "truth." His fullest historical treatment is of sexuality—specifically, the shift from the ancient Greek model, where sexuality is an unbounded element of human existence, an expression of the goddess Aphrodite, to the modern understanding of sexuality as a thing to be controlled.

Part of this shift obviously came from Protestantism with its emphasis on individual righteousness and redemption. But an important part was also played by the Counter-Reformation, a reform movement in the Catholic Church. Confession and penance are sacraments in the Catholic Church. They are ways through which salvation is imparted to Christians. The Counter-Reformation increased the frequency of confession and guided confessioners to specific kinds of self-examination, designed to root out the sins of the flesh down to the minutest detail. Sex thus became "a badly exorcised complicity between the body's mechanics and the mind's complacency: everything had to be told" (Foucault, 1976/1990a, p. 19). This was the beginning of the Western idea that sex is a deeply embedded power, one that is intrinsic to the "flesh" (the vehicle of sin par excellence, as compared to the Greek idea of bodily appetites) and one that must be eradicated through inward searching using an external moral code and through outward confession.

While these Christian doctrines would have influenced culture generally, they could have remained connected to the fate of Christianity alone had it not been for other secular changes and institutions beginning in the eighteenth century, most particularly in politics, economics, and medicine. With the rise of the nation-state and science, population control became an economic and political issue. Previous governments had always been aware of the people gathered together under its banner or in its name, but conceiving of the people as the *population* is a significant change. The idea of population transforms people into a nameless object that can be analyzed and controlled.

In this transformation, science provided the tools and the nation-state the motivation and control mechanisms. The population could be counted and analyzed statistically, and those statistics became important for governance and economic pursuit. The population represented the labor force, one that needed to be trained and, more fundamentally, born. At the center of these economic and political issues was sexuality—"It was necessary to analyze the birthrate, the age of marriage, the legitimate and illegitimate births, the precocity and frequency of sexual relations, the ways of making them fertile or sterile, the effects of unmarried life or of the prohibitions, the impact of contraceptive practices"—and so on (Foucault, 1976/1990a, pp. 25–26).

Medicine and psychiatry took up the sex banner as well. Psychiatry set out to discover the makeup of the human mind and emotion, and it began to catalog mental illnesses, especially those connected with sex. It conceptualized masturbation as a perversion at the core of many psychological and physical problems, homosexuality as a mental illness, and the maturation of a child in terms of successive sexual issues that the child must resolve on the way to healthy adulthood. In short, psychiatry "annexed the whole of the sexual perversions as its own province" (Foucault, 1976/1990a, p. 30). Law and criminal justice also bolstered the cause, as society sought to regulate individual and bedroom behaviors. Social controls popped up everywhere that

> screened the sexuality of couples, parents and children, dangerous and endangered adolescents—undertaking to protect, separate, and forewarn, signaling perils everywhere, awakening people's attention, calling for diagnoses, piling up reports, organizing therapies. These sites radiated discourses aimed at sex. (pp. 30–31)

All of these factors worked to change the discourse of Western sexuality. Sex went from the Greek model of a natural bodily appetite that could be pleased in any number of ways, to the modern model of sex as the insidious power within, something separate from the inner or whole person. At the heart of this change is the confession, propagated by Catholicism and Protestantism and picked up by psychiatry, medicine, educators, and other experts. Confessional rhetoric is found everywhere in a society that uses Victorian prudence as its backdrop for incessant talk in magazines, journals, books, movies, and reality television shows. Here, repression is used as a source of discourse, and sex has become the topic of conversation, a central feature in Western discourse, and the defining feature of the human animal. Sex is suspected of "harboring a fundamental secret" concerning the truth of mankind (Foucault, 1976/1990a, p. 69).

Concepts and Theory: The Importance of Being Critical

What is Foucault's point in constructing counter-histories? Part of what he wants to do is expose the contingencies of what we consider reality, but to what end? Many critical perspectives are based on assumptions of what would make a better society. Most social movements are like this; there is a definite goal toward which the movement is aimed. But that isn't the case with Foucault. He doesn't have a vision of what society ought to be like. Part of the reason for this is his view of history: History isn't linear, but is characterized by ruptures and discontinuities. Predicting or steering a course for society is thus impossible. Another reason is that Foucault rejects the idea of truth, both in terms of its existence and in terms of our ability to express it (even if one did exist). Thus, there's no ultimate goodness toward which to guide society, and it's impossible to steer history in the first place. So why upset the applecart with counter-histories?

There are two reasons. First, upsetting the applecart is its own purpose. Or, put another way, the critical perspective has its own intrinsic value.

In counter-histories, Foucault (1966/1994) wants us "to discover that these orders are perhaps not the only possible ones or the best ones" (p. xx). He wants to free up the possibility of thinking something different. The power of knowledge is that it presents itself to us as transparent, as if it were only what it is, a reflection of the reality of the world. But for Foucault, knowledge is simply a **truth game**: the rules, resources, and practices that go into making something true for humans. In counter-histories, then, Foucault is interested only in setting our thinking free from the limitations of *im*possibility (at least as far as it's possible). Foucault doesn't necessarily have a place he is taking us; he doesn't really have a utopian vision of what knowledge and practice ought to be. His critique is aimed at freeing knowledge and opening it up to possibility; it's aimed at creating an empty space that is undetermined. Undetermined space is creative space.

The second reason I think Foucault does this is based on my reading of Foucault and others like him. There's a shift in the focus of ethics when we move from truth-as-truth to truth-as-game. Quite simply, under truth-as-truth, our ethical obligation is to the truth; however, with truth-as-game, our ethical focus shifts. Perhaps an example might help. Let's say you and your partner are arguing over an event. He or she sees it one way, and you see it totally differently. Most arguments revolve around whose claim is more accurate: The truth of the event is used to claim a superior position in the argument. On the other hand, if both of you firmly believe that the truth or actuality of what happened is unavailable, impossible to get at, then what you are left with is trying to understand what the other's version of truth is doing for him or her. Here's the important point: Arguing about what really happened—fighting about the truth—prevents you from getting at what matters, and it sets up destructive poles of conflict.

Understanding truth as a game changes the ground rules, practices, and outcomes. In societal situations, discourse comes to be seen for what it is: a truth game, not a statement of fact or existence. Let's take the discourses that create gender and racial differences as examples. Historically, much of the debate was centered upon the veracity of the essentializing discourses. In other words, claims were being made about how women were essentially different from men, and blacks were different from whites, biologically, genetically, and religiously. After prolonged conflict, the discourses have changed somewhat, but imagine a world where those discourses and others like them are seen as truth games—there is no truth of race, no truth of gender, no truth of sexuality. The only thing that matters is what those discourses accomplish. The question then becomes, what are those discourses accomplishing for those that hold them?

The Craft of Citizenship   Power

The Basics: Comprehension and Explanation

- How would you phrase Weber's, Dahrendorf's, and Foucault's central questions?
- With those questions in mind, write a two- to three-sentence statement that captures their theoretical response.

  > *Helpful hints:* For example, you could phrase Weber's question as "What are the foundations of power in modern society?" His answer might be something like this: "Power is the legitimated ability to realize one's own goals, despite the efforts of others. There are three power bases in modern society: class, status, and political associations. More often than not, power in modernity is legitimated as rational legal and is usually exercised through bureaucratic position."

- Identify and define all the important concepts from each theorist. Again, I've only placed concepts in bold without the supporting concepts in italics, and again, there's a lot going on under each main concept.
- How are class, status, and party related to power?
- What are bureaucracies, and what effects do they have?
- How do groups move from quasi-groups to interest or conflict groups?
- When would we expect conflict to become more violent and intense?
- How does modern knowledge and discourse work to control individuals?
- Explain the process through which sex became governed through modern knowledge. How did the individual's relationship to his or her own sexuality change?

Skill Set 1: Inference and Application

- Why is Weber's theory of class specifically important today in your country?
- Why would social movements and change be more difficult today? What implications does bureaucratic management have for democracy?
- Where do race and gender fit in with these analyses of power?

  > *Helpful hints:* Start by thinking about the kind of groups that the various races and genders are, and then how organizations and modern knowledge work to exclude or oppress.

- Using Dahrendorf and Foucault, speculate about the place of the Internet in democracy.
- Elaborate on how the bureaucratic personality is formed by including Goffman's ideas of deference and demeanor rituals.

- Using Foucault's ideas about episteme and discourse, speculate about how you are participating in the domination of your life.
  - ➢ *Helpful hints:* In order to do this, you will have to think historically. Think of ways you are being controlled that your parents or grandparents weren't. Remember, these controls will probably seem "reasonable" because they are based in modern knowledge. Start by thinking of obvious issues, like smoking and drinking.

Skill Set 2: Interpretation, Analysis, Evaluation, Synthesis

- There are two models of intentional social change in this chapter: Dahrendorf's and Foucault's. Analyze and critique each in terms of applicability to this day and age. Which do you think is more fitting and why? How would Parsons' theory of revolutionary change augment these theories?
- Using Alexander and Dahrendorf, explain why tension and conflict are unavoidable and necessary in democracy.
- How do Dahrendorf's conditions of conflict violence and intensity complement or expand the conditions of religious terrorism? In what ways are religious terrorist groups different from the interest groups that Dahrendorf is directly considering?
- Using elements from Weber, Dahrendorf, and Foucault, how does power work in modern society?
- Analyze the model of democracy presented in Chapter 1 using Foucault's ideas, specifically his ideas about counter-histories and the reasons behind a critical perspective.

7

Gender

Y ou'll recall that the social project of modernity is based on the idea, value, and belief in equality, and that this belief comes from a more fundamental assumption about human beings: Every individual is capable of discerning truth, born with the capacity to reason, and not only able but required to make decisions that guide his or her life and contribute to the welfare of society at large. However, you also know that the social project fell well short of the mark—the belief in equality was in truth founded upon practices of *in*equality. Western capitalism, for example, was built on black slave labor as well as upon the free labor that women provided and continue to provide. Women were also excluded from owning property in Western societies until the middle of the nineteenth century, and they didn't have the right to vote in democratic elections until well into the twentieth century. Gender continues to be the basis for the unequal distribution of income: In 2008, the median income for women in the United States with a college degree was 26 percent less than for men (U.S. Bureau of Labor Statistics, 2009). Gender is also a factor in violence: Women in the United States are 6 times more likely to suffer violence from a partner than men are (Bureau of Justice Statistics, n.d.). In addition, it's estimated that 91 percent of rape victims are female versus 9 percent that are male (UCSC Rape Prevention Education, 2009).

When compared to other systems of inequality, gender has unique characteristics. It is the oldest system of economic and political discrimination and was quite likely the first. Gender is also ubiquitous: It's found in virtually every situation and thus crosscuts every other system of stratification. Further, gender is structured in such a way as to keep group members from connecting, sharing grief, and building solidarity—there is no neighborhood or ghetto for gender. Moreover, gender is required of every single person; thus, children are intentionally and thoroughly trained in gender, sometimes even before birth. Finally, gender is the social category that is most powerfully linked by most people to biological, genetic, and religious causes and legitimations.

In this chapter, we will consider how and why gender inequality started— Charlotte Perkins Gilman will explain the evolutionary roots of patriarchy and how women's bodies changed to accommodate patriarchy. We'll also find out how gender inequality is patterned structurally in society today— Janet Chafetz will explain the workings of gender stratification at four different levels: in the individual, situation, organization, and the economy. In addition, we'll see that gender is more than a system of prejudice; it's also a way of being—Dorothy E. Smith will explain how women's awareness of the world is different from men's, and how women are systematically excluded from legitimated knowledge.

The Root Causes of Gender Inequality—Charlotte Perkins Gilman

Charlotte Stetson Perkins Gilman (1860–1935) was born Charlotte Perkins in Hartford, Connecticut. Her father was related to the Beecher family, one of the most important American families of the nineteenth century. Gilman's parents divorced early, leaving Charlotte and her mother to live as poor relations to the Beecher family, moving from house to house. Gilman's adult life was marked by tumultuous personal relationships; her first marriage, in 1884, to Charles Stetson, ended in divorce, but it also yielded Gilman's feminist novella, *The Yellow Wallpaper*—an important work that is still taught in women's studies courses today. Gilman was a prolific writer and journalist. Among her best-known works are *Concerning Children, The Home, The Man-Made World,* and *Herland* (a feminist utopian novel). Gilman's most important theoretical work is *Women and Economy*. In Gilman's lifetime, the book went through nine editions and was translated into seven different languages. Gilman was also politically active. She often spoke at political rallies and was a firm supporter of the women's club movement, which played a vital part in the progress toward women's rights in the United States. Finally, suffering with cancer, Charlotte Gilman died by her own hand on August 17, 1935.

Concepts and Theory: The Evolution of Gender

Gilman's main theoretical question focuses on the origins of gender inequality, and she draws on evolutionary theory to explain the root causes. Darwinian evolution is based on several ideas. First, the fundamental relationship is between the biological species and the environment in which it lives. Second, within that environment, there is a struggle for existence, with different species competing for environmental niches. Third, biological species are not fixed but exist in a permanent state of change. Genetic variation within the species comes about because of changes in the environment and through species' competition; some variations are successful, while others are not. The struggle for survival also weeds out the weaker, less adaptive variations, leaving the fittest to carry on. Both these processes are determined through natural selection. Fourth, the results of natural selection are genetically passed on from parent to offspring. Variations that are less adaptive leave few or no descendants, and the stronger ones multiply over generations.

Gilman doesn't use evolution as an analogy; she is interested in the actual, genetic evolution of the human species and how that both influences and is affected by social evolution. But Gilman isn't concerned with the entire human evolutionary process, only a specific element: how women and women's bodies have changed in response to patriarchy. In order to understand this, Gilman adds some ideas to general evolutionary theory. First, like Marx, she sees the economy as our evolutionary adaptation. The economy is basic; our use of it is the result of natural selection pressures. Our genetic patterns and bodies are built for economic production. It's the reason we have hands, brains, and vocal cords; the reason we walk upright; and so forth. Second, Gilman makes a distinction between self- and race-preservation. Natural selection related to self-preservation develops those characteristics in the individual that are needed to succeed in the struggle for self-survival. Race-preservation, on the other hand, develops those characteristics that enable the species as a whole to succeed in the struggle for existence. The relationships between self- and race-preservation should be balanced in order to be adaptive: Individuals need to be selfish enough to fight for their own survival, and selfless enough to fight for the good of the whole species.

The next element in Gilman's theory is much like that given to us by Spencer and others. Along with the genetic and biological changes, humans developed society. Because of our overwhelming dependency on social organization for survival, we create cultural meanings and behavioral guidelines that in turn support the equilibrium between self- and race-preservation. Over time, culture and behavioral patterns become institutionalized— Gilman calls this "accumulation of precedent." Gilman has in mind such things as art and religion—habits of mind and behavior that are separate from the economy and tend to reinforce and legitimate the current pattern of economic production. With the accumulation of precedent, humans create their own environment. We thus have two environments that affect our evolution—the physical and the social.

General Problems for Human Evolution

In the transition from usual primate behavior to economy and society, there were some obstacles to overcome. One obvious problem is the move from a symbiotic relationship with the environment to one of control. Generally speaking, every species is well suited to its environment. This means that an animal will suffer and most likely die if you put it in an environment that is radically different from its own; a polar bear would not survive in the Serengeti, a fish won't survive out of water, and so on. Fully developed Homo sapiens, however, occupy "a peculiar position in the animal kingdom. Unlike the other higher mammals, he has no species-specific environment, no environment firmly structured by his own instinctual organization. . . . [Thus,] man's relationship to his environment is characterized by world-openness" (Berger & Luckmann, 1966, p. 47). Humans can thus live just about any- and everywhere. We have lived in outer space and at the bottom of the ocean, and millions of us have lived for generations in the middle of deserts that barely support even the most basic of plant and animal life. This level of adaptability is our specific niche and is fundamentally related to the economy. However, this level of control didn't appear suddenly; it developed over a long period of evolutionary history, and up until fairly recent history, it was an all-consuming struggle.

Another issue that has faced human survival is the problem of social connections. If you consider society today, you'll see that almost all of your connections to other people are socially and culturally produced. This way of patterning relationships and behaviors gives us incredible adaptation potential. Because our patterns aren't instinctually driven, we have an enormous range of possibilities that can be modified to suit the various issues confronting human survival. Like control of the environment, this ability to create social connections developed over time and involved struggle. Here, we had to overcome the genetic social programming we inherited from our closest relatives.

The problem was that the last common ancestor (LCA) of humans—that is, the last species that existed before the line that would lead to Homo sapiens developed—had a disposition for limited and weak social ties, rather than a natural tendency toward sociability. "This pattern of weak tie formation, low sociality, high mobility, and strong individualism was to pose . . . a difficult problem for hominoid species, especially those on the human line, once they moved from a forest to an open-range habitat" (Maryanski & Turner, 1992, p. 13). In other words, in order to create society, our species had to overcome its genetic programming against strong, lasting, and extensive social ties.

The Problems With Men

To the general problem of sociability that we just discussed, Gilman adds the issue of intrinsic male energy. According to Gilman (1911/2001), there are distinct, natural male and female dispositions. The basic masculine characteristics are "desire, combat, self-expression; all legitimate and right in proper use" (Gilman, 1911/2001, p. 41). The problem is that the male tendency toward aggression, individuality, and objectification were at odds with the need for social organization. As long as "the male savage was still a mere hunter and fighter, expressing masculine energy . . . along its essential line, expanding, scattering" (Gilman, 1899/1975, p. 126), social organization of any complexity was impossible.

Female energy, on the other hand, is naturally more conservative and is characterized by maternal instincts—the love and care of little ones. Notice that in terms of social relationships, females naturally form a bond, whereas men do not. For Gilman, then, women are the general race type for humans, not men. In order to begin to create the social ties necessary for society to exist, the "giant force of masculine energy" had to be tamed, and men had to connect socially as women did naturally. This evolutionary pressure probably created any number of options, but two patterns came to the forefront through natural selection: monogamy and patriarchy. Monogamy would obviously help establish the kin connection between men and children. But in order to accomplish this, the sexual behavior of women had to be controlled. There had to be strong safeguards and sanctions in place to assure the man that the child was indeed his. This need for control created pressures for patriarchy to evolve.

However, monogamy wasn't enough to socialize male energy. There's nothing in monogamy itself that would make a man less independent and more committed to caretaking social relations; thus, another pressure was created to select patriarchy. Through patriarchy, men not only subjugated women, but also had to provide for dependent women and children. Prior to patriarchy, both men and women produced economically, but as men dominated women, they also removed them from the economic sphere. Women could no longer provide for themselves, let alone their children. Men had to take on this responsibility, and as they did, they took on "the instincts and habits of the female, to his immense improvement" (Gilman, 1899/1975, p. 128). Therefore, men became more social as a result of patriarchy, and kinship became the foundation upon which every other social institution was built.

Yet patriarchy and monogamy did more than give society a foundation from which to build. Remember, the other problem facing human survival was controlling the environment. The fundamental defining feature of economic production is the utilization or dominance of the environment. Economic production does not occur if a species is simply gathering or hunting what is naturally present in its surroundings. What we mean by economy is the manufacture of something that does not naturally occur. If humanity was to survive and adapt through an economy, then the environment had to be subjugated and made to yield something that it naturally wouldn't. Survival as humans was dependent upon this happening as rapidly as possible. The gender best suited naturally for aggressive control was the male. By taking women out of the productive sphere, and therefore forcing men to be more productive, "male energy ... brought our industries to their present development" (Gilman, 1899/1975, pp. 132–133). According to Gilman, then, patriarchy and monogamy thus solved two of the most basic problems facing human existence.

Concepts and Theory: Modern Dysfunctions of Patriarchy and Monogamy

We have long since achieved a level of economic production equal to maintaining the entire human race. Our level of affluence is unmatched in human history. Yet it is also true that our control of the environment has gone so far that we are now in danger of destroying it. We can also look around us and behold the extent of social connections. People living in modern societies at the beginning of the twenty-first century are able to connect with others all around the globe. Yet, as with the economy, there are plenty of dysfunctions in our social relationships. In turning her gaze to modernity, Gilman notes dysfunctions as well, especially in gender relations.

Gilman characterizes the current overall system and its effects as sexuo-economic. In sexuo-economic relations, two structures overlap: the social structure of the economy and the private sphere of sexual relationships. The basic issue here is that because women are dependent upon men economically, these two structures, which ought to be somewhat separate, intertwine. The interlacing of the economy and sex is due to evolutionary changes in women. When workforce participation is denied to women, they are deprived of interaction with the natural environment through economic production. Under patriarchy and monogamy, women's relationship to the natural environment, with all of its laws and effects, is thus replaced by another. Rather than a woman's survival being dependent upon her economic production, she is economically dependent upon a man. Men thus became women's economic environment, and, just as any organism responds to its environment, woman changed and adapted to the new environment.

All animals that have two sexes also have what we call secondary sex characteristics. The specific function of secondary sex characteristics is to attract mates. Humans have these as well. However, humans have what Gilman calls morbid excess in sex distinction. In other words, the visual cues used to attract a mate have become accentuated in humans to the point that they are morbid or gruesome. Further, these morbid sex distinctions are found in women more than men, which is a reversal of what is usually found in nature—in most animals, the male is the most flamboyant. The need to attract a man has changed the natural form of women's bodies, according to Gilman. In addition to exaggerated breasts and buttocks, women are smaller, softer, and physically more dependent. In addition, rather than improving her skills in economic pursuits, under monogamy and patriarchy a woman must improve her skills at attracting a man. In fact, expertise in attraction skills constitutes her basic economic skill. She devotes herself to cosmetics, clothes, primping, subtle body language techniques, and so on. "It is what she is born for, what she is trained for, what she is exhibited for. It is, moreover, her means of honorable livelihood and advancement" (Gilman, 1899/1975, p. 87). Moreover, the increase in sex distinctions leads to greater emphasis on sex for both men and women. Further, in this sexuo-economic structure, women develop an overwhelming passion for attachment to men at any cost.

Obviously, the economic dependency of women will have economic results as well. Women are affected most profoundly as they become "nonproductive consumers." According to Gilman, in the natural order of things, productivity and consumption go hand-in-hand, and production comes first. It's part of what we do as a species, and there is a natural balance to it when everybody contributes and everybody consumes. The balance shifts, however, as women are denied workforce participation. The consumption process is severed from the production process, and the whole system is therefore subject to unnatural kinds of pressures. Noneconomic women are focused on noneconomic needs. In the duties of her roles as wife, homemaker, and mother, she creates a market that focuses on "devotion to individuals and their personal needs" and "sensuous decoration and personal ornament" (Gilman, 1899/1975, pp. 119–120). The economy, of course, responds to this market demand and creates a feminized market.

Evolution to Democracy

Taken together—the morbid excess in secondary sex characteristics, the obsession with sex, the feminization of the market, and women's unhealthy emotional attachment to men and relationships—these dysfunctions have created an imbalance between self- and race-preservation, which in turn has resulted in an accumulation of precedent. In other words, our economic, religious, familial, educational, mass media, and health care structures have institutionalized the emphasis on the self over the collective. But humanity has also evolved to the point where the initial issues—economic survival and establishing social relations—are no longer evolutionary pressures. Relieving these pressures has truly given us freedom to choose. We are no longer shackled by "rudimentary forces." What's more, "The development of democracy . . . [h]as so strengthened, freed, emboldened, the human soul . . . that we have thrown off slavery, and with the same impulse have set in motion the only struggle toward securing woman's fuller equity" (Gilman, 1899/1975, pp. 147–148).

It is Gilman's position that just as technical progress is our heritage, so is ever-expanding equality. Evolution of the species involves not only economic advancement, but increasing compassion as well; ethical and technical evolutions are inexorably linked. At the present evolutionary moment, we are only hindered by our own blindness: "We do not, as a rule, know how to read the most important message to humanity—the signs of the times" (Gilman, 1899/1975, p. 146). We can afford the luxury of complete equality, but we fail to see the problem:

> Being used to them, we do not notice them, or, forced to notice them, we attribute the pain we feel to the evil behavior of some individual, and never think of it as being the result of a condition common to us all. (p. 84)

Structuring Gender Inequality—Janet Chafetz

Janet Saltzman Chafetz (1942–2006) received her BA in history from Cornell University and her MA in history from the University of Connecticut (UConn). While at UConn, she began graduate studies in sociology and then completed her PhD at the University of Texas at Austin. She taught at the University of Houston beginning in 1973. Chafetz served as president of Sociologists for Women in Society (SWS) from 1984 to 1986, and as chairperson of the American Sociological Society (ASA) Theory Section from 1998 to 1999. Chafetz was also honored as the first invited lecturer for the Cheryl Allyn Miller Endowed Lectureship Series, sponsored by SWS; her book *Gender Equity* won the American Educational Studies Association Critic's Choice Panel Award (1990) and was selected by *Choice Magazine* for their list, Outstanding Academic Books (1990–1991). Chafetz wrote a total of 11 books, which helped shape the field of gender studies in the twentieth century. Janet Chafetz died of cancer on July 6, 2006.

Concepts and Theory: Structures of Gender Inequality

While Gilman is concerned with how gender inequality came about, Chafetz is interested in explaining how social structures maintain gender inequality in modern societies. Her theory is particularly powerful because she theorizes at four structural levels, and she brings her theory full circle. Sociologists tend to think about society on four levels: macro, meso, micro, and individual. Macro-level analysis is of the institutions and structures that form the largest factors and processes that make up society, meso phenomena are at the level of the organization, micro-level phenomena are those that occur in face-to-face interactions, and individual analysis is of the person. In addition to hitting all four levels, Chafetz explains how gender inequality works—how gender stratification is patterned over time—and uses the same theoretical elements to explain how gender disparity can be changed. Thus, Chafetz offers perhaps the most comprehensive structural explanation of gender stratification.

The Core Structure

Like Marx, Chafetz argues that the economy determines class stratification. In this case, Chafetz is looking at how a basic property of capitalism pushes for the use of gender as a stratifying factor. As you know, capitalism requires exploitation and is motivated to achieve the highest profit possible in order to accumulate additional capital to invest. This generally brings about low wages in the job market, but it also drives the search for groups that can be systematically exploited. If capitalism can create or identify a group that can legitimately be exploited as a whole, then profits will not only be higher but will also be most easily gained.

Under patriarchy, much of what women do in our society is done for free. No wages are paid for the wife's domestic labor—this work constitutes the unpaid labor force of capitalism. Without this labor, capitalism would crumble. Paying women for caring for children and domestic work would significantly reduce profit margins and the capitalists' ability to accumulate capital. In addition, a man's ability to devote his time entirely to a job or career is dependent upon the woman's exploitation as a woman. When women are allowed in the workforce, they tend to be kept in menial positions or given lower wages for the same work as men. All of this, of course, is legitimated through a system of belief in the natural differences of men and women: Women are "built for" childcare and nurturing.

In brief, then, Chafetz argues that the initial and most important macro-level factor in gender discrimination is the workforce participation of women: The lower the level of women's workforce participation (involvement in the job market), the greater will be the amount of inequality found at the three other structuring levels. Conversely, the more women are able to gain and keep jobs and careers, particularly in high-paying segments, the less will be the general level of gender inequality.

Organizational Structures of Gender Inequality

To explain how organizations contribute to gender inequality, Chafetz uses Rosabeth Kanter's (1977) work. Kanter gives us a social-psychological argument in which the organizational position of the person influences her psychological states and behaviors. Kanter points to three factors related to occupational position that influence work and gender in this way: the possibility of advancement, the power to achieve goals, and the relative number of a specific type of person within the position. Each of these factors in turn influences the individual's attitudes and work performance—or what we could call her organizational personality.

Most positions in an organization fall within a specific career path for advancement. The path for a professor, for example, goes from assistant, to associate, to full professor. The position of dean doesn't fall within that path. A professor could aspire to become dean, but he or she would have to change career trajectory. Kanter argues that women typically occupy positions within an organization that have limited paths for advancement. We can think of the occupational path for women as constricted in two ways: (1) The opportunities for advancement in feminized occupations, such as administrative assistant or nursing, are limited by the nature of the position; and (2) women who are on a more open career path often run into a glass ceiling that hinders their progress.

Positions also have different levels of power associated with them. As with career paths, we typically find that across the labor market, women hold organizational positions with less power attached to them than do men. Clearly, there are some women who transcend this situation, but women who are in positions of power are typically seen as "tokens," because there are no similar others in those positions within the company. This is Kanter's (1977) third organizational variable: relative numbers—the number of a group or identity in an organization as compared to others. There are generally fewer women in economic organizations.

For both Kanter and Chafetz, the importance of these organizational structures is that they provide a context for sense making, attitudes, and behavior. A basic tenet in social psychology states that people will manage and evaluate their behavior based on different roles available in diverse situations. For example, you evaluate your performance differently at home than at school because there are different roles available. And your evaluation of yourself will be different depending on how well you live up to the role expectations. Repeated similar evaluations form the basis of how you feel about yourself in these different situations and dispose you to different levels of motivation. (You'll be more highly motivated in roles where you are certain of positive evaluations.) Chafetz is arguing that within organizations, the most important social contexts include power and opportunity. If a person's available roles are associated with power and opportunity, then the individual will feel and act empowered. On the other hand, if the roles are limited in terms of control and prospect, the person will feel ineffectual and act likewise.

The problem in organizations is that women are systematically excluded from positions of power and opportunity. In response, many women are much less willing to exhibit positively aggressive behaviors at work. They feel ineffectual and limited in what they can achieve within the organization. The worker herself as well as others around her, including supervisors, are left to make sense out of these behaviors and sentiments. While these differences in behavior and attitude are clearly linked to organizational position, people generally attribute them to gender differences. These negative stereotypes of gender and work are used to reinforce gender inequality within the organization.

Micro-Level Structures of Gender Inequality

Chafetz (1990) asserts that for gender inequality, the most significant micro-level structure in face-to-face relations is exchange (p. 22). There are two issues that are important for seeing the effect that exchange has on gender. First, social exchanges are different from economic ones in that they lack specificity. All economic exchanges take place under the contract model. In other words, almost all of the elements of the exchange are laid out and understood in advance. For example, if you are buying a car on credit, you know exactly how much you have to pay every month and when your debt will be paid off. However, in social exchanges, the terms of the exchange cannot be clearly stated or given in advance. Imagine a situation where a friend of yours invites you over for dinner and tells you when and how you will be expected to repay. Thus, social exchange is implicit rather than explicit, and it is never clear when a debt has been paid in full.

Second, exchange theory argues that when alternatives are present, people will gravitate toward exchanges among equals. We tend to look for someone with whom we can balance out costs and benefits in the long run. Friendship is based on an equal exchange relationship: All parties feel that they give about as much as they take. This equal reciprocity among friends leads to a social bond built on trust and a high level of discretion in repayment. However, if an exchange isn't balanced—if one of the participants has more resources than the other—the person who has less will first seek out other exchange relations. In the absence of alternatives, the person with fewer resources will balance the exchange by offering compliance and deference, thus granting power to the other.

Because of their systematic exclusion from specific workforce participation and the subsequent structuring of economic organizations, women typically come into intimate relationships with fewer resources than men. This imbalance is offset by the woman offering deference and compliance to the man. The man's power in this exchange relationship is insidious precisely because it is based on social exchange. As we've seen, social exchanges are characterized by implicit agreements rather than explicit ones, with no clear payoff date or marker. Obviously, social exchange theory predicts the inverse as well: "The higher the ratio of women's material resource contribution to men's, the less the deference/compliance of wives to their husbands" (Chafetz, 1990, p. 48).

Gender is also structured at the micro level through performance. Recall that Goffman (Chapter 3) explains that selves are hidden, and the only way others know the kind of self we are claiming is by the cues we send out. Others read these cues, attribute to us the kind of self that is claimed, and then form righteously imputed expectations. These expectations are pressures to conform. If we don't, that part of our self will be discredited and stigmatized. Because gender is arguably the very first categorization that we make of people, gender is thus an extremely important part of impression management and self-validation: "[T]he 'doing' of gender is undertaken by women and men whose competence as members of society is hostage to its production" (West & Zimmerman, 1987, p. 126). As such, Goffman (1959) would see gender as a form of idealized performance in that we "incorporate and exemplify the officially accredited values of the society" (p. 35). In other words, social norms, ideologies, and stereotypes are used more strongly in gendered performances than in most others.

Thus, gender is an especially meaningful and risky performance that is produced in almost every situation. We tend to pay particular attention to the cues we give out about our gender and the cues others present. Goffman (1959) further points out that we look to the opposite gender to affirm our managed impression. Our gendered performances, then, are specifically targeted to the opposite sex and tend to be highly stereotypical. According to Chafetz (1990), "For men, this quest [for affirmation] entails demonstrations of strength and competence. However, for women it entails demonstrations of weakness, vulnerability, and ineptitude" (p. 26).

Personal Structures of Gender Inequality

Gender inequality generally functions without coercion. That is, "people of both genders tend to make choices that conform to the dictates of the gender system status quo" (Chafetz, 1990, p. 64). The question is, why do women voluntarily cooperate in their own oppression? Chafetz draws on several theoretical traditions to explain how individuals become gendered, the most powerful of which is psychodynamic theory. As it's used in theory, *psychic* refers to the basic energies that are the core of your inner life. In Freudian theory, these energies get structured as the id, ego, and superego. It's important to keep in mind that these are structures within the person and that they accomplish the same thing any structure does. This implies that when we use the idea of intrapsychic structures to talk about gender, we are making a much stronger statement than simply saying that boys and girls are socialized differently. Intrapsychic structures are at the core of the person, and much of what happens at this level is unconscious.

Nancy Chodorow's work forms the basis of Chafetz's psychodynamic theory. Chodorow (1978) argues that men's and women's psyches are structured differently due to dissimilar childhood experiences. The principal difference is that the majority of parenting is done by the mother. Both boys and girls thus grow up with their chief emotional attachment being to their mother. Girls are able to learn their gender identity from their mothers, but boys have to sever their emotional attachment to their mother in order to form their gender identity. The problem, of course, is that in capitalism the father is absent. Remember, we learned from Marx that capitalism lifted out economic production from every other institution. Girls' intrapsychic structure, then, is one that is built around consistency and relatedness—they don't have to break away to learn gender, and their social network is organically based in their mother. Women thus value relationships and are intrapsychically oriented toward feelings, caring, and nurturing.

However, in order to become gendered, boys have to separate from their mother, but there isn't a clear model for them to attach to and emulate. The male psyche, then, becomes one that is disconnected from others, that values and understands individuality, that is more comfortable with objective things than relational emotions, and that has and values strong ego boundaries. According to Freud, this male psyche also develops a fear and hatred of women (misogyny). As the boy tries to break away from his mother, she continues to parent because of the absent father. The boy unconsciously perceives her continued efforts to "mother" as attempts to smother his masculinity under an avalanche of femininity. He thus feels threatened and fights back against all that is feminine.

These intrapsychic differences play themselves out not only in male–female relationships, but also in the kinds of jobs men and women are drawn to. Generally, men are drawn to the kinds of positions that demand individualism, objectification, and control. Women, on the other hand, are frequently drawn to helping occupations where they can nurture and support. While there have certainly been changes in occupational distribution over the past 30 years, most of the stereotypically gendered fields continue to have disproportionate representation. The important point Chafetz is making is that the personal preference individuals feel to be in one kind of occupation rather than another is strongly informed by gendered intrapsychic structures. These personal choices, then, perpetuate gender structures of inequality.

Chafetz thus argues that gender inequality is initially produced and stabilized through the economic structure and the division of labor. A gendered division of labor gives men and women different resource levels, and because men have superior material resources, women at the micro level must balance the exchange by offering deference and compliance. Wifely compliance means that women are either kept at home, and thus utterly dependent upon the man for material survival, or are allowed to work but must also carry the bulk of the domestic duties (double workday). Wives' absence or double workday thus feeds back to and reinforces the gendered economic division of labor.

As a result of men's economic and micro-level power, men have the greatest influence on society's definitions of gender. These definitions include stereotypes, norms, and ideologies that devalue women's work, legitimate unequal opportunities and rewards, and place higher value on masculine traits than on feminine ones. These definitions are internalized and are used for and reinforced in gender performance. Moreover, because men are generally absent in parenting, due either to being the sole support of the family or to women's double workday, gender differences occur in a person's psychic structure, which in turn predisposes men and women to seek out specific kinds of jobs and careers: "[W]omen, therefore, choose to place priority on family responsibilities, and, where financially possible, this priority often includes the choice to forgo other forms of work altogether" (Chafetz, 1990, p. 75).

The division of labor by gender also patterns opportunity at the organizational level. The initial gender inequality in the division of labor with men holding the positions of greater power, plus gendered stereotypes of work expectations, imply that there will be a strong tendency for men to guard and keep the positions of power for other men. This incumbency in turn creates an unequal distribution of opportunities and rewards, which helps create male resource supremacy at the micro level as well as produce negative worker attributes for women and positive ones for men at the meso level of organizations.

Concepts and Theory: Changing Gender Inequality

Chafetz (1990) argues that any change in gender inequality begins at the macro-level structure, apart from the intent of social actors. Put differently, initial changes in gender stratification are involuntary. These structural changes then work back through the micro and meso levels to spur additional changes. As these structural factors engage, women are able to form conflict groups intentionally directed toward changing gender inequality, which in turn help gain elite support. Chafetz lists four different kinds of processes that can unintentionally produce changes in the structure of gender inequality: population growth or decline, changes in the sex ratio of the population, technological innovations, and changes in the economic structure.

Population changes: If the number of jobs that need to be filled remains constant, then the greater the growth in the working age population, the lower will be women's workforce participation. The inverse is true as well: As the size of the working population declines, women will gain greater access to the job market, if the number of jobs remains constant.

Sex ratio changes: The sex ratio of a population, the number of males relative to the number of females, tends to change under conditions of war and migration. If in the long run there is a reduction in the sex ratio of a population (thus, more women than men), women will gain access to higher-paying and more prestigious work roles. Conversely, if there is an increase in the sex ratio (more men than women), then women's workforce participation will tend to decrease.

Economic and technological changes: There are two general features of men's and women's bodies that can influence women's workforce participation: Men on average tend to be stronger than women, and women carry, deliver, and nurse babies. Women will tend to gain employment if new technologies reduce strength, mobility, and time requirements. In addition to work requirements, technology can also change the structure of the job market. As the economy expands due to technological innovations, women will tend to achieve greater workforce participation, holding population growth constant. If women's role in the workforce increases, then women's level of material and political resources will increase as well, thus decreasing males' relative micro power and the level of gender differentiation, as well as weakening gender stereotypes, ideologies, and normative expectations of gender performance. In addition, as women's resources and thus their micro power increase, they are more able to influence the household division of labor and men's contribution to familial and domestic work. And, as men contribute more to domestic and familial work, women are more able to gain resources through increased workforce participation.

When any social change occurs, society usually experiences adjustment problems. Change to the social system brings a kind of disequilibrium that has to be solved so that actions and interactions can once again be regulated by generally accepted roles, norms, and values. In the case of gender, the short-term problems are related to women having greater levels of resources and thus higher levels of independence and power. Examples of problems/issues stemming from this shift include increases in the divorce rate and women's demands for control over their own bodies. Social disruptions such as these tend to motivate elite support of women's rights in order to restore social order. The elite not only pass laws and oversee their enforcement, but they can also lend other material or political support, such as money and social capital (networks of people in powerful positions).

Consciousness and the Relations of Ruling—Dorothy E. Smith

Dorothy E. Smith (1926–) was born in Northallerton, Yorkshire, England. She earned her undergraduate degree in 1955 from the London School of Economics, and her PhD from the University of California, Berkeley, in 1963. She has taught at Berkeley, the University of Essex, and the University of British Columbia, and is currently a professor emeritus at the University of Toronto, where she has been since 1977. In recognition of her contributions to sociology, the American Sociology Association honored Smith with the Jessie Bernard Award in 1993 and the Career of Distinguished Scholarship Award in 1999. Her book *The Everyday World as Problematic* has received two awards from the Canadian Sociology and Anthropology Association: the Outstanding Contribution Award and the John Porter Award, both given in 1990. Other important works by Smith include *The Conceptual Practices of Power: A Feminist Sociology of Knowledge,* and *Institutional Ethnography: A Sociology for People.*

So far, we've seen that gender inequality involves the body and social structures. In this section, we want to consider the idea that gender stratification also involves consciousness—specifically, a break in the consciousness of women between their lived experience and the ruling texts that purport to explain their lives. To talk about this issue we'll first consider feminist epistemology in general. As we've seen, the idea of modernity is founded on a specific kind of knowledge, positivism. Yet we've also seen from Marx (1859/1994) that "it is not the consciousness of men that determines their existence, but their social existence that determines their consciousness" (p. 211). In spite of this insight concerning the sociology of knowledge, sociology continues to principally use and value positivism, as if knowledge and consciousness exist independently of a situated knower. Feminist epistemology critiques this position.

Ways of Knowing: A Feminist Critique of Positivism

Very briefly, there are four characteristics of positivistic knowledge that are important here. First, according to the positivistic approach, true or correct knowledge only comes when the observer separates him- or herself from that which is being studied. You undoubtedly came across this idea in your methods class: The researcher must take an objective stand in order to safeguard against bias. Second, personal emotions must be set aside in the pursuit of pure knowledge. Third, no personal ethics or values must come into the research. Social science is to be value-free, not passing judgment or trying to impose values on others. And, fourth, knowledge progresses through cumulation and adversarial debate.

In contrast to positivistic epistemology, Patricia Hill Collins (2000) gives us four characteristics of alternative epistemologies, ways of knowing and validating knowledge that challenge the tenets of positivism and the status quo. First, alternative epistemologies are built upon lived experience, not upon an objectified position. Social science argues that to truly understand society and group life, one must be removed from the particulars and concerns of the subjects being studied. This distancing turns subjects into objects of study. In contrast, feminist epistemology claims that it is only those women and men who experience the consequences of living under an oppressed social position who can select "topics for investigation and methodologies used" (p. 258).

Second, rather than emotional withdrawal, feminist epistemology requires personal accountability. Because feminist knowledge is built upon lived experience and not an objective observation, the assessment of knowledge is a simultaneous assessment of an individual's character, values, and ethics. Third, feminist knowledge is built around the ethics of caring rather than a belief in value neutrality. According to this critical perspective, the appearance of value-free knowledge is a tenet of positivistic faith rather than an actual characteristic of knowing: All knowledge is intrinsically value-laden and should thus be tested by the presence of empathy and compassion. The fourth and last dimension of feminist epistemology is the use of dialogue rather than adversarial debate to further knowledge. Dialogue rather than debate implies the presence of at least two subjects, not a subject and an objective observer.

Together, these four characteristics imply that feminist epistemology is holistic: It doesn't require the separation of the researcher from his or her own experiences, nor does it require separation of thoughts from feelings, or even assume that it is possible to do so. In feminist epistemology, the story is told and preserved in narrative form and not "torn apart in analysis" (P. Collins, 2000, p. 258). As we'll see, this is precisely the approach that Smith applies in her standpoint theory.

Concepts and Theory: The New Materialism

As we've seen, Marx's ideas about materialism put forth that economic manufacturing creates a mirror of production that is the basis of consciousness. If that mirror is constructed through means and relations of production that are in harmony with humankind's species-being, then the mirror is true and unblurred. Capitalist production, however, creates a reflection that gives a misleading image, which is the basis of false consciousness and ideology. Yet, as we've seen, some argue that advanced capitalist economies are now postindustrial, which implies changes in the class structure and its corresponding consciousness.

Smith proposes a new materialism for postindustrial society, one where facts and texts rather than commodification produce alienation and objectification. With Marx, capitalist production, commodities, and money mediate the relationships people have with themselves and others. Smith, however, argues that Marx's theory was specific to industrialized capitalism. With the shift toward service and technological innovation driven by theoretical knowledge, social relationships and power are mediated more through texts and "facts" than commodities and money. Further, just as people misrecognized the reality in back of money and commodities, so today most people misrecognize the relations of power in back of texts and facts. This new materialism and its basis in power are true for all people. However, Smith (1987) argues, the way in which text operates has ramifications specific to gender. Obviously, men have always had a significant hand in producing knowledge throughout the ages. But there is a "singular coincidence" between the way men look at the world and the particular way in which knowledge is produced in modernity (p. 2)—positivism creates objectified, controlling observers.

Texts and Facts

Smith is specifically concerned with texts that are officially or organizationally written and read. She gives us the example of two different texts that came out of an incident in 1968 involving police and street people in Berkeley, California. One text came in the form of a letter to an underground newspaper and was written by someone who was marginally involved in the altercation. His text was "written from the standpoint of an actual experience" (D. Smith, 1990, p. 63) and contained specific references to people, places, times, and events. It was embedded in and expressed actual life experiences as they happened. This was a personal account of a personal experience that reflexively situated the writer in the event.

The other text was the official incident report that came from the mayor's office. The standpoint of this second text is organizational. Rather than being an account of a personal experience, it was written from the point of view of anonymous police officers who are portrayed as trained professionals and organizational representatives. In addition, the official report embedded the text within "sequences of organizational action extending before and after them" (D. Smith, 1990, p. 64) using reports from police, courts, and probation officers. In other words, the official text brought in many elements that existed outside of the actual situation and experience. Through this text, the actual experience was objectified and given meaning through extra-local concepts rather than the experience itself.

Most people not only accept such texts as authoritative, but also have a tendency to believe "facts" at face value. Facts, however, are dependent upon theory for their existence:

> Facts and theories are much more intimately connected than is admitted. . . . Not only is the description of every single fact dependent on *some* theory . . . but there also exist facts which cannot be unearthed except with the help of alternatives to the theory to be tested. (Feyerabend, 1988, p. 27)

Think about this: What are the conditions necessary for the flu virus to exist as a fact? Most of us would respond to such a question by thinking or saying, "The flu just *is* a virus." But how would doctors in the early 1800s have viewed something like the flu? At that time, medical science had determined that all disease is created by an imbalance of bodily fluids, or the four humors: yellow bile, black bile, phlegm, and blood. In order to heal the patient, then, doctors would try to balance out the humors, which is why they would purge or bleed their patients. Why don't doctors do that today? Because the facticity (a thing or event's ability to exist as a fact) of the human body and its pathologies has changed. The flu's facticity as a virus came into existence because of changes in medical theories and instruments. If medical theories change again, so will the "facts" concerning the flu.

Concepts and Theory:
Readers and the Relations of Ruling

Smith's point with the story about the incident in Berkeley is that official accounts and facts can differ quite a bit from how people actually experience life. Differing accounts aren't surprising. We know that eyewitness accounts can vary and, if you've ever played the game Telephone, you know that stories can break down simply in the telling and retelling. But Smith has something more significant in mind than differences in perspective and the atrophy of information. Quite simply, the kind of knowledge that is seen as authoritative is built from a perspective that is intentionally objective and is used to govern and control women.

Smith (1990) refers to this as the relations of ruling and has in mind the "total complex of activities, differentiated into many spheres, by which our kind of society is ruled, managed, and administered" (p. 14). In technologically advanced societies that are bureaucratically organized and centered on theoretical knowledge, ruling and governing take place specifically through text. As we've seen with Foucault, the social sciences turn people into populations that can be reduced to numbers, measured, and thus controlled. Through abstract concepts and generalized theories, the social sciences empty the person of individual thoughts and feelings and reduce him or her to concepts and ideas that can be applied to all of a general type.

Much of this literature in the social sciences is related to data generated by the state, through such instruments as the U.S. Census or the FBI's Uniform Crime Reporting Program. These data are accepted without question as the authoritative representation of reality because they are seen as facts—data that correspond to the assumptions of science. These data are then used to test theories and hypotheses that are generated, more often than not, by previous work found in the literature (most of which has been produced by men), not from questions and concerns coming out of the real lives of women, which, as we'll see, are distinct from those of most men. This type of approach to understanding human behavior:

> is a systematically developed consciousness of society and social relations . . . [that] claims objectivity not on the basis of its capacity to speak truthfully, but in terms of its specific capacity to exclude the presence and experience of particular subjectivities. (D. Smith, 1987, p. 2)

Smith (1992) argues that such text forms "the bridge between the actual and discursive. It is a material object that brings into actual contexts of reading a fixed form of meaning" (p. 92). Notice the distinction that Smith is making between the "fixed form" of the text and the "actual context of reading." The actual context is the place of lived experiences. It's a place where life is unfixed, spontaneous, meaningful, and subjective. The text, however, is fixed, not simply because it is presented as fact, but also because it is open to revision only by experts. Moreover, the relationship between texts and experts is itself mediated by the rules of scientific research, another form of text.

Professional social scientists, then, are trained readers. The entire graduate experience is one that consistently requires the student to dissect the social world as a dispassionate, objective observer. Sociologists are trained to begin research in the literature, to use abstract theories to categorically see the people they study, and then to objectively measure and make statistical inferences. As sociologists "work with standard methods of thinking and inquiry, they import the relations of ruling into the texts they produce" (D. Smith, 1992, p. 91).

Yet professional social scientists aren't the only trained readers—if they were, texts would have no power to rule. When women become aware of the texts that surround their lived reality, the text directly enters their everyday life and makes an authoritative claim to be the voice of true knowledge gained through scientific or organizational inquiry. It is this appearance that prompts women to privilege the objective voice above their own. Notice something here: Through higher education, mass media, counseling, politics, and so on, all of us are trained to privilege this voice over our own. In a postindustrial, bureaucratized society, we believe in the moral authority of texts and facts.

One of the consequences for women of this kind of knowledge is the experience of a fault line. The idea of a fault line comes from geology where it refers to the intersection between a geologic fault (a fracture in the earth's crust) and the earth's surface. Women discover "a point of rupture in my/our experience as woman/women with the social forms of consciousness" that is "located in a relation of power between women and men" (D. Smith, 1987, pp. 49, 51). Men usually do not sense a disjuncture between what they live and what they know of the world. Part of the reason for this is that many of the activities of men match up with or correspond to abstract, objectifying knowledge. A male sociologist "works in the medium he studies" (D. Smith, 1990, p. 17). Another reason that men don't usually experience a disjuncture between objective knowledge and the everyday world is that women have traditionally negotiated that break for them.

To understand this, let's think about the usual distinction between boss and secretary. Generally speaking, the secretary (typically a woman) is there to do the menial labor, to take care of the mundane details through which an organization functions, and to keep the boss (typically a man) free from intrusions from the outside world by screening all calls and visitors. Now think about the traditional division of labor in the home. Men go to work while women take care of the "small details" of running a household: grocery shopping, cooking, cleaning, and taking care of the kids. Both of these examples illustrate the mediation role that Smith tells us women play— women intervene between men and the actual, lived world, and they take care of the details that make real life possible. In doing so, they shelter men from the "bifurcation of consciousness" that women experience (D. Smith, 1987, p. 82). Note that the woman tends to do this even if both she and the man are working outside the home.

The Standpoint of Women

To counter the general way that social knowledge is produced by and reproduces ruling relations, Smith advocates a method of inquiry she calls "standpoint." Standpoint is used to mean that groups standing outside the place of privilege actually have a more authentic knowledge of the social system than the ruling individuals. This is true first because the disenfranchised are in a better position to see the whole system at work. For example, most white people aren't aware that they are not the subject of police scrutiny. Most blacks, on the other hand, have firsthand knowledge of how surveillance works in the shopping malls and streets of America.

The second reason standpoint is more authentic is that it intrinsically recognizes the political nature of all knowledge and ways of knowing. Rather than seeing information as pure and free from ethical considerations, the feminist standpoint recognizes that all knowledge exists because of a specific kind of sociopolitical configuration of social structures and interests. As a form of critical knowledge, then, standpoint seeks to privilege the lived experiences of those who are outside the relations of ruling, represent the social world from the view of the oppressed, make the studies and accounts of disenfranchised groups accessible to those who are the subjects of the studies, and create knowledge that can be used by the oppressed to subvert and change their social world.

Rather than producing readers and objects, standpoint inquiry creates spaces for translators and subjects. In standpoint, the lives of women aren't simply read; that is, they aren't textually determined. A researcher using standpoint inquiry is situated in a never-ending dialogue with the actual and the textual. There is a constant moving back and forth among the voice of the subject, the voice of authoritative text, and the interpretations of the researcher. Smith (1992) sees this back-and-forth interplay as a dialectic:

> The project locates itself in a dialectic between actual people located just as we are and social relations, in which we participate and to which we contribute, that have come to take on an existence and a power over [and] against us. (pp. 94–95)

In this way, sociology becomes a living language and dialogue rather than an objective and objectifying text.

A significant goal of standpoint inquiry is to reveal how texts are put together with practices at the level of women's lived experience. "Making these processes visible also makes visible how we participate in and incorporate them into our own practices" (D. Smith, 1992, p. 90) and how we involve ourselves in creating forms of consciousness "that are properties of organization or discourse rather than of individual subjects" (D. Smith, 1987, p. 3). Specifically, Smith is interested in finding out just how the relations of ruling pervade the lives of women. These relations, as we've seen, come through texts and researchers. But in most cases, the relations of ruling are misrecognized by women. They are rendered invisible by the normalcy of textual and factual legitimacy.

Smith is also interested in how actual women incorporate, respond to, see, and understand the texts that are written from a feminist or standpoint perspective. This reflexive move—examining feminist texts in relation to lived experience—places emphasis on the realities of daily life rather than on knowledge per se. That is, in positivism the purity of knowledge is the driving force, and the criterion of validity is whether or not knowledge is objectively true, with truth being a function of methodology. With feminist standpoint, the motivation for research is to understand the lives of women, and the criterion of validity is whether or not the knowledge resonates with women and improves their lives. It's an ethical move from the supremacy of knowledge to the significance of lived lives.

Disregarding the actual lived lifeworld where women encounter text is how "the very intellectual successes of the women's movement have created their own contradictions" (D. Smith, 1992, p. 88). In other words, without this continual connection to the lived experiences of women, even feminist knowledge can become objective text. The contradictions arise, according to Smith, as feminism believes its own theory—a theory that is seen to exist apart from the lived experiences of the women it attempts to describe. For Smith, resistance and revolution do not—indeed, cannot—begin in theory or even sociology. Such a beginning would simply replace the ruling ideas with another set of ruling ideas. In order to create a sociology of women, or to bring about any real social change, it is imperative to begin and continue in the situated perspectives of the people in whom we are interested.

The Craft of Citizenship   **Gender**

The Basics: Comprehension and Explanation

- Identify the main concerns and questions of each theorist. With those questions in mind, write a two- to three-sentence statement that captures their theoretical response.
- Make a detailed list of the primary theoretical concepts each theorist employs. Then, define the most important concepts in Gilman's evolutionary theory, Chafetz's structural theory of gender inequality, and Smith's theory of texts and gendered consciousness.

  > *Helpful hints:* You undoubtedly have noticed that no concepts are placed in bold. Part of critical thinking is the ability to identify these yourself. The best way to begin is to deal with each section under "Concepts and Theory" separately. Each section presents a theoretical explanation about how one specific thing works or came into existence. Usually, you can find this in the title. For example, the first Concepts and Theory section for Gilman is about the evolution of gender. So, that's the issue being explained, and it's your first important concept. Then, you want to search for causes or dynamics, things that push for gender evolution to happen. In this case, you'll find those under the subsection "General Problems for Human Evolution." These problems push for evolution to occur. Go into those sections and pick out the terms that most clearly express these issues. In this case, "no species-specific environment" and "the problem of social connections" are among the first. You'll also find issues that push for evolutionary change under the subsection "The Problems With Men." Then ask yourself, what effects come out of these pressures? The immediate answer is monogamy and patriarchy. So, go through the chapter section by section and follow the logic of each argument, looking for the most important concepts.

- Explain how gender inequality evolved.
- Explain the dysfunctions of gendered evolution for modern, democratic society.
- Explain how gender inequality is structured in modern societies.

(Continued)

(Continued)

- Explain how structured gender inequality can change.
- Explain how texts replicate the relations of ruling and thus objectify and control women.
- Explain how standpoint can be used to challenge texts and address gender inequality.

Skill Set 1: Inference and Application

- Evaluate your participation in gender inequality using Gilman's dysfunctions of patriarchy and monogamy. In other words, how are you in your daily life challenging or conforming to these dysfunctions?
- In the same way, evaluate your participation in gender inequality using Chafetz's micro and individual levels. Put another way, how do you in face-to-face situations and personal choices challenge or perpetuate gender inequality?
- Do the same with Smith's theory of text.
  - ➤ *Helpful hints:* In some ways, this might be the most difficult. As members of this society and associates in university culture, we tend to believe and take for granted the place that text has in our lives. With Smith, we have to question the facts we accept, especially as they concern women and men, and we have to examine the practices through which we try to understand ourselves and our relationships. (We usually do this through some form of text.)

Skill Set 2: Interpretation, Analysis, Evaluation, Synthesis

- How could Dahrendorf's theory of interest group formation inform or supplement Chafetz's theory of changing gender inequality?
- Synthesize Gilman's, Chafetz's, and Smith's theories of gender into a robust theory that explains how gender inequality works generally and can be changed.
  - ➤ *Helpful hints:* Usually, the theories you'll be working with won't have been intended to go together, so synthesis will always entail imagination. In this case, however, these theories actually fit together well, so you won't have to do too much stretching and bending. Think first about the big idea that each brings; then look for theoretical inroads, places where you can connect the theories.

- Drawing specifically on the discussion in Chapter 1, Habermas, Foucault, and now Smith, write a position paper on the issue of knowledge (epistemology) in modern society. What kind of knowledge is most useful for participatory democracy and civic sociology, and why?

  > *Helpful hints:* Because of the way the issue is framed in terms of democracy, it would probably be beneficial for you to think about and integrate what you've learned about the way democracies are supposed to work (civil society, civil religion, civil sphere, and so on). That will give you a framework for understanding and evaluating the kind of knowledge you'll be focusing on.

Race

While gender is more universal, the use of race as a category of distinction has historically been more destructive. Though women have been seen as less than men, in general their essential humanity hasn't been denied. The modern category of race, however, is based on such a distinction. While people have obviously always been aware of differences of skin tone and facial features, in premodern societies race wasn't an important way that people used to mark difference. Religion, territory, and eventually being civilized versus uncivilized were much more important categories for most of human history. Race, as such, only became important with the dawn of modernity and specifically capitalism. Capitalism provided the motivation (accruing profit at the least possible expense) and the means (commodification) to make race the primary marker of difference in modern nations. While slavery had always existed, it wasn't until the advent of capitalism that *chattel* slavery—people seen as property—could exist. It was also modernity that brought to the forefront the issue of human nature as a political concern. You'll recall that political rights in modernity exist for the individual simply because of his or her humanity. Thus, one's standing as a human became an issue of concern and definition.

We are without a doubt at a significant moment of change in U.S. race relations. In 2008, the country elected its first black president. But are we now in a "post-racial" society, one in which race no longer makes a difference? Current statistics appear to say no. The 2008 median income for white families was $55,530, while black family median income was $34,281 (DeNavas-Walt, Proctor, & Smith, 2009). The U.S. Department of Justice (2008) reports that at midyear 2008 there were 4,777 black male inmates per 100,000 U.S. residents being held in state or federal prison and local jails, compared to just 727 white male inmates per 100,000 U.S. residents. The National Urban League (2009) has an overall statistical index of African American equality as compared to whites: The 2009 Equality Index was 71.1 percent.

The three theorists in this chapter will explain how race matters. Each of our theorists will have a somewhat different way of understanding how racial inequality works. In considering W. E. B. Du Bois' theoretical work, we'll see how and why the dividing line of race defined the separation between human and subhuman. With Du Bois, we'll also think about how culture and identity are used to subjugate black people, and he will show us that there are social psychological effects stemming from economic and cultural oppression. William Julius Wilson, on the other hand, focuses solely on structures, specifically the structural arrangements among government, capitalist economy, and the division of labor. In doing so, we will look at race relations in the United States over three historical periods. In the end, Wilson argues that race as such plays a lesser role today than in previous periods in black oppression. Finally, Cornel West's work brings us back to the issues of culture and social psychology, as he argues that increasing market saturation has created black nihilism, a denial of the intrinsic meaning and value of human life.

Double Consciousness—W. E. B. Du Bois

William Edward Burghardt Du Bois (1868–1963) was born in Great Barrington, Massachusetts. His mother was Dutch African and his father French Huguenot–African. Du Bois' education in the abject realities of blackness in America came during his college years at Fisk, a historically black university in Nashville, Tennessee; it was his first visit to the southern United States during the "Jim Crow" era. During his life, Du Bois advocated a two-pronged approach in overcoming oppression. He encouraged blacks to work together to create their own culture, art, and literature, and to create their own group economy of black producers and consumers. Du Bois also advocated active protest, which at times put him at odds with Booker T. Washington, another significant black leader of the time. Du Bois was also a principal force in the Pan-African movement, which was founded on the belief that all black people share a common ancestry and should therefore work collectively around the globe for equality. Du Bois died in 1963 at the age of 95.

Probably more than any other single person, Du Bois was responsible for black consciousness in America and possibly the world during the twentieth century. His book, *The Souls of Black Folk,* defined the problem of the color line. He was a founding member of the National Association for the Advancement of Colored People (NAACP) and its chief spokesperson during its most formative years. Du Bois also produced the first scientific studies of the black condition in America. Among Du Bois' other important books are *The Philadelphia Negro, The Negro, John Brown, Black Reconstruction,* and *Darkwater.*

Concepts and Theory: The Expanding Economic Base

Following Marx, Du Bois argues that the basic force behind racism is the economic structure of capitalism. As we've seen, capitalism is dependent upon a cheap labor force to exploit, and at the outset capitalism used chattel slavery as a way to get the most profit from the least investment. However, as we've seen, democracy is an expanding, unfinished project. Thus, over the years, slavery was defeated and blacks were ultimately freed. But, as we all know, that wasn't the end of the story. Legally abolishing slavery did little to change the culture of racism that had provided the legitimation for slavery. Du Bois sees that this cultural authority is still being used as the basis of exploitation in global capitalism. Due to the nature of exploitation, workers in places like the United States push for and gain higher wages, which obviously reduces profits. Along with increasing worker rights, technological growth in core economies helps to create the middle class and with it, increasing levels of affluence—but only in the core nations and only at a price.

Writing in the first half of the twentieth century, Du Bois saw the beginnings of what we now call globalization. Du Bois also saw that the affluence of the American middle class was based upon exploiting other nations and peoples—dark nations and dark peoples. Du Bois (1920/1996a) explains, "There is a chance for exploitation on an immense scale for inordinate profit, not simply to the very rich, but to the middle class and to the laborers. This chance lies in the exploitation of darker peoples" (pp. 504–505). He goes on to say, "This labor is kept cheap and helpless because the white world despises 'darkies'" (p. 507), and finally, "This exploitation of the 'dark lands' has "only one test of success—dividends!" (p. 505). Thus, even as political and economic structures in the United States change, the culture of racism continues, not only so blacks in this country can be oppressed, but even more so that dark nations can be used as fields of exploitation.

Concepts and Theory: The Defining Power of Culture

While he draws on Marx to explain the economic base, Du Bois turns to Weber's theory of legitimation to explain how the power of racism continued into the twentieth century. In terms of oppression, the problem with distinctions made using premodern social categories is that they were by definition temporary. People within oppressed groups could become civilized, could convert to the dominant religion, and could move and thus claim different territorial identities. There was also a problem with premodern slavery: Even at its worst, it was based on social relationships. For most of human history, slavery was used either primarily as a method of controlling and punishing a conquered people or criminals, or as a way of paying off debt or getting ahead. The latter is referred to as indentured servitude. People would contract themselves into slavery, typically for 7 years, in return for a specific service, like passage to America, or to pay off debt. Notice that whether this type of slavery was used as a result of war or crime or economic need, it maintained and was based upon social relationships, but not so with chattel slavery. Under the capitalist notion of property, it became possible for people to be defined as property, and there are no associated obligations. The key, then, to black slavery was to define race as a natural, God-given distinction that was immutable and characterized blacks as less than human.

This sort of thing was distinctly possible at the dawn of modernity. Remember that modernity brought a fundamental shift in the way people were viewed. Prior to modernity, people were subjects under the rule of emperors and monarchs. While rule was absolute in such systems, subjects were also seen as charges—people who needed to be cared for and guided like children. Subjects were not only ruled over; they were also *seen as incapable of ruling themselves*. Modernity changed all that. People began to be understood as having rights as well as having the mental and ethical capabilities to make reasoned decisions for themselves and thus society. It's out of this caldron of new beliefs and values that true freedom could arise—humankind is free, not because some government makes it so, but because God endowed humans with inalienable rights. Notice how spiritual, biological, and social forces come together here: Because of our biological birth as humans, God bestowed upon us the spiritual gift and responsibility of free will, which is to be used to enrich human existence. Notice also how these biological and spiritual narratives are legitimations. You'll recall from Weber that legitimations are stories that undergird power relations; they provide an ethical basis for belief in authority. These same sorts of narratives were used to deny blacks their human nature and thus their rights. Du Bois sees these narratives at work in history and representation (defined below). The insidious thing about historical legitimation is that it can work through omission.

History as Ideology

The first historian was Thucydides (460 BCE–395 BCE), who wrote *The History of the Peloponnesian War,* but history took on added significance under modernity. Before the advent of the nation-state, people were loyal to immediate local groups or to their religion. Nation-states break these distinctions down: They cover large territories, embrace diverse peoples, and de-center religion. One of the things that defines a nation and creates a sense of identity and solidarity is a common history. National histories, then, act as narratives that bring people together, create national identities, and legitimate common values and institutional arrangements.

In this way, history plays an important role in legitimation and creating a sense of reality. For example, why does marriage exist? No one subjectively knows—none of us was there when it was instituted and thus we don't have firsthand knowledge. Instead, we have historical accounts and stories of how and why it came about. Because we weren't there, history takes on objective qualities and thus feels like fact. This facticity legitimates our institutions and social arrangements unquestionably. But, Du Bois tells us, current national history is written from a politicized point of view. Because people of color were not seen as having the same status and rights as white people, our history did not see them. We have been blind to their contributions and their place in society. Du Bois calls this kind of ideological history "lies agreed upon." Du Bois, however, holds out the possibility of a scientific history. This kind of history would be guided by ethical standards in research and interpretation, and the record of human action would be written with accuracy and faithfulness of detail. Du Bois envisions this history acting as a guidepost and measuring rod for national conduct. Du Bois (1935/1996b) presents this formulation of history as a choice: We can either use history "for our pleasure and amusement, for inflating our national ego," or we can use it as a moral guide and handbook for future generations (p. 440).

Representation

History is a kind of representation. To represent means to depict, describe, image, interpret, portray, render, or express. As we saw in Chapter 2, our social world is a symbolic, represented world. In that chapter, we also saw that the meaning any sign or symbol conveys isn't an intrinsic characteristic of the sign or the object. So, for example, the meaning of money isn't part of the paper we use to represent money, just as history doesn't represent a chronological record of facts and events. The question becomes, then, what do cultural symbols and practices represent? The short answer is that they represent the social world, along with its values and relationships. Sometimes what's represented are cultural images that can be bought and sold. For example, the image of the woman on this month's *Cosmopolitan* magazine doesn't reflect what real women look like, nor does it represent their lifeworld, but it does represent and stimulate a desire to be such a woman. This representation, however, isn't simply this empty image of capitalism. There are cultural structures and discourses of power that lie beneath the gloss.

In speaking about the representations of his time, Du Bois (1920/1996c) says, "The whites obviously seldom picture brown and yellow folk, but for five hundred centuries they have exhausted every ingenuity of trick, of ridicule and caricature on black folk" (pp. 59–60). The effect of such representation is cultural and psychological: The disenfranchised read the representations and become ashamed of their own image. Du Bois gives an example from his own work at *The Crisis* (the official publication of the NAACP). *The Crisis* put a picture of a black person on the cover of the magazine. When the readers saw the representation, they perceived it (or consumed it) as "the caricature that white folks intend when they make a black face." Du Bois queried some of his office staff about the reaction. They said the problem wasn't that the person was black; the problem was that the person was *too black*. To this, Du Bois (1920/1996c) replied, "Nonsense! Do white people complain because their pictures are too white?" (p. 60).

Du Bois is seeing the differences between denotative and connotative meanings. One of the definitions of denote is to announce. So, the denotative meaning is that which the sign clearly announces. The literal meaning of connote is to mark; words can thus be marked by additional, connotative meanings. A good illustration is our *Cosmo* woman: The surface meaning is woman, but behind the image is an entire world of beliefs, ideas, values, behaviors, and relationships that have been generated—or encoded—to induce people to buy into the image. This connotative meaning then acts as a myth that delineates gender: Women must be attractive and sexually available, women are the objects of gaze, women are to be pursued and conquered, and so on.

Du Bois is marking these sorts of distinctions here for race. We use the term *white* to analogously refer to everything that is good, pure, and decent. The term *black* is likewise reserved for things or people that are despicable, ignorant, and depressing. In our cultural language, we also perceive these two categories as mutually exclusive. For example, we will use the phrase "this issue isn't black or white" to refer to something that is undecided, that can't fit into simple, clear, and mutually exclusive categories. The area in between is a gray, no-person's land. It is culturally logical, then, to perceive unchangeable differences between the black and white races, which is also the logic behind the "one drop rule" (as mentioned in Chapter 4, a historical slang term used to capture the idea that a person is considered black if he or she has any black ancestor). Du Bois (1920/1996a) refers to this as the theory of human culture that has worked its way into our daily thought: "Everything great, good, efficient, fair, and honorable is 'white'; everything mean, bad, blundering, cheating, and dishonorable is 'yellow'; a bad taste is 'brown'; and the devil is 'black'" (p. 505).

The Importance of Identity

Du Bois saw the importance of culture in the formation of identity long before we had theoretical terms to talk about such things. We can define identity simply as a sort of correspondence between the individual and types of persons, or roles and status positions, available in culture and social networks. For example, you identify yourself as a student. Student is a type of person that is available to you and others culturally and socially. It exists apart from you, and will continue to exist long after you're gone. When you identify yourself as a student, you're accepting the status position and roles that come with that kind of person. You're saying that part of you corresponds to that identity. Identities, then, are about existence. You exist as a student, as a male, as a bisexual, as a Christian, as a son, as an African American, and so on. You would be hard-pressed to name a part of you that isn't tied to some identity—identities give you a way of understanding and guiding your existence. Your subjective experience can only become objectively real as you locate it within an already existing identity framework. Identities are also how you understand and make meaningfully real the actions, thoughts, and feelings of others.

Now, imagine a situation where the strongest identities available to you were constructed by people who denied some or all of your humanity. Imagine a culture that deprived you of all that we just said; your very existence as a vibrant, living human being with full potential for expression was denied by the culture you found yourself in and by the social practices and relations of those who held power. In speaking to such a situation, an African living under colonial rule, Franz Fanon (1952/1967), cries out, "Out of the blackest part of my soul, across the zebra striping of my mind, surges this desire to be suddenly *white*. I wish to be acknowledged not as *black* but as *white*" (p. 63, emphasis added). W. E. B. Du Bois (1903/1996d), living as a black man in the United States, echoes, "Between me and the other world this is ever an unasked question. . . . How does it feel to be a problem?" (p. 101).

Double Consciousness

Double consciousness comes out of the interplay of identity and representation. As you know, consciousness is the distinctly human awareness of the world. It is, in fact, self-awareness, a reflexive move through which you situate your self in the social context. One way to understand this—one that fits in well with Du Bois' work—is through Charles Horton Cooley's (1902) theory of the looking glass self. A looking glass is another term for mirror. Cooley's use of that phrase helps us see that the self is reflexive, or, put differently, the self is born and exists in the reflections that others give it.

Cooley (1902) argues that there are three steps to this mirroring process. First, we imagine what we look like to other people. This is obviously the reflection of the looking glass. Note that Cooley didn't say we actually perceive how others see and judge us; rather, we imagine their perceptions and judgments. Yet this imagination is not based on pure speculation. It is based on commonly available social identities that contain images and scripts associated with a cultural identity. Second, we imagine how they feel about how we look. Identities always have expectations and evaluative standards associated with them. When people identify us as a certain kind of person, they then expect us to behave accordingly. These evaluations are not disinterested but are laced with emotional investment because all identities come in clusters, not individually. Thus, identities are always dependent upon the other identities in a set, as the identity of professor is dependent upon that of student, or, more pointedly, the identity of racial superiority is dependent on the existence of inferiors. Third, we have an emotional response to their evaluative feelings. That emotional response is either pride or shame.

For blacks in America, Du Bois argues, there are two looking glass selves—a double consciousness. On the one hand, there is the identity mirror that exists due to legal status and citizenry, that of being an American. However, there is also the mirror that white superiority holds up to blacks. This mirror's reflection is clearly inferior to that of American. Those two mirrors thus form a double consciousness in African Americans,

> [a] sense of always looking at one's self through the eyes of others, of measuring one's soul by the tape of a world that looks on in amused contempt and pity. One ever feels his twoness,—an American, a Negro; two souls, two thoughts, two unreconciled strivings; two warring ideals in one dark body, whose dogged strength alone keeps it from being torn asunder. (Du Bois, 1903/1996d, p. 102)

Race and Class—William Julius Wilson

William Julius Wilson (1935–) was born in Derry Township, Pennsylvania. Wilson attended Wilberforce and Bowling Green Universities before completing his PhD in sociology at Washington State University in 1966. His first professorship was at the University of Massachusetts at Amherst, and he joined the faculty of the University of Chicago in 1972. There he held the position of professor and was the director of the Center for the Study of Urban Inequality. He moved to Harvard in 1996, where he currently holds the Lewis P. and Linda L. Geyser University Professorship. Wilson has received many top honors in his career, including the 1998 National Medal of Science (the highest such honor given in the United States), and he was named by *Time* magazine as one of America's 25 Most Influential People in 1996. He has authored several groundbreaking and significant books including *The Declining Significance of Race, The Truly Disadvantaged,* and *When Work Disappears: The World of the New Urban Poor.*

Wilson gives us a unique and complex way of seeing racial inequality. Obviously, his concern is the oppression of black people in the United States, but to simply see this inequality as a product of racism is too simplistic. Wilson argues that racism as such requires a particular kind of structural configuration among the state, the economy, and social relations. This triangle of relations comes from Marx. Wilson's approach is to first understand the state as a relatively independent actor that can limit capitalism as well as support it. Wilson also questions whether racism is always the causal force in the oppression of blacks. In order to answer that question, Wilson analyzes black inequality in the United States from slavery to the current system.

In the end, Wilson argues that racism as a causal factor in determining the overall condition of blacks in the United States has been declining in significance since the Civil War. To document the causal force of racism, Wilson tracks the changing relationships between the economy and the state. We'll see that to be effective, racism needs a particular kind of institutional configuration. In its absence, other factors become important for influencing the position of blacks in the United States—in particular, a split labor market and class. As we discuss Wilson's theory, keep in mind that he is not arguing that racism is no longer present or important. Racism is still a problem, but Wilson is pointing out that because of shifts in the relationship between the economy and the state, the *relative importance* of race has declined over time and has been replaced by class-based issues.

Concepts and Theory: American Racial History

Wilson divides U.S. history into three economic phases and demonstrates that different theories are best at explaining different kinds of economic race relations. There's an important insight into theory that we can glean from Wilson's approach. Most theories contain scope conditions; very few are claimed to be a "theory of everything." Scope conditions limit the applicability of any theory, and understanding the scope conditions is a part of evaluation in critical thinking. Most students understand that scope conditions can be set by topic. So, for example, Mead's social psychological theory is probably not good for explaining globalization. But scope conditions can also include issues of time or historical change. In Wilson's case, he uses three different theories—Marx's state-capitalist collusion, split labor market theory, and his own class-state theory—to explain race relations for the three different time periods: pre–U.S. Civil War, post–Civil War through the 1930s, and post–World War II.

The Plantation Economy

You'll recall that Marx's theory argues that capitalists as the dominant class use their power to exploit workers and to enlist the state's active support. In this model, the state and economy are in collusion to exploit the worker. Wilson argues that Marx's theory is best for explaining the racial caste system that worked under the American plantation economy, at least in the South. This type of non-manufacturing, agrarian society is characterized by a simple division of labor and a small aristocracy. In such a society, there is very little if any job market competition. During this period in the southern United States, working whites were either craftspeople or serfs, and blacks were generally held as slaves. In addition, in a plantation economy there is a vast distance between the upper and lower classes. Because of this distance, there is little contact between classes, and what contact does happen is highly ritualized and subject to strong social norms of manners and etiquette. These conditions result in little to no class conflict, with the white workers having "little opportunity to challenge the control of the aristocracy" (Wilson, 1980, p. 13).

In such systems of production, the aristocracy dominates both economic and political life. In the United States, the white, landed elite were able to secure laws and policies that were extremely favorable to their economic interests, and they were able to propagate a ruling ideology concerning the differences between the races. As in classic Marxist thought, the system of production and the state formed a mutually reinforcing cycle. As a result, "the system of slavery severely restricted black vertical and horizontal mobility" (Wilson, 1980, p. 24), and race relations with elite whites took the form of paternalism (the care and control of subordinates as a father). An important issue to notice is who benefits from the system: In this case, it's the capitalist class.

Post–Civil War to New Deal Politics

After the U.S. Civil War, the industrialization of the economy grew quickly and the Southern economy in particular expanded rapidly. In addition, the Thirteenth and Fourteenth Amendments to the Constitution abolished slavery and granted civil rights to the black population. As a result, from the latter part of the nineteenth century through the 1930s, there were massive changes in the system of production and race relations. This period marks a shift from race relations based on a paternal, racial caste system to a more class-based labor market. In the South, economic expansion greatly increased the political power of the white working class. Blacks were freed but had very little economic or political power, as white workers attempted to control the newly available skilled and unskilled positions. The outcome was an elaborate system of Jim Crow segregation that was reinforced with a strong ideology of biological racism. The name "Jim Crow" doesn't refer to an actual person but to the stereotypical characterization of blacks in minstrel shows at the time. The idea of Jim Crow segregation references the laws that many states enacted after the Civil War in order to control blacks and preserve white privilege. Jim Crow segregation generally benefited the higher-paid white working class by keeping blacks out of the competition for jobs, especially in the South.

The North experienced a different configuration. Due to high levels of migration of blacks from the South and high immigration rates of European whites, blacks most often entered the job market as strikebreakers. White workers would strike for better wages or working conditions, and management would bring in black workers to keep production going. In some cases, management would preempt a strike by hiring black workers on permanently. This move obviously created high tension between black and white workers, which culminated in a number of race riots in 1917 and 1919. The Great Depression of the 1930s shifted things considerably for both black and white workers in the North. During the Depression, there was a strong movement toward unionizing. The unions themselves began to recruit black workers. As a result, black antagonism toward the unions was reduced, black and white workers saw themselves as united in their stand for economic reforms, and the practice of employers using blacks as strikebreakers was eliminated.

Wilson (1980) argues that race relations in this time period are best explained using split labor market theory. This theory assumes that, in general, business would support a free and open market where all laborers compete against one another regardless of race. This kind of competition would result in an overall higher level of exploitation because capitalists could pit blacks against whites. In addition, split labor theory proposes three key classes, rather than the two of orthodox Marxist theory: the capital business class, higher-paid labor, and cheaper labor. Understanding that there is another interest in the labor market besides capitalists, and knowing that capitalists would benefit from an open rather than restricted job market, we see that segregation benefited the white working class rather than capitalists.

Race, then, became a tool of the higher-paid working class to preserve its own economic interests. The white higher-paid working class promoted racist ideologies and discriminatory practices in order to monopolize skilled labor and management positions, prevent blacks from obtaining necessary skills and education, and deny blacks political resources. Thus, while race was still an issue, it originated with white workers rather than collusion between capitalists and the state. Also notice that class became increasingly important during this time. Labor markets are primarily split over class, not race. Race thus became a marker for class antagonisms rather than for racism itself.

World War II and Beyond

Before describing this time period, let's be clear about Wilson's theoretical argument. It's a structural argument, which means that structural arrangements are seen as determining social relations. For Marx, the driving structure is the economy: The means of production determine the relations of production. As we've seen, Wilson adds an independent state to this theory. This means that the interrelations between the state and the economy structure our social relationships, in this case race relations and black inequality. Wilson argues that the role of the state continued to change from the classic Marxist model. World War II brought a ban on discrimination in defense and government agencies. This move also provided for on-the-job training for blacks. Black workforce participation continued to expand under the equal employment legislation of the 1950s and 1960s and growing affirmative action programs. These changes obviously didn't come as a result of the government's desire for equality, but in response to the civil rights movement, which also boasted black political involvement. But regardless of the source, the state took successive steps to address black inequality.

In addition, the trend toward industrialization that began in the North prior to the Civil War expanded geographically and exponentially from the 1940s onward. This facilitated a shift in the black population toward urbanization, away from rural, agricultural settings and low-paying farm jobs and toward cities and industries with better-paying jobs. A large black population thus began to develop in urban centers, which in turn prompted an increase in the number of black business owners and black professionals oriented toward serving the needs of the growing black community. As a result of affirmative action and these economic and population shifts, more and more businesses were seeking black employees. For example, during the 10-year period between 1960 and 1970, the average number of corporate recruitment visits to traditionally black colleges jumped from 4 to 297; in some southern colleges, the number rose from zero to 600 corporate visits. During this time, there was also a jump in the percentage of blacks working in government jobs, rising from 13 percent to almost 22 percent, and the overall percentage of black males in white-collar positions rose from 16 percent to 24 percent (Wilson, 1980, pp. 88–109).

However, the United States began to noticeably shift toward a postindustrial economy beginning in the 1970s. This move away from manufacturing and toward service- and knowledge-based goods brought the decentralization of U.S. businesses, further expansion in government and corporate sectors, and demographic shifts from urban to suburban settings (sometimes referred to as "white flight"). These economic and population changes created a situation in which city tax resources either declined, or increased at slower-than-necessary rates. At the same time, and due to the same social factors, cities experienced a sharp increase in expenditures. This situation obviously created problems for municipal services, such as public assistance and urban schools.

The picture that Wilson gives us of the time following World War II involves two opposing forces. On the one hand, political and economic opportunities for blacks increased dramatically. Through the 1930s, 1940s, and 1950s, the black working class experienced increasing opportunities and urbanization, which at the time was a positive move. On the other hand, from the 1970s on, there was the decentralization of American business, decreases in manufacturing and increases in government and corporate jobs, and white flight from urban to suburban settings. These overlapping yet opposing forces fragmented the black labor force and resulted in "vastly different mobility opportunities for different groups in the black population" (Wilson, 1980, p. 121).

Those African Americans who were already moving toward the middle class were poised to take advantage of the economic and political shifts. They continued to experience upward mobility and "unprecedented job opportunities in the corporate and government sectors" (Wilson, 1980, p. 121). These middle-class blacks, like their white counterparts, have been able to move to more affluent neighborhoods. The other segment of the black labor force, however, has become locked into the cycle of inner-city problems: declining city revenues in the face of increasing social needs. These are "the relatively poorly trained blacks of the inner city, including the growing number of younger blacks emerging from inferior ghetto schools" (Wilson, 1980, p. 121) who are locked into low-paying jobs with high turnover rates and little hope of advancement.

Based on this theoretical understanding of race relations and black inequality, Wilson (1997) argues that our very best efforts at ending such inequality should be aimed at improving the class opportunities of Americans as a whole, especially as we move into a postindustrial, globalized economy. While these efforts would alleviate the economic suffering of many,

> Their most important contribution would be their effect on the children of the ghetto, who would be able to anticipate a future of economic mobility and share the hopes and aspirations that so many of their fellow citizens experience as part of the American way of life. (p. 238)

Market Moralities and Black Nihilism—Cornel West

Cornel West (1953–) was born in Tulsa, Oklahoma. He began attending Harvard University at 17 and graduated 3 years later, magna cum laude. His degree was in Near Eastern languages and literature. West obtained his PhD at Princeton, where he studied with Richard Rorty, a well-known pragmatist. West has taught at Union Theological Seminary, Yale Divinity School, the University of Paris, and Harvard, and is currently at Princeton. Among his most significant works are *Race Matters* and *Democracy Matters: Winning the Fight Against Imperialism*. His recent works include *Keeping Faith: Philosophy and Race in America* and a rap CD, *Never Forget: A Journey of Revelations*.

West picks up Wilson's theme but moves it into the realm of culture. West, then, can be seen as furthering Du Bois' analysis into the beginning of the twenty-first century. Since the 1960s, the upwardly mobile black population in the United States has increasingly become the target of capitalist markets. Capitalists have spent over two centuries marketing to whites, but blacks have constituted a strong and viable market for only the past 40 years or so. Given the historical background of the black community in the United States, this concentrated marketing has had unique effects on African Americans of all classes. In order to see into this distinctive process, West creates a unique theoretical perspective by blending critical Marxism, pragmatism, existentialism, and Christianity.

Concepts and Theory: Market Forces—Market Moralities

As a way of distributing goods and services, markets have been a part of human history for millennia. Capitalist markets, however, have a couple of unique characteristics. Modern capitalism, you'll remember, is defined by the endless accumulation of capital to create more capital. This drive implies that the need for profit is insatiable and thus continues to increase. Because markets are the mechanism through which profit and capital are gained, modern capitalist markets are intrinsically expansive: They expand vertically (through accessories for an existing product), horizontally (producing new products within a market), and geographically (extending existing markets to new social groups). A second unique characteristic of modern capitalism is an essential aspect of markets: Capitalists are driven to create a never-ending stream of new or different commodities. Keep in mind that commodification is a process that converts more and more of the human lifeworld into something that can be bought and sold, and it creates new "needs" within the consumer. Human beings are not just the only animal capable of economic production; we are also the only species able to create new psychological drives and needs for the new products. The primary tools through which these needs are created are mass media and advertising.

In our current society, expansive markets, commodification, and advertising have dramatically affected culture. In order to see this, let's set up a kind of ideal type we'll call "grounded culture." The primary functions of grounded culture are communication and the formation of social bonds. In traditional social groups, grounded culture was the norm; it emerged out of face-to-face interactions and was generally unmediated. There were few if any written texts and most if not all communication took place in real social situations. There was then a strong correlation between culture and social reality: All communicative acts—including speech, gift giving, rituals, exchanges, and so on—were directly related to and expressive of social relationships.

Expanding markets, commodification, advertising, and mass media have emptied grounded culture of this type of social reality. In order to expand, markets and commodification reach into our lifeworld and create products where there used to be symbolic value. Let me give you an example: Back in the 1960s, hippies began wearing tie-dyed T-shirts. These shirts were handmade, and only hippies wore them. The shirts also had very specific meanings attached to them: They most directly represented the experience of taking hallucinogenic drugs and the free-flowing nature of hippie life. As a piece of culture, the tie-dyed T-shirt did exactly what culture is intended for: It communicated meaning and social connections that arose out of real group experiences. Today, however, you can buy a tie-dyed shirt at Wal-Mart, and it has no clear meaning. The meaning has been emptied out because the shirt is now a commodity, rather than a group-specific sign. Markets and commodification thus trivialize meaning.

Advertising generally, and most specifically in postindustrial society, reduces commodities from their use-value to pure sign-value. Use-value is how much a product is actually worth in real-life terms—the value of a product is its use in your life. Exchange-value, on the other hand, is how much we pay for products. As you can imagine, we pay more for commodities in market exchange then they're worth in real terms. But Marx didn't live in a society utterly given over to commodification and advertising. "Today what we are experiencing is the absorption of all virtual modes of expression into that of advertising" (Baudrillard, 1981/1994, p. 87). Advertising does not seek to convey information about a product's use-value; rather, advertising places a product in a field of unrelated signs in order to enhance its cultural appearance. As a result of advertising, we tend to relate to the fragmented sign context rather than the use-value. Think about the example of clothing. The actual use-value of clothing is to cover us and keep us warm. Yet right now I'm looking at an ad for clothing in *Rolling Stone*, and it doesn't mention anything about protection from the elements or avoiding public nudity. The ad is interesting in that it doesn't even present itself as advertising at all. It looks more like a picture of a rock band on tour. The advertising, then, is selling the sign-value of these articles of clothing as part of the rock-and-roll lifestyle (which is mythical in its own right).

Thus, in the consumer society, social relations are read through a system of commodified signs rather than symbolic exchange. Commodities become the sign-vehicles in modernity that carry identity and meaning (or the lack thereof). For example, in modern society, the automobile is a portable, personal status symbol. Driving an SUV means something different from driving a Volkswagen Beetle, which conveys something different from driving a hybrid. As this system becomes more important and elaborated, a new kind of labor eventually supplants physical labor: the labor of consumption. This doesn't mean the work involved in finding the best deal. The labor of consumption is the work a person does to place him- or herself within and read the signs of an identity that is established and understood in a matrix of commodified signs.

All of this has a general, overall effect. Cultural signs are no longer moored to any social or physical reality; all of them are fair game for capitalism's manipulation of desire. Any cultural idea, image, sign, or symbol is apt to be pulled out of its social context and used to advertise and to place the individual in the position of sign-consumer. As these signs are lifted out of the social, they lose all possibility of stable reference. They may be used for anything, for any purpose. Moreover, the more media that are present, and the faster information is made available (via cell phones, texting, instant messaging, DSL computer connections, and so forth), the faster the signs will circulate and the greater will be the appropriation of indigenous signs for capitalist gain, until there remains no sign that has not been set loose and colonized by capitalism run amok. All that remains is a yawning abyss of meaninglessness—a placeless surface that is incapable of holding personal identity, self, or society.

Black Nihilism

While the description of capitalist culture holds for everyone in it, it is especially significant for black Americans. Since civil rights and the rise of the black middle class, the African American community as a whole has been subject to what West calls "market saturation." West argues that being a focus for market activity, commodification, and advertising has changed black culture in America. Prior to market saturation, blacks had a long history of community and tradition. They were equipped with a kind of cultural armor that came in large part via black civic and religious institutions. This armor, used to survive first under slavery and then under segregation, consisted of clear and strong structures of meaning and feeling that "embodied values of service and sacrifice, love and care, discipline and excellence" (West, 2001, p. 24). However, as a result of the twin structural influences of civil rights and upward mobility, blacks moved out of black communities and churches, and the structural bases for cultural armor were thus weakened.

In place of cultural armor, blacks have since been inundated with the market moralities of conspicuous consumption and material calculus (value established through material goods rather than ethical or intrinsic characteristics). The culture of consumption orients people to the present moment and to the intensification of pleasure. This culture of pleasure uses seduction to capitalize "on every opportunity to make money" (West, 2001, p. 26). It overwhelms people in a moment where the past and future are swallowed up in a never-ending "repetition of hedonistically driven pleasure" (p. 26). Further, the material calculus argues that the greatest value comes from profit-driven calculations. Every other consideration, such as love and service to others, is hidden under the bushel of profit.

As I've mentioned, most of these cultural ramifications of markets and commodification have also been present in other groups. But in West's (2001) opinion, two issues make these effects particularly destructive for blacks. First, black upward mobility and the presence of the black middle class affect only a small segment of the population. Most of the black citizens of the United States still suffer economically, yet are still subject to market saturation. The other issue that makes the black experience of market saturation distinct is the "accumulated effect of the black wounds and scars suffered in a white-dominated society" (p. 28). In other words, there is a historical and cultural heritage, no matter how much the immediacy of market saturation and pleasure tries to deny it: Much of the history and economic prosperity of the United States was built on over the 188 years of black oppression, from 1776 to 1964.

Obviously, these two factors influence one another. Healing from past wounds can only take place in a present that is both nurturing and repentant, a place that does not replicate hurts from the past. According to West (2001), this isn't happening for blacks in America: Cultural beliefs and media images continue to attack "black intelligence, black ability, black beauty, and black character in subtle and not-so-subtle ways" (p. 27). Furthermore, as noted earlier, black upward mobility is still limited. In the abstract, West's argument so far looks like this: black upward mobility + increased civil rights → weakening of civic and religious community base → substitution of market moralities for cultural armor—all of which takes place within the framework of the black legacy in the United States and continued oppression. "Under these circumstances, black existential angst derives from the lived experience of ontological wounds and emotional scars" (p. 27). The "ontological wounds" that West is speaking of come from the ways in which black reality and existence have been denied throughout the history of the United States.

In general, existential angst refers to the deep and profound insecurity and dread that comes from living as a human being—basically, our anguish over life and death: What is the meaning of life; and what happens after we die? In traditional societies, this angst was addressed through religion, faith, and deeply embedded social structures. In contemporary society, it is left to the person to resolve. West employs the idea of angst to describe the uniquely black experience of living under American capitalism and democracy. Black experience is intensely historical, yet the past and the future are buried under the market-driven pleasures of the moment; black experience is fundamentally communitarian, yet that civic and religious base is overwhelmed by market individualisms; black experience is painfully oppressive, yet it is countered only by increasing target marketing and consumerism. Thus, West argues that the result of market saturation and moralities for blacks is a spiritual condition of despair and insecurity. West refers to this as "black nihilism."

Concepts and Theory: Black Cultural Armor

Because blacks no longer have the necessary culture, community, or leadership, this angst cannot be used productively. Righteous anger, turned against the oppressor in hopes of liberation, becomes increasingly difficult to muster and express. Black nihilism denies the hope in which this anger would be founded. With no viable path, righteous anger is turned inward and expressed in black-against-black violence, especially against black women and children. However, nihilism can be treated. West argues that it is a disease of the soul, one that cannot be cured completely as there is always the threat of relapse. This disease must be met with love and care, not arguments and analysis. What is required is a new kind of politics, a politics of conversion, which reaches into the subversive memory of black people to find modes of valuation and resistance—a politics centered on a love ethic that is energized by concern for others and the recognition of one's own worth. This kind of politics requires prophetic black leaders who will bring "hope for the future and a meaning to struggle" (West, 2001, p. 28). There is, however, a crisis in American black leadership.

For West, strong leaders come out of vibrant communities. With the breakdown of the black community, black leaders don't have a social base that is in touch with the real issues. There is thus no nurturing of a critical consciousness in the heart of black America. Rather, much of the new black leadership in America comes out of the middle class, and black middle-class life is "principally a matter of professional conscientiousness, personal accomplishment, and cautious adjustment" (West, 2001, p. 57). West maintains that what is lacking in contemporary black leadership is anger and humility; what is present in overabundance is status anxiety and concerns for personal careers.

West (2001) argues that there are three kinds of black leaders in society today: race-effacing managerial leaders, race-identifying protest leaders, and race-transcending prophetic leaders. The managerial/elitist model is growing rapidly in the United States. This style of leadership is one that conforms fully to bureaucratic norms. The leader navigates the political scene through political savvy and personal diplomacy, and race is down-played in the hopes of gaining a white constituency. The second type of leader, the protest leader, capitalizes on the race issue but in a very limited way, resulting in racial reasoning—a way of thinking that is more con-cerned with clearly black issues rather than social justice. In racial reason-ing, the discourse of race centers on black authenticity: the notion that some black experiences and people are really black while others aren't. Racial reasoning results in Black Nationalist sentiments that "promote and encourage black cultural conservatism, especially black patriarchal (and homophobic) power" (West, 2001, p. 37). Closing the ranks thus creates a hierarchy of acceptability within a black context.

These two kinds of black leaders have promoted political cynicism among black people, and have dampened "the fire of enraged local activists who have made a difference" (West, 2001, p. 68). Part of black nihilism is fed by this sense of ineffectuality, of being lost in a storm too big to change. In this context, the liberal focus on economic issues is rejected as simplistic. Likewise, the conservative critique of black immorality is dismissed as ignor-ing public responsibility for the ethical state of the union. In their places, West proposes a democratic, pragmatically driven dialogue. West doesn't propose absolutes; instead, he gives a prophetic call to radical democracy and faith, to finally take seriously the declaration that all people are created equal.

What is needed, according to West, is black leadership founded on moral reasoning rather than racial reasoning. Moral reasoning is the ethical center of race-transcending, prophetic leaders. Prophetic leadership does not rest on any kind of racial supremacy, black or white. It uses a coalition strategy, which seeks out the antiracist traditions found in all peoples. It refuses to divide black people over other categories of distinction and rejects patriarchy and homophobia. Prophetic, moral reasoning is also based on a mature black identity of self-love and self-respect that refuses to put "any group of people on the pedestal or in the gutter" (West, 2001, p. 43). Moral reasoning also uses subversive memory, "one of the most precious heritages [black people] have" (West, 1999, p. 221). It recalls the modes of struggling and resisting that affirmed community, faith, hope, and love, rather than the contemporary market morality of individualism, conspicuous consumption, and hedonistic indulgence.

Both the coalition strategy and mature black identity are built at the local level. West (1999) sees local communities as working "from below and sometimes beneath modernity" (p. 221); socially embedded networks mitigate the effects of market saturation. It is within vibrant communities and through public discourse that local leaders are held accountable and earn respect and love. Such leaders merit national attention from the black community and the general public, according to West. Together, moral reasoning, coalition strategy, and mature black identity create the black cultural armor. West's use of "armor" is a biblical reference. Christians are told in Ephesians 6:13 (New International Version) to "put on the full armor of God, so that when the day of evil comes, you may be able to stand your ground, and after you have done everything, to stand." There, the threat was the powers of darkness in heavenly places; here, the threat is black nihilism in the heart of democracy. These two battles are at least parallel if not identical for West. The fight for true democracy is a spiritual battle for the souls of humankind that have been dulled by market saturation, especially the souls of black America. West (2001) exhorts black America to put on its cultural armor—a return to community life and moral reasoning along with coalition strategy and mature black identity—so as to "beat back the demons of hopelessness, meaninglessness, and lovelessness" and create anew "cultural structures of meaning and feeling" (p. 23).

The Craft of Citizenship	Race

The Basics: Comprehension and Explanation

- Identify the main concerns and questions of each theorist. With those questions in mind, write a two- to three-sentence statement that captures their theoretical response.
- Make a detailed list of the primary theoretical concepts each theorist employs. Then define the most important concepts in Du Bois' theory of cultural oppression, Wilson's theory of race and class, and West's theory of black nihilism.

(Continued)

(Continued)

- According to Du Bois, how does culture work to oppress blacks?
- Explain how class is becoming increasingly important in U.S. race relations. Be certain to explain how racism works in each time period.
- Explain how market saturation is affecting African Americans today. Don't forget to explain how market saturation came about.
- How is black nihilism overcome?

Skill Set 1: Inference and Application

- What is it about early modern structures and culture that provided the basis for racism?
- If you're African American, explore how your values and sense of self are impacted by market moralities. If you're not African American, how have market moralities affected you?
  - ➢ *Helpful hints:* Like the implications about religious beliefs, this requires you to make a problem out of something you may take for granted and feel as if it were natural. However, while this is difficult, it is also the most authentic use of civic sociology and what C. W. Mills (1959) calls the sociological imagination: "The first fruit of this imagination—and the first lesson of the social science that embodies it—is the idea that *the individual can understand his own experience* and gauge his own fate only by locating himself with his period" (p. 5, emphasis added).
- In what ways do your buying practices perpetuate racism globally?
- Du Bois holds out the hope that history can be told in a way that doesn't deny the experience, existence, or contribution of any group. Describe the perspective from which such a history could be written.
  - ➢ *Helpful hints:* Go back in the text and consider the ideas of any who theorized about culture in modernity. What kind of culture do those theorists see as necessary for modern democracy? Apply those values and ideals to writing history.
- Explain the policy implications of Wilson's theory.
- What does West's critique of political leadership imply generally about what we should expect from leaders in a democratic society? Analyze the current national leadership using West's criteria. Think especially about Barack Obama. Where would you place him in West's scheme? Search the Internet to discover West's opinion of Obama.

Skill Set 2: Interpretation, Analysis, Evaluation, Synthesis

- Evaluate Wilson's class-based proposals using West's theory of black nihilism.
- Interpret and evaluate Wilson's state-economy model using Habermas' theory of organized capitalism. According to these two theories, what is gained and lost as the state becomes more involved in the economy?
- Using Dahrendorf's theory of bureaucratic society, explain why the number of race-effacing managerial leaders is growing rapidly in the United States.
- Explain West's notion of race-transcendent leadership and moral reasoning using the theoretical explanation of generalized culture found in Parsons and Durkheim (and implicit in Bellah).
- Synthesize Du Bois, Wilson, and West into a general theory of racial inequality.

  ➢ *Helpful hints:* As in our work with gender, these theories have fairly clear theoretical inroads, or connections, that you can develop. Think in big terms about what each theory brings, and you should see the connections. It should be especially helpful to keep in mind the distinction between culture and structure.

- Compare and contrast Foucault's and West's theories of subjective experience. How can these theories be brought together to give us greater insight into how individual, subjective experiences are formed in this period of modernity?

9

Globalization

One of the things you have probably noticed as we've moved through this book is that the forces of modernity that were set in motion 200 to 300 years ago continue to influence our lives today, mostly in ways that were unforeseen or undesirable in terms of the original social project of modernity. In the last two chapters, we especially saw that modernity created the categories of race and gender that we use today in the unequal distribution of resources. Other challenges and critiques have come out of those same forces as well. Through our journey, we've seen how capitalism, which was intended as the great equalizer, has created class inequities and ideologies. The civil sphere, wherein the great debates of democracy were to be held, has been colonized by consumerism and a sense of entitlement. Religion on the one hand has become a source of terrorism on the world stage, and on the other has become privatized to the point of meaninglessness. And modern power, which was to rest in the masses in the free exercise of individual will, is found rather as the individual objectifies and controls him- or herself in the interest of governmentality. We've also seen how modern knowledge itself has been instrumental in oppression and derailing the social project of equality.

In this final chapter, we take a look at one of the foundation stones of the social project: the existence of society. In Chapter 2, we set the parameters of such an entity—society as an objective, independent system bounded by the nation-state, with specific structures and institutions that together could be guided to greater levels of social justice. In this chapter, we consider the possibility that as a result of globalization, those ideas of society no longer hold. At this point in time, globalization is a contested concept, but that simply means we haven't figured out all that goes into defining the process—it's that new. It is clear, however, that "[t]he term globalization applies to a set of social processes that appear to transform our present social condition of weakening nationality into one of globality. At its core, then, globalization is about shifting forms of human contact" (Steger, 2009, p. 9). Globalization by definition, then, challenges our concepts of society (weakening nationality) and, by extension, democracy (human contact).

We'll take a look at three sociological theories of globalization. We start with Anthony Giddens. He'll give us a basic way of understanding globalization in terms of extending social relationships beyond national boundaries. Giddens also gives us eyes to see that modernity always implied globalization; the globalizing tendencies of modernity have been present since the beginning. And he'll give us our first way of thinking about politics in a global age. Like Giddens, our second theorist, Immanuel Wallerstein, argues that the seeds of globalization were contained in the institutional arrangements of modernity, but Wallerstein focuses exclusively on the economic system of capitalism. He argues that the reason contradictions within capitalism haven't yet played themselves out is that they have yet to be played out globally. While Marx understood that capitalism created the first true world markets, he also thought the system itself was contained within the boundaries of the nation-state. Thus, capitalism would fall nation by nation in Marx's scheme. Wallerstein, however, points out that as long as capitalists could shift exploitation to less developed nations, the contradictions of capitalism could be mitigated and the system would survive. With the globalization of all the dynamics of capitalism—commodity production, the division of labor, and exploitation—the inherent contradictions of capitalism will shortly play themselves out and bring an end to modern capitalism as we know it.

We'll spend an extended amount of time considering our last theorist, Manuel Castells. By now, you have sufficient background in the basic ideas that both Giddens and Wallerstein employ to be able to grasp their basic arguments. Castells, on the other hand, opens up a new horizon of thought, and we'll need to spend a bit more time exploring his ideas. Your background in systems will help, but Castells proposes that an entirely new system has replaced the social systems of modernity. Rather than systems of institutions and social relations, Castells argues that globalization is built on networks of communication, mostly structured through the Internet. These networks not only transcend the boundaries of nation, but also completely redefine human connections. The globalized network society, then, can only be understood through the logics of computer networks, and in this network society, class, power, politics, meaning, and identities are radically redefined.

Runaway Modernity—Anthony Giddens

Anthony Giddens was born January 18, 1938, in Edmonton, North London, England. He received his undergraduate degree with honors from Hull University in 1959, studying sociology and psychology. Giddens did his master's work at the London School of Economics, finishing his thesis on the sociology of sport in 1961. From then until the early 1970s, Giddens lectured at various universities including the University of Leicester, Simon Fraser University, the University of California at Los Angeles, and Cambridge. Giddens finished his doctoral work at Cambridge in 1976. He remained there through 1996, during which time he served as dean of social and political sciences. In 1997, Giddens was appointed director of the London School of Economics and Political Science. Giddens is the author of some 34 books, which have been translated into over 20 languages. He is also a member of the Advisory Council of the Institute for Public Policy Research (London) and has served as advisor to former British prime minister Tony Blair.

Concepts and Theory: Time–Space Distanciation

Giddens argues that globalization should be understood at the most basic level as the stretching out of social relationships across time and space. He calls this "time–space distanciation." In one way, this technical-sounding term simply refers to the basic question of sociability we've been aware of since Chapter 2: How are human behaviors patterned over time and space? One of the things that Giddens wants us to know is that at its core, modernity is about creating and managing greater and greater distances between social actions. Think about the definition of society from Chapter 2, and you'll see that such stretching out allows us to create and manage society—large-scale social institutions and structures exist only because of time–space distanciation. The fundamental way in which this happens is by emptying time and space of their natural attributes. Up until the beginning of modernity, time and space were seen as closely linked to natural settings and cycles. The cycle of the sun set the boundaries of the day, the cycle of the moon marked the month, and the year was noted by the cycles of the seasons. But the week—which is the primary tool we use to organize ourselves today—exists nowhere in nature; it's utterly abstract in terms of the natural world. In fact, it's precisely because the week is abstract that it can be used in countless ways to organize (stretch out) actions.

The same is true about the mechanical clock. Previous to the invention and widespread use of the mechanical clock, people regulated their behaviors around the moving of the sun. Time was inexorably understood with reference to place and the concrete arc of the sun across the sky. The first step in emptying the day of time was the invention of the mechanical clock, and that was soon followed by institutionally established time zones. These advances allowed people to control time and to schedule events and actions over vast expanses of space, as with train travel. In recent years, computer and Internet technologies have further emptied time. We can now conduct business and communicate with people halfway around the world in "real time." However, this thing we call real time doesn't exist anywhere, really. Real-time communication is utterly symbolic; it means that we can communicate instantaneously with others who are perhaps living in a different day (across the international dateline).

The emptying of time and space means that time–space distanciation can be increased almost without limit, and globalization accelerates the process. It continues to push the process through the modern institutions of capitalism, industrialism, the nation-state, and the world military order. Each of these four factors tends to create social relations at a distance that can in turn influence local events. For example, the industrialization of textiles in

Asia led to plant closings and job loss in North Carolina. Through capitalism, the division of labor has been extended globally, so that we now depend on workers in other countries to manufacture the goods we need. Nation-states and the military complex are by definition globalizing factors; nations and international wars are only understood and possible within a global order. Keep in mind that Giddens sees these as processes, not lifeless historical events. Thus, the world military order continues to create more and more distant events that affect local involvements, as the increasing number of wars the United States has been involved in since World War II demonstrates. Moreover, time and space are further emptied with every advance in communication technologies.

Modernity Out of Control

For Giddens, then, globalization has been inherent within modernity since the beginning. But globalization has also pushed time–space distanciation past the point of being able to fulfill some of the Enlightenment's most treasured goals: control and the belief in progress were founded on the idea of contained systems. Remember our discussion in Chapter 2: In modernity, society is seen as a separate entity, a system of interrelated parts whose functions and dynamics could be discovered and controlled. By definition, systems have explicit boundaries, at least controllable ones do. The possibility that modern society could be controlled was based on the assumption that it was a system with "a nation-state at its centre that organizes the rights and duties of each citizen" (Urry, 2006, p. 168). As we saw in Chapters 2 and 5, this nation-state was to be guided through an identifiable civil society. Globalization by definition transgresses those boundaries and sets up distant social relationships that influence local order, but those distant relations aren't contained within or governed by any regulatory system like the nation-state. So, what began as attempts to control social life through time–space distanciation has in the long run made control more difficult, as social relations have expanded past any single system.

Giddens (1990) further tells us that "this is a dialectical process because such local happenings may move in an obverse direction from the very distanciated relations that shape them" (p. 64). In other words, because of the complexity of globalization, it is impossible to predict outcomes of actions. Furthermore, as the world becomes increasingly globalized, it becomes increasingly decentered, "not under the control of any group of nations, and still less of the large corporations" (Giddens, 1994, p. 34). In the end, modernity becomes "a runaway engine of enormous power which, collectively as human beings, we can drive to some extent but which also threatens to rush out of our control and which could rend itself asunder" (Giddens, 1990, p. 139).

Concepts and Theory:
From Emancipatory to Lifestyle Politics

The social project of modernity was founded on emancipatory politics—processes of liberating individuals and groups from the constraints that adversely affect their lives. It was the hope that democratic nation-states could bring equality and justice for all. But emancipatory politics is founded on there being a center, a steering mechanism that allows society to be directed. Giddens argues that as the four dynamics of modernity continue to push globalization, it becomes increasingly obvious that what we mean by society is something that cannot be contained within the boundaries of a single nation. Further, emancipatory politics presumes a central political identity, one around which people can rally and push for reform. That, too, is becoming increasingly difficult to achieve.

Life politics, by way of contrast, is the politics of choice and lifestyle. Unlike emancipatory politics, it is not based on group membership and characteristics; rather, it is based on personal lifestyle choices. We have come to think of choice as a freedom, but choice in a global society is more than freedom—it's an obligation, a fundamental element in contemporary living. Part of this obligation is due to innate characteristics of modern knowledge. Remember, at its core the modern way of knowing is founded on doubt and skepticism. Because of this core, the hope of progress never materializes—the ideal of progress means that we never truly arrive. Every step in our progressive march forward is examined in the hopes of improving what we have achieved. Progress thus becomes a motivating value and a discourse of modernity, rather than a goal that is ever reached. This way of knowing continually overturns everything we know, not only about science and technology but also our political sensibilities, how to construct identities and how to guide a life course. Progress then becomes extremely difficult to map. Knowledge that is founded on doubt can have no signposts, no reference points that convey a sense of rightness or progress, particularly in terms of personal growth (life, liberty, and the pursuit of happiness). The construction of a self (Chapter 3)—of a cohesive narrative that conveys a sense of solidity—is left up to the individual *who must choose among competing claims*. These claims to the good life are made against the unlimited horizon of globalized media and information.

By definition, a globalized world is a mediated world. Most of our social connections outside local relationships are mediated; they happen through communication technologies like mass media, the Internet, and telecommunications. Mediated experiences are created as we are exposed to multiple accounts of situations and diverse others with whom we have no direct association. Every time we watch television or read a newspaper, we are exposed to lives, ideas, and worldviews to which we have absolutely no real connection, and like so many other features of modernity, this stretches out co-presence, but it also creates a collage effect. The pictures and stories that we receive via the media do not reflect any essential or social organization. Instead, stories and images are juxtaposed that have nothing to do with one another in the hopes of stimulating an audience. The picture we get of the world, then, is a collage of diverse lifestyles and cultures, not a direct representation.

As a result of being faced with this collage, what happens to us as individuals? One implication is that the plurality of lifestyles presented to us not only allows for choice, but also necessitates it. In other words, what becomes important in constructing identities is not the issue of group equality, but rather, the insistence on personal choice. What is at stake in this milieu, the issue of personhood of which we are most aware, is not political equality (as with emancipatory politics) but rather, inner authenticity. In a world that is perceived as constantly changing and uprooted, it becomes important to be grounded in and to express one's self. Life politics creates such grounding and expression. It creates "a framework of basic trust by means of which the lifespan can be understood as a unity against the backdrop of shifting social events" (Giddens, 1991, p. 215).

However, it would be wrong to conclude that life politics is powerless because it does not result in a social movement. Quite the opposite is true. Life politics springs from and focuses attention on some of the very issues that modernity represses. What life politics does is to "place a question mark against the internally referential systems of modernity" (Giddens, 1991, p. 223). In traditional society, morality was provided by the institutions, especially religion. Modernity has wiped away the social ground upon which this kind of morality was based. Life politics "remoralizes" social life and demands "renewed sensitivity to questions that the institutions of modernity systematically dissolve" (p. 224). Rather than asking for group participation, as does emancipatory politics, life politics asks for self-realization, a moral commitment to a specific way of living. Rather than being impotent in comparison to emancipatory politics, life politics "presage[s] future changes of a far-reaching sort: essentially, the development of forms of social order 'on the other side' of modernity itself" (p. 214).

Global Capitalism—Immanuel Wallerstein

Immanuel Wallerstein (1930–) was born in New York City and attended Columbia University where he received his bachelor's (1951), master's (1954), and PhD (1959). His primary teaching post was at the State University of New York, Binghamton, where he taught from 1976 to his retirement in 1999. He has also held visiting professor posts in Amsterdam, British Columbia, and the Chinese University in Hong Kong, as well as several other locations. In addition to many professional posts, he has served as president of the International Sociological Association and director of the Fernand Braudel Center for the Study of Economies, Historical Systems, and Civilizations. Wallerstein's major works include *The Modern World-systems,* volumes 1–3. For more recent and perhaps more accessible pieces, read *The End of the World as We Know It* and *World-Systems Analysis: An Introduction.* Wallerstein focuses on one aspect of Giddens' four dimensions of globalization: the capitalist economy. But rather than being concerned with time–space distanciation, Wallerstein centers his discussion on the structural contradictions of global capitalism.

Concepts and Theory: World-Systems

Capitalism has always had a global aspect. Marx and Engels (1848/1978) saw that the world market was one of the factors that destroyed the remnants of feudalism and pushed for the development of the modern nation-state, over which the bourgeoisie exercised "exclusive political sway" (p. 475). The current system, however, goes far beyond what Marx supposed. Today's global capitalism is structured through a worldwide division of labor: World economies are defined "quite simply as a unit with a single division of labor and multiple cultural systems" (Wallerstein, 2000, p. 75). The basis for this division of labor is twofold: the exportation of exploitation and a state-facilitated cycle of leading products.

We're familiar with exploitation from Marx: It is represented by the difference between what a worker gets paid and the amount he or she produces. We've also seen that this exploitation by capitalists can then be leveraged by labor in order to raise wages for workers and obtain other benefits, like safe working conditions and health insurance. This means that in advanced capitalist countries, the average wage is high and the opportunity for profit based on exploitation is low. In response, capitalists export exploitation. Manufacturing is moved to other countries where there aren't guaranteed worker benefits and protections and the hourly wage is miniscule. While there may not be the level of collusion between capitalism and the state that Marx thought, the state is certainly involved in supporting capitalist enterprise through two channels: subsidizing externalized costs and guaranteeing quasi-monopolies. There are three kinds of externalized costs that the state subsidizes: transportation, toxicity, and the exhaustion of raw materials. Firms rarely, if ever, pay the full cost of transporting their goods (via road and rail systems, waterways, etc.); the bulk is paid by the state.

Almost all production produces toxicity, whether noxious gases, waste, or some kind of change to the environment. How and when these costs are incurred and who pays for them is always an issue. The least expensive methods are short-term and evasive (dumping the waste, pretending there isn't a problem), but the costs are eventually paid and quite often by the state. For example, according to the U.S. Environmental Protection Agency, funding for hazardous waste site cleanup from 1993 through 2005 was well over $19 billion (U.S. Environmental Protection Agency, 2009). Capitalist production also uses up raw materials, but again, firms rarely pay these costs. When resources are depleted, it's generally the state that steps in to restore or recreate the materials:

> The basic (and not very well publicized) fact is that *by its nature, capital is bad at preserving things. . . . There is no profit in maintenance or preservation. . . . The profit is in expansion, accumulation, and marketing something old or new at lower costs.* (O'Connor, 1998, p. 317, emphasis original)

However helpful these externalized costs are to the pursuit of accumulation, states that contain the most successful capitalist enterprises do more: They provide a structure for quasi-monopolies. We know that modern capitalism is defined by the endless pursuit of capital and that this type of accumulation is fueled by the drive for expanding markets and ever-increasing profits. We assume that those markets are free and that competition results in the best product for the money while at the same time ensuring capitalist profit. However, Wallerstein argues that truly free markets would make the endless accumulation of capital impossible. Free markets imply that all factors influencing the means of production are free and available to all firms, that goods and services flow without restriction, that there is a very large number of sellers and a very large number of buyers, and that all participants have complete and full knowledge. "In such a perfect market, it would always be possible for the buyers to bargain down the sellers to an absolutely minuscule level of profit," which would destroy the basic underpinnings of capitalism (Wallerstein, 2004, pp. 25–26). True open competition, then, results in low profits and would thus make modern capitalism (endless accumulation) impossible. There is therefore pressure for states to provide some basis to mitigate the effects of free markets.

The most important way in which states facilitate quasi-monopolies is through patent laws that grant exclusive production rights for an invention for a certain number of years. The state guarantee allows companies to gain high levels of profit in a monopolistic market for long enough to obtain considerable accumulation of capital. The practice of granting patents also results in a cycle of leading products. The largest and most successful firms actively market a patented product as long as the profit margin is high. As soon as the product becomes less profitable through more open competition (once the patent runs out), the product is given over to less profitable companies, with the original firm creating new leading products. Producers of the unpatented product engage in freer competition but with less profit.

Thus, the world economy is linked through production and a never-ending cycle of leading products. This cycle of products accentuates a problem already inherent within capitalism: overproduction. Recall from Marx that the drive for profit and capital, coupled with humanity's ability to create new needs, naturally leads to overproduction—too much production for the market to bear. Opening the world market up to this cycle of leading products relieves the pressure of overproduction for a short time. But in the long run, the state's guarantee of quasi-monopolies acts like a supercharger on this contradiction of capitalism. The result is that cycles of overproduction and market turndown occur globally, resulting in a much more powerful engine for economic crises.

The worldwide division of labor created through the movement of products and labor from advanced capitalist nations to rising capitalist nations creates relationships of economic dependency and exploitation. These capitalist relationships are expressed through three basic types of economic states: core, periphery, and semi-periphery. Briefly, core states are those that export exploitation; enjoy relatively light taxation; have a free, well-paid labor force; and constitute a large consumer market. The state systems within core states are the most powerful and are thus able to provide the strongest protection (such as trade restrictions) and capitalist inducements, such as externalizing costs, patent protection, tax incentives, and so on. Peripheral states are those whose labor is forced (i.e., there are very few occupational choices or worker protections) and underpaid. In terms of a capitalist economy and the world system, these states are also the weakest— they are able to provide little in the way of tax and cost incentives, and they are the weakest players in the world-system. The peripheral states are those to which capitalists in core states shift worker exploitation and more competitive, less profitable products. These shifts result in "a constant flow of surplus-value from the producers of peripheral products to the producers of core-like products" (Wallerstein, 2004, p. 28).

The relationship between the core and the periphery is thus one of production processes and profitability. There is a continual shift of products and exploitation from core to peripheral countries. Yet there are cycles in both directions: Peripheral countries are continually developing their own capitalist-state base. As we've seen, profitability is highest in quasi-monopolies, and these, in turn, are dependent upon powerful states. Thus, changing positions in the capitalist world economy is dependent upon the power of the state.

Over time, peripheral economies become more robust and peripheral states more powerful: Worker protection laws are passed, wages increase, and product innovation begins to occur. The states can then begin to perform much like the states in core countries—they create tax incentives and externalize costs for firms, they grant product protection, and they become a more powerful player in the world-system economy. These nations move into the semi-periphery. Semi-peripheral states are those that are in transition from being a land of exploitation to being a core player, and they both export exploitation and continue to exploit within their own country.

Concepts and Theory: The Demise of Global Capitalism

Since 1450, world economies have moved through four distinct phases. Each phase consists of a two-part wave that repeats itself dialectically, each time precipitating deeper economic crises. I'm not going to go into much historical detail here; you can read Wallerstein's (1974, 1980, 1989) three-volume work for the specifics. But briefly, Phase 1 occurred roughly between 1450 and 1640, which marks the transition from feudalism and world empires to the nation-state. Both the Ottoman Empire and the Hapsburg Dynasty began their decline in the sixteenth century. As the world empires weakened, Western Europe and the nation-state emerged as the core, Spain and the Mediterranean declined into the semi-periphery, and northeastern Europe and the Americas became the periphery. During this time, the major form of capitalism was agricultural, which came about as an effect of technological development and ecological conditions in Europe.

The second phase lasted from 1640 to 1750 and was precipitated by a systemwide recession that lasted approximately 80 years. During this time, nations drew in, centralized, and attempted to control all facets of the market through mercantilism, the dominant form of capitalism in this phase. Mercantilism was designed to increase the power and wealth of the emerging nations through the accumulation of gold, favorable trade balances, and foreign trading monopolies. These goals were achieved primarily through colonization. As with the previous period, there was a great deal of struggle among the core nations, with a three-way conflict among the Netherlands, France, and England.

The third phase began with the Industrial Revolution. England quickly took the lead in this area. The last attempt by France to stop the spread of English power was Napoleon's continental blockade, which failed. Here, capitalism was driven by industry, and it expanded geographically to cover the entire globe. Wallerstein (2000) places the end of the third phase at the beginning of World War I and the beginning of the fourth phase at the Russian Revolution of 1917. The Russian Revolution was driven by the lack of indigenous capital, continued resistance to industrializing from the agricultural sector, and the decay of military power and national status. Together, these meant that "the Russian Revolution was essentially that of a semi-peripheral country whose internal balance of forces had been such that as of the late nineteenth century it began on a decline towards a peripheral status" (Wallerstein, 2000, p. 97). During this time, the British Empire receded due to a number of factors including decolonization, and two states in particular vied for the core position: Germany and the United States. After World War II, the United States became the leading core nation, a position it enjoyed for two decades.

The Costs of Leadership

Leading states always have a limited life span. Becoming a core nation requires a state to focus on improving the conditions of production for capitalists, but staying hegemonic (dominant) requires a state to invest in political and military might. Over time, other states become economically competitive, and the leading state's economic power diminishes. In attempts to maintain its powerful position in the world system, the hegemonic state will resort first to military threats and then to exercising its military power. The "use of military power is not only the first sign of weakness but the source of further decline," as the capricious use of force creates resentment first in the world community and then in the state's home population as the cost of war increases taxation (Wallerstein, 2004, pp. 58–59).

Thus, the cost of hegemony is always high, and it inevitably leads to the end of a state's position of power within the world-system. For the United States, the costs came from the Cold War with the USSR; competition with rising core nations, such as Japan, China, and an economically united and resurgent Western Europe; and such displays of military might as the Korean, Vietnam, Gulf, and Afghanistan and Iraqi Wars. The Iraq War, in response to the terrorist attacks of September 11, 2001, has been particularly costly. The terrorist attacks energized politically right-wing groups in the United States that used the fear of terrorism to cut ties with the political center and "to pursue a program centered around unilateral assertions by the United States of military strength" (Wallerstein, 2004, p. 87). This, along with attempts to do away with many of the geopolitical structures set in place after 1945 (like the United Nations), has "threatened to worsen the already-increasing instability of the world-system" (p. 87).

Marking the End

There are several key points in time for world-systems, such as the Ottoman defeat in 1571, the Industrial Revolution around 1750, and the Russian Revolution in 1917. Each of these events signaled a transition from one capitalist regime to another. Wallerstein (2004) argues that one such event occurred in 1968, when revolutionary movements raged across the globe involving China, West Germany, Poland, Italy, Japan, Vietnam, Czechoslovakia, Mexico, and the United States. So many nations were caught up in the mostly student-driven social movements that, collectively, they have been called the "first world revolution."

Wallerstein tells us that the upheavals of 1968 were directed at the contradictions of society and its failure to fulfill the hope of modernity. Students by and large rejected many of the benefits of technological development and proclaimed society had failed at the one thing that truly mattered: human freedom. The material benefits of technology and capitalism were seen as traps, things that had blinded people to the oppression of blacks, women, and all minorities. "In country after country of the so-called Third World, the populaces turned against the movements of the Old Left and charged fraud. . . . [The people of the world] had lost faith in their states as the agents of a modernity of liberation" (Wallerstein, 1995, p. 484). The 1968 movements in particular rejected American hegemony because of its emphasis on material wealth and failure to extend equal rights and social justice to all people.

The upheavals of 1968 occurred at a time when the world was standing at the brink of an economic downturn or stagnation, which lasted through the 1970s and 1980s. According to Wallerstein (2004), while the world-system has put effort into making an economic rebound, there are at least three structural problems hindering it. First, 400 years of capitalism have depleted the world's supply of cheap labor. Every wave has brought continued geographic expansion, and it appears that we have reached the limit of that expansion. Inevitably, this will lead to a sharp increase in the costs of labor and production and a corresponding decrease in profit margins.

Second, there is a squeeze on the middle classes. Typically, the middle classes are seen as the market base of a capitalist economy. A standard method of pulling out of a downturn is to increase the available spending money for the middle classes, either through tax breaks or through salary increases. This additional money spurs an increase in commodity purchases and subsequently in production and capital accumulation. However, this continual expanding of middle-class wages eventually becomes too much for firms and states to bear. One of two things must happen: Either these costs will be rolled back, or they will not. If they are not reduced, "Both states and enterprises will be in grave trouble and frequent bankruptcy" (Wallerstein, 1995, p. 485). If they are rolled back, "There will be significant political disaffection among precisely the strata that have provided the strongest support for the present world-system" (p. 485).

Third, as we've noted, accumulation is based on externalizing costs. Two of those costs—raw material depletion and toxicity—have natural limits, and it appears that we might be reaching them. Global warming, ozone rupture, destruction of the rain forests, and land degradation from waste are themes with which we are all familiar. James O'Connor (1998) sees the problem with raw resources and toxicity as a second contradiction of capitalism, a contradiction based on the *conditions* of production rather than the *means* of production. This contradiction is called *underproduction*. While overproduction occurs with exchange-value, underproduction is more clearly associated with use-value. While there is obvious exchange-value in a raw material such as oil, its use-value in this case is more important—fossil fuels are depleted in their use, and they are nonrenewable. Because these issues are limited by use-value, they constitute the ultimate reality of capitalism. According to O'Connor, "The closer we get to use-value theoretically, the closer we get to real places and real, live people practically" (p. 128).

With overproduction, the crisis comes from the demand side of the production equation; with underproduction, the crisis comes from the supply side. The supply side of capitalism entails the ecosystems from which raw materials are taken and toxins dumped; the mental and physical well-being of the labor force, which is influenced by the state of the ecosystem; and the state-supplied infrastructure. Thus, underproduction occurs when capitalist firms and states fail to renew or protect the conditions of production.

Concepts and Theory:
Political Involvement in an Age of Global Transition

What will follow the 400-year reign of capitalism is uncertain. Nevertheless, our opportunity to make a difference is greater than ever: "[F]undamental change is possible. . . . and this fact makes claims on our moral responsibility to act rationally, in good faith, and with strength to seek a better historical system" (Wallerstein, 1999, p. 3). According to Wallerstein (1999), the world-system is in a period of transition. During transition periods, systems become unstable and take on the attributes of complex or chaotic systems, which are ordered, but the ordering is unpredictable and the system as a whole can't be directed. However, one characteristic of complex systems is what has become known as the "butterfly effect"—an analogy that was used to understand weather systems, which many meteorologists now believe are best explained through chaos theory. The idea of the butterfly effect is that small inputs can have large outputs—a butterfly beating its wings in Brazil could set off a tornado in Texas. What this implies socially is that "every small action during this period is likely to have significant consequences" (Wallerstein, 2004, p. 77). Wallerstein exhorts us to make diligent efforts to understand what is going on; we must make choices about the direction in which we want the world to move, and we must bring our convictions into action. "None of us can opt out of any of these tasks. If we claim we do, we are merely making a hidden choice" (p. 90).

The Network Society—Manuel Castells

Manuel Castells (1942–) was born in La Mancha, Spain, and grew up in Valencia and Barcelona. In college, he studied law and economics and received his PhD in sociology and another in human sciences from the University of Paris–Sorbonne in 1967. While in Paris, he was a political activist, fighting against Franco's dictatorship. He taught sociology at the University of Paris from 1967 to 1979. In 1979, he took a professorship at the University of California, Berkeley; then, in 2003, he moved to the University of Southern California Annenberg School for Communication. Castells has written 22 books, has coauthored 21, and has had over 100 articles published in academic journals. His most influential works are his trilogy, *The Information Age: Economy, Society, and Culture,* which has been translated into over 23 languages. Among his many awards and distinctions is the C. Wright Mills Award from the American Society for the Study of Social Problems, the Robert and Helen Lynd Award from the American Sociological Association, the National Medal of Science from Catalonia, and the Lifelong Research Award from the Committee on Computers and Information Technology of the American Sociological Association.

In his work, Castells intends his theory to be used as an analytic heuristic. This approach implies two things. First, unlike Wallerstein, Castells' theory isn't meant to be predictive; rather, it's a way of seeing and analyzing the social world. Second, the theory is a "work in progress open to rectification by empirical research" (Castells, 2000a, p. 6). His work, then, is quite literally intended to provide ideas and concepts "to be used in the building of a sociological theory able to grasp emerging forms of social organization and conflict" (p. 6).

Concepts and Theory: Information Technology

Castells' idea is that the information revolution that began in the 1980s has restructured capitalism and created a global society that is connected via networks. Prior to World War II, the capitalist system had played out its Marxist dynamics and was in a worldwide, inexorable depression—there was no way out. Socialist movements were gaining power globally, and there was a good chance that capitalism would have collapsed had it not been for the war. During the Great Depression of the 1930s, John Maynard Keynes published a new theory of economics. The basic tenet of Keynesian economics is that the state can moderate the effects of free market capitalism through controlling interest rates and by investing in the economic infrastructure, thus becoming a major consumer. But, Castells argues, Keynesian economics, just like laissez-faire capitalism before it, had built-in contradictions and limitations, which came to a head by the 1970s and resulted in rampant inflation.

From the 1970s into the 1990s, massive efforts at restructuring capitalism were under way. There were four goals: (1) Deepen the logic of profitability; (2) improve the profitability of both capital and labor; (3) globalize commodity and labor markets; and (4) use the state to maximize the profitability of the national economy, even at the cost of social programs and education. Essential to this project was flexibility, such as "just-in-time" (JIT) inventory strategies, and adaptability. Castells (2000b) argues that this attempt at restructuring would have been extremely limited without the new information technology.

By new information technology, Castells has in mind computer technologies, both hardware and software, which, when coupled with the Internet, have connected humanity in a way that was up to this point unthinkable. As Giddens points out, space and time have become more abstract and infinitely less meaningful in terms of patterning and organizing social connections. Further, and perhaps more importantly, information has become the focal point of economic practices and growth. As the name indicates, information technologies act on information. In industrial societies, technologies act on the production process. For example, Ford's assembly-line technology, along with mass-produced, interchangeable parts, broke down the process of making a car into a series of simple tasks that unskilled workers could perform. So profound was the effect of this technology on economic production that it became known as "Fordism."

Information technologies, however, act upon information. As an example, let's consider something that falls a bit outside of Castells' concerns, but that most of us can relate to: music recording and playback. Before the digital age, music was recorded using analog technologies. Analog recording stores music as a continuous wave in or on the media (phonograph record or magnetic tape). It's called analog because the waves imprinted on the media are *analogous* to the sound waves of the music (the same basic idea applies to video recordings). In digital recording, the music is translated into discrete numbers or data. The first step in this information technology was developed in 1937 by British scientist Alec Reeves (he invented pulse-code modulation [PCM], one of the platforms upon which today's digital technology is based) and every step since then has involved innovations in how technology can store, transmit, and play back information. The production of these technologies for consumption is a secondary move: In a network society, technical innovation is focused primarily on producing and reproducing information—commodification comes later.

The most important informational technologies have focused on computers and communication. Ever since the first digital computer was invented in the early 1940s, each new technology has been directed at storing and using information. Castells (2000b) argues that this move to information technologies is having and will continue to have pervasive effects because human activity is based on information. There have been three major technological advances that have fundamentally influenced knowledge and information: the alphabet (written language), the printing press, and the computer. We know that the effects of the first two advances were tremendous. Civilization itself is indebted to written language, and the advent of the printing press led to the rise and spread of the Protestant Reformation, the Renaissance, and the Scientific Revolution. In addition, because the first commercially viable printed book was the Bible, and there was no comparable text in Asian countries, mechanized printing did not take hold as rapidly there, which in turn facilitated the European advantage over the East in the Industrial Revolution and technological domination. The printing press also influenced the way in which people think. The transmission of information changed from artistic expression (with hand printing) to chiefly textual. This shift facilitated the conversion from metaphorical to linear thinking. Castells is concerned with the third technological advancement in communication and information—the computer—and its influence in structuring society.

The Network Society

The most significant effect of computer technology that Castells sees is that the logic of networks will be the basis of the new social system. The idea of a network is rather straightforward. It is a set of interconnected points or "nodes," and nodes are simply places where the threads or paths of the network cross. Networks can be made up of any number of things, like networks of exchange. Castells is concerned with information networks, the nodes of which are points where information is held or processed. This kind of network is possible because of computer and communication technologies, and it is defined by those technologies.

Let's think for a moment about a computer network. Because the basic properties of networks are the same, you can choose any online network, such as AIM, the network at your place of work, the Internet as a whole, and so on. Networks are open and extremely flexible structures. They can be of almost any size and can change without threatening the balance of the whole. Networks have no center, and they work on the binary inclusion/exclusion model: That is, a node is either in the network or not; if a node ceases to function, it's eliminated and the network is rearranged—for example, your computer can move into or out of a network without affecting the network as such. There is no distance between nodes and no time element; rather than distance, such as between my computer and yours, what matters in networks are restrictions on the flow of information, and time, if used at all, is simply a marker of flow (e.g., when you sent your email). A node becomes important in a network either because it can hold and process information more efficiently, or because it functions as a switch that connects different networks. Once programmed, networks function automatically and impose their logic on all the social actors using it.

Such computerized informational networks have redefined the material basis of life in our society. All animals, including humans, are fundamentally related to time and space, but computing and network technologies have changed that relationship. Rather than the biological clock of human existence, or the mechanical clock of the industrial age, new communication technologies "annihilate time" (Castells, 2000b). Rather than the essentialness of place, new information technologies have reoriented us to a space of flows, where exists the "organizational possibility of organizing the simultaneity of social practices without geographic contiguity" (Castells, 2000a, p. 14). Thus, social organization is set free from the confines of time and space. This freedom is so profound in its implications that Castells (2000b) marks the information age as the beginning of human history, "[i]f by history we understand the moment when . . . our species has reached the level of knowledge and social organization that will allow us to live in a predominantly social world" (pp. 508–509).

Power in any such network is dramatically reorganized from the hierarchical model of bureaucracies and social inequalities. Power in networks is a function of a node's ability to find, hold, and process information. Nodes that can act as switches between informational networks are power-holders: "Since networks are multiple, the inter-operating codes and switches between networks become the fundamental sources in shaping, guiding, and misguiding societies" (Castells, 2000b, p. 502). More importantly, the informational network has provided the structure for the core activities of a global economy. Currently, the bulk of capital accumulation results from financial flows rather than production. Profit from production and consumption, from organizations and institutions, is extracted and reverted to the financial flows. Capital is then invested globally, following interests of greatest return, which are increasingly based on speculation and money markets rather than real goods and services. Financial flows are thus based on theoretical knowledge and timeliness of information. This "electronically operated global casino" decides the "fate of corporations, household savings, national currencies, and regional economies" (Castells, 2000b, p. 503).

The network society has dramatically affected class as well. It results first in capitalism without capitalists. The legal owners of any large business—Marx's definition of capitalists—are found in investment funds and individual portfolios, both of which are subject to networks of speculative management. The corporate managers don't make up a capitalist class either, because they do not control, nor do they know about, the movements of capital in networks of financial flows. Rather than a class that holds and uses capital, the global capital network is a network of networks that "are ultimately dependent upon the non-human capitalist logic of an electronically operated, random processing of information" (Castells, 2000b, p. 505).

The working class has likewise been redefined by the logics of networks. Labor has become exceedingly general. Rather than the specified labor of production, it's labor as a generic part of speculative capitalism—labor becomes a piece on the global chessboard of capital flows. Capital and labor increasingly exist in different spaces and times: capital in the space of flows and the instant/constant time of computerized communication, and labor in the space of places and the time of clocks and daily life. "At its core, capital is global. As a rule, labor is local" (Castells, 2000b, p. 506). What becomes organized through networks is work, rather than labor. The work of organizations is carried on in network fashion. Each contributing member is a node, and the network as a whole can be made up of individuals, segments of businesses, or entire companies, large or small. They can be dispersed over thousands of miles and exist in different clock-time zones. All this and more can be coordinated for a single project, thus forming an informational network. As soon as the project is finished, the nodes are disconnected and reorganized for other work. The work process is thus globally integrated but fragmented locally, resulting in the individuation of labor, increased flexibility, and instability of work.

The organizational logic of communication and informational technologies has reformed politics as well. In most places around the world, people now get their information about political candidates through the media, which has become the platform for politics. In a media-saturated environment, capturing attention becomes the single most important scarce resource. Politics thus becomes personalized in the cult of personality, "and image-making is power-making" (Castells, 2000b, p. 507). In the spectacle of image, with a public (an audience) dulled by a constant barrage of images and information, the most effective messages are negative: "assassination of opponents' personalities, and/or of their supporting organizations" (2000a, p. 13). Thus, the information of value in politics is anything that will spark a scandal. An entire network revolves around finding, protecting, and leaking this valued information. "Politics becomes a horse race, and a tragicomedy motivated by greed, backstage manoeuvres [sic], betrayals, and, often, sex and violence—a genre increasingly indistinguishable from TV scripts" (2000a, p. 13).

Politics cannot but influence the state, and the politics of spectacle and reliance on the media undermine its legitimacy and power. In response, personalities begin to build informational networks and systems of deference around themselves, further challenging the legitimacy of the state. State power is also challenged by the global flows of money and information. Part of this has to do with the pure size of capital flows and the volatility of money markets, but more basically, since the nation-state has always been defined in terms of "subordinating to orderly domination . . . a 'territory'" (Weber, 1922/1968, p. 901), the breakdown of time and space (territory) by the network society deeply undermines the power of the state. In response, states partner with other nations and build multinational and international organizational, informational networks, such as the World Trade Organization, NATO, the International Monetary Fund, and so on. The result is that "the new state is no longer a nation-state" (Castells,

2000a, p. 14); rather, it is a network state created out of negotiated decision making and power sharing.

Concepts and Theory:
Networks, Identities, and Democracy

For Castells, identities are clusters of cultural traits that function to provide meaning for people. In order to see the implications of this, think back to the fundamental attributes of meaning from Chapter 3. Meaning isn't any *thing*—it isn't in an action or a word, it isn't inherent within an experience, nor is it located in any object. Rather, meaning is that which actions, words, and so on express or sign, and signs always point away from themselves—therefore, *meaning is never the thing-in-itself*. And meaning constitutes our reality: "No longer can man confront reality immediately. . . . [It] seems to recede in proportion as man's symbolic activity advances. Instead of dealing with the things themselves, man is in a sense constantly conversing with himself" (Cassirer, 1944, p. 42).

If meaning isn't the actual thing or event, then meaning is achieved or created, and one of the functions of identity is to provide a basis for the construction of biographical narratives of meaning. Castells (2004) defines three different types of identities: The first type, the legitimizing identity, is the kind found in the dominant institutions of society. You remember that legitimations are stories or narratives that provide a moral or ethical basis for social power. Meaning needs to be legitimated, too, but for a different reason. The connection between an event, object, or experience and the meaning it conveys is constructed and thus tenuous. There was no biological, physical difference between the deaths of North Vietnamese soldiers during the Vietnam conflict and the likely impending deaths of three American astronauts on *Apollo 13*. The different meanings that those issues of life and death evoked were culturally and socially constructed, and they were legitimated. Thus, legitimizing identities are those around which individuals construct meaning and a sense of self that are related to and legitimate civil society.

The second type in Castells' scheme is resistance identity. This type of identity normally comes out of a sense of exclusion from the institutions of civil society and is bound up with the formation of communities of resistance that give members a sense of solidarity and the ability to form countercultures and ideology. These communities and identities can center around such issues as religious views and other status inequities, such as race and gender. Because they are resistance identities, they create strong boundaries of inclusion and exclusion and thus work to "exclude the excluders." It's important to note that resistance identities aren't concerned with social change; they are reactionary and seek to establish an identity where identity has been denied.

This is where the issue of meaning that we talked about above becomes important. Identities provide a meaningful ordering and framework for life. As we saw in Chapter 8, when identities are denied, or controlled to the point of redefining the person, the existential questions of life and purpose come to the forefront—conversely, when identities are unproblematic, the questions of existence are effectively silenced. Under conditions of exclusion, resistance identities function as cultural, emotional, and psychological strongholds. Their purpose isn't to change, but to proclaim. Often these identities are born out of "the pride of self-denigration" (Castells, 2004, p. 9) and shout back at institutions with proclamations such as "black is beautiful" or "I am woman, hear me roar."

The third type of identity that concerns Castells is the project identity. This is an identity associated with social projects of change: "In this case, the building of identity is a project of a different life" (Castells, 2004, p. 10). Project identities produce subjects, but subjects, Castells is very clear about, are not individuals. Merriam-Webster (2002) defines *subject* variously as "the material from which a thing is formed," "the theme of a discourse or predication," "something that sustains or is embodied in thought or consciousness," or "something that forms a basis (as for action, study, discussion, or use)." Castells' use of the term subject captures all of the above. Subjects are collective actors that form the material of our sense of self and our involvement with the world. These subjects are the themes of the discourse of social change; they are the mental and emotional focus through which identity and meaning are sustained in consciousness; and, especially in the case of project identities, the subject forms the basis for action, study, and discussion.

The Crisis in Democracy

Castells (2004) defines *civil society* as "a set of organizations and institutions, as well as a series of structured and organized social actors, which reproduce . . . the identity that rationalizes the sources of structural domination" (p. 8). While civil society isn't identical with the state, it exists in relation to the state; and the state is the "object of citizenship" (p. 402). However, the state is suffering a crisis of legitimation in the network society. Its sovereignty has been undermined by "global flows and trans-organizational networks of wealth, information, and power" (p. 402); by the spectacle of politics; and by the state's increasing inability to fulfill its commitments to the safety net of minimal benefits, including unemployment, retirement income, health care coverage, insuring bank deposits, and so forth. These effects of the network society have created a crisis of legitimation for the nation-state and, by extension, legitimizing identities and democracy.

There are two important effects growing out of this legitimation crisis. First, "A growing majority of citizens do not feel that democracy will help them very much in addressing the issues that confront them in their daily lives" (Castells, 2004, p. 413). One measure of this is what is commonly called voter apathy. In 1960, about 61 percent of the television sets in the United States were tuned to the October presidential debates, and voter turnout for the presidential election was almost 65 percent of the adult population. By the year 2000, fewer than 30 percent of the televisions tuned to the presidential debates, and voter turnout had dropped to 51 percent (Patterson, 2002).

The second outcome of the legitimation crisis is the ascent of resistance identities. Remember how Castells conceptualizes identities: They function to create meaning. In this case, resistance identities are created to counter the loss of meaning and direction that accompanies the legitimation crisis. To help us get a clear sense of resistance identities in the network society, let's think through the example of gender in Western nations. Prior to the women's suffrage movement of the 1800s and early 1900s, being a "woman" was by and large a legitimizing identity. The identity bound all women together and situated them in the discourse of patriarchy. The identity thus legitimated the family structure as well as the unequal power relations between men and women. The suffrage movements worked to create a project identity committed to gaining equal rights for women, in particular, the right to vote and the right to higher education. In the 1960s, a second wave of feminism emerged to address the unofficial discrimination and inequalities that still existed for women. Equal opportunities for work and political power, equal pay, cultural representations, and control over their bodies were some of the issues. Both the first and second waves of feminism had project identities.

Beginning in the early 1990s, another wave of feminism arose, mostly among young women who had grown up with benefits achieved by the first two waves of feminism. These women also were most affected by the new information and communication technologies. Feminism for these women is different. Rather than having specific political, economic, or social goals, third wave feminism challenges the definitions of woman, femininity, and feminism, which are seen as creating a sense that all women are essentially the same. All essentializing theories are rejected, including feminist theory, gender theory, conflict theory, and so on. The focus is on deconstructing such totalizing identities and discourses and insisting on diversity. Rather than either a legitimizing or project identity, third wave feminism denies the possibility of a woman's identity: "Since no monolithic version of 'woman' exists, we can no longer speak with confidence of 'women's issues'; instead, we need to consider that such issues are as diverse as the many women who inhabit our planet" (Dicker & Piepmeier, 2006, p. 107).

While being able to trace the history of feminist identity is enlightening, most resistance identities don't have this evolving background. Today, most resistance identities are formed around such things as religious fundamentalism, geographic region, music styles, and so on. An example that has both geographic region and music is found in Jeff Foxworthy's comments at the 2007 Country Music Television awards ceremony, held in Nashville, Tennessee. Here are a few lines from his speech:

> I like country music because it's about the things in life that really matter. . . . It's about love, family, friends, with a few beers. . . . It doesn't take political sides even on things as ugly as war. Instead, it celebrates the men and women who go to fight 'em. . . . It's about kids and how there ain't nothing like 'em. . . . Country folks love their kids and they will jack you up if you try to mess with 'em. . . . Country music doesn't have to be politically correct. We sing about God because we believe in Him. . . . It's real music, sung by real people for real people. The people that make up the backbone of this country. . . . You can call us rednecks if you want, we're not offended, 'cause we know what we are all about. We get up and go to work, we get up and go to church, and we get up and go to war when necessary. (Foxworthy, quoted in Martin, 2007)

Foxworthy defined the country music identity by "building trenches of resistance and survival on the basis of principles different from, or opposed to, those permeating the institutions of society" (Castells, 2004, p. 8). Without specifically saying so, the statement builds strong boundaries of exclusion for anyone outside country music or the values proclaimed, and it simultaneously builds a sense of community and solidarity for country music fans. Within that solidarity, it allows little if any diversity: "In contrast to pluralistic, differentiated civil societies, cultural communes display little internal differentiation" (p. 70). That is one of the qualities of resistance identities: They provide a strong cultural center, a clear sense of right and wrong, a solid ground for meaning.

Resistance identities in the network society are acts of cultural resistance, with no real political or economic goals. Much like a third wave feminist concerned with expressing gender, Foxworthy's country music fan is concerned with the meanings surrounding identity. They both draw a line in the sand and proclaim, this is who I am. Moreover, as you can see with both examples, resistance identities are individualized. There's a sense of cultural community that accompanies these identities, and there are clear meanings associated with them, but neither of them requires or implies that members actually group together. You can be a country music fan and believe in the boundaries that Foxworthy proclaims, and never once get together with other fans. Further, if and when you do get together, the focus will probably be on music and beer, "With a cheap woman and two timin' man thrown in for spice" (Foxworthy, quoted in Martin, 2007). The center of discussion would probably not be political activism. If you do talk about ideas or values with which you disagree, it likely won't be with any intent of creating a project to bring about change. It will simply be a ritual that generates high levels of emotional energy that will make your identity and beliefs feel more sacred. Resistance identities thus create a strong sense of meaning in a world where meanings are becoming delegitimized and fragmented.

With the sources of legitimizing identities weakened or gone, the shared identities necessary for democracy are no longer present. Further—and this is extremely important to note—project identities in and of themselves are suffering the same fate as legitimizing identities, because both share the same social basis: the civil sphere and democratic government defined by the nation-state. What Castells' theory implies is that that form of society is gone or receding; social connections are now being made through the network society that is not bounded or limited by the state. The structural, systemic bases of participatory democracy as understood from the eighteenth century through the last decades of the twentieth are gone, and resistance identities by themselves are nothing more than emotional constructs that give individuals and small groups a sense of meaning and purpose.

However, resistance identities can form the basis of new project identities. In fact, Castells (2004) argues that resistance identities could "be *the main potential source* of social change in the network society" (p. 70, emphasis added). These new project identities do not come out of the industrial era's "identities of civil society" (p. 422) but may emerge from the intense interactions around cultural resistance. For example, while there's an emphasis on choice in what passes as gender (expressions of femininity) in third wave feminism, there are also a good number of third wavers who are deeply involved in political activism, not always for women's rights. So, for instance, a third wave feminist may have a project identity built around environmental issues—specifically feminist-as-environmentalist—yet at the same time, she expresses her gender identity as resistance. However, there is nothing about resistance identities that necessarily implies project identities.

Resistance identities thus represent a further danger to the idea of participatory democracy: Rather than creating new project identities, these resistance communes could simply maintain their inward gaze, occupied only with keeping the meaningfulness of their own identities. Castells (2004) ironically characterizes such narcissism as "inducing a process that might transform communal heavens into heavenly hells" (p. 70).

Among the resistance identities Castells (2004) lists as possibilities for project identities are religious communes, nationalism, ethnicity, gender, territorial identities, environmentalism, and so on. Again, please notice that the content—what the identity is about—is virtually unimportant, in terms of it being the basis of a project identity. The deciding factor between resistance and project identities is the intent to bring change. In other words, project identities have projects. Project identities in the network society, however, don't generally work the same as in industrial society. As we've seen, the network society implies a new form of power. Rather than the political power of civil society, network power resides in codes of information and images of representation. Conflict over power in the network society is a battle for people's minds: "Whoever, or whatever, wins the battle of people's minds will rule, because mighty, rigid apparatuses will not be a match, in any reasonable timespan, for the minds mobilized around the power of flexible, alternative networks" (Castells, 2004, p. 425).

According to Castells, there are two types of "symbol mobilizers," those social actors able to influence information and imagery. First, there are the Prophets, symbolic personalities that can create information and imagery and mobilize the network. Recent examples include Bono of U2 (and his work on AIDS and developing nation debt forgiveness), Angelina Jolie (protesting use of landmines, helping refugees), and Sting (and his work with Amazonia, helping to save the Amazon rainforests). The second and more important avenue for mobilizing symbols and information around project identities is the decentralized activity of the network itself. The Internet can of course be used to gather people together for rallies, demonstrations, and so on. But its greatest impact is on people's awareness, thinking, and feelings about the project issue. In contrast to the Prophet motif, this "impact on society rarely stems from a concerted strategy, masterminded by a center" (Castells, 2004, p. 427). Decentralized, flexible networks of information and communication around issues of environmentalism, women's lives, sweatshop working conditions, refugees, human rights violations, and so on, produce and distribute news, ideas, insights, explanations, strategies, and images around the world, thus impacting the way people see and interface with the world.

This network of social change is the breeding ground for a new democracy. Its form is different, without the "orderly battalions, colorful banners, and scripted proclamations" (Castells, 2004, p. 428) of civil society, and it's thus difficult to recognize. But for the same reason, there is a continuing

> subtle pervasiveness of incremental changes of symbols processed through multiform networks, away from the halls of power. It is in those back alleys of society, whether in alternative electronic networks or in grassrooted networks of communal resistance, that I have sensed the embryos of a new society, labored in the fields of history by the power of identity. (p. 428)

The Craft of Citizenship | **Globalization**

The Basics: Comprehension and Explanation

- Identify the main concerns and questions of each theorist. With those questions in mind, write a two- to three-sentence statement that captures the essence of their theoretical response.
- Make a detailed list of the primary theoretical concepts each theorist employs. Then define the most important concepts.
  - > *Helpful hints:* Identifying and defining terms is always important in theoretical work. It is especially so here because we are using new sets of ideas, many of which challenge the ideas we've been working with since the beginning of the book. So, before working with the entire theory, make certain that you understand the concepts.
- Explain how time–space distanciation is first emptied of time and space and then stretched out through global dynamics. How did time–space distanciation form a foundation for modernity? How is that foundation now challenged? Spell out how life politics is an effect of both time–space distanciation and modern knowledge. In other words, why is emancipatory politics less feasible today than lifestyle politics?
- Explain the economic dynamics in back of the relationships among the core, semi-periphery, and periphery, and explain how they are related to the demise of capitalism. In your explanation, be sure to describe why Wallerstein argues that we are in the last stages of capitalism. Outline the impact that the current global system has on participatory democracy.

(Continued)

(Continued)

- Explain how the logic of networks structures and creates a new global society. How have power, politics, class, and the core activities of a global economy been impacted as a result of the network society? What are the implications of the network society for identities?

Skill Set 1: Inference and Application

- List the practices and meanings in your life that would fall under life politics. How do these express your authenticity in the social world? How do they remoralize social life? How could they potentially affect others?
- What are the implications of Wallerstein's "end-time politics" for your civic sociology?
  - ➢ *Helpful hints:* Be certain to think through the implications of the small-input scenario (the butterfly effect). Use your sociological imagination.
- In what ways does Castells' portrayal of the legitimation crisis characterize you? In what ways can you overcome this crisis and move toward project identities?
- Propose a project that would fit into Castells' notion of the new democracy. The project topic can be anything, so pick something you really care about. Using Castells' theory, explain how your project could potentially influence society.
- Speculate about possible effects of Castells' idea of the network society on sociology and other social disciplines.

Skill Set 2: Interpretation, Analysis, Evaluation, Synthesis

- Compare and contrast the three theories of globalization in this chapter. What are the dynamics that drive each? What are the effects? At what points can these three theories be brought together to form a more powerful explanation of globalization?
- Using Giddens, Wallerstein, and Castells, explain how democracy and politics have changed as a result of globalization. How has the state been decentered from the social project of modernity? How have political identities and personal practices been redefined?
- Draw elements from Perinbanayagam, Bellah, the discussion in Du Bois, and Castells to create a theoretically robust definition of identity. How are identities important for democracy?

- In Chapter 5, I had you write a theoretically robust definition of civil society and explain its importance for democracy. Castells argues that the network society implies that civil society can no longer be the basis for participatory democracy. Using your definition, explain and evaluate Castells' conclusion.
- Using Castells' theory, evaluate the theory of power I had you synthesize in Chapter 6. In your opinion, how does power work in our current society? Theoretically explain your position.
- How is Giddens' notion of life politics similar to Perinbanayagam's artful ethics?
- How is the modern idea of society (from Chapters 1 and 2) challenged by the theorists in this chapter? How would you now define society?
- How has capitalism changed as a result of the network society? Focus your discussion on capital and class.

References

Addams, J. (2002). *Democracy and social ethics.* Chicago: University of Chicago Press. (Original work published 1902)

Alexander, J. C. (2006). *The civil sphere.* Oxford, UK: Oxford University Press.

Alexander, J. C., & Smith, P. (2001). The strong program in cultural theory: Elements of a structural hermeneutics. In J. H. Turner (Ed.), *Handbook of sociological theory.* New York: Kluwer Academic.

Barker, C. (2008). *Cultural studies: Theory and practice* (3rd ed.). Thousand Oaks, CA: Sage.

Baudrillard, J. (1994). *Simulacra and simulation* (S. F. Blaser, Trans.). Ann Arbor: University of Michigan Press. (Original work published 1981)

Bellah, R. N. (1970). *Beyond belief: Essays on religion in a post-traditional world.* New York: Harper & Row.

Bellah, R. N. (1985). *Religion, citizenship and the crisis in public education.* Retrieved January 2, 2008, from http://www.robertbellah.com/lectures_3.htm

Bellah, R. N. (1987). Conclusion: Competing visions of the role of religion in American society. In R. N. Bellah & F. E. Greenspahn (Eds.), *Uncivil religion: Interreligious hostility in America.* New York: Crossroad.

Bellah, R. N. (1995, March 7). *Individualism and commitment: "Americans' cultural conversation."* Lecture delivered at Portland State University, Portland, OR. Retrieved January 2, 2008, from http://www.robertbellah.com/lectures_6.htm

Bellah, R. N., Madsen, R., Sullivan, W. M., Swidler, A., & Tipton, S. M. (1992). *The good society.* New York: Vintage Books.

Berger, P. L. (1967). *The sacred canopy: Elements of a sociological theory of religion.* New York: Anchor.

Berger, P. L., & Luckmann, T. (1966). *The social construction of reality: A treatise in the sociology of knowledge.* New York: Anchor.

Blumer, H. (1969). *Symbolic interactionism: Perspective and method.* Berkeley: University of California Press.

Bourdieu, P. (1984). *Distinction: A social critique of the judgment of taste* (R. Nice, Trans.). Cambridge, MA: Harvard University Press. (Original work published 1979)

Bourdieu, P. (1989). Social space and symbolic power. *Sociological Theory, 7*(1), 14–25.

Bourdieu, P. (1991). *Language and symbolic power* (J. B. Thompson, Ed.; G. Raymond & M. Adamson, Trans.). Cambridge, MA: Harvard University Press.

Browne, M. N., & Keeley, S. M. (2007). *Asking the right questions: A guide to critical thinking* (8th ed.). Upper Saddle River, NJ: Pearson Education.

Bureau of Justice Statistics. (n.d.). Retrieved September 2, 2009, from http://www.ojp.usdoj.gov/bjs/cvict_c.htm

Butler, J. (1993). *Bodies that matter: On the discursive limits of "sex."* New York: Routledge.

Calhoun, C. (2003). Pierre Bourdieu. In G. Ritzer (Ed.), *The Blackwell companion to major contemporary social theorists.* Malden, MA: Blackwell.

Cassirer, E. (1944). *An essay on man.* New Haven, CT: Yale University Press.

Castells, M. (2000a). *End of millennium* (2nd ed.). Malden, MA: Blackwell.

Castells, M. (2000b). *The rise of the network society* (2nd ed.). Malden, MA: Blackwell.

Castells, M. (2004). *The power of identity* (2nd ed.). Malden, MA: Blackwell.

Chafetz, J. S. (1990). *Gender equity: An integrated theory of stability and change.* Newbury Park, CA: Sage.

Chodorow, N. (1978). *The reproduction of mothering: Psychoanalysis and the sociology of gender.* Berkeley: University of California Press.

Collins, P. H. (2000). *Black feminist thought: Knowledge, consciousness, and the politics of empowerment* (2nd ed.). New York: Routledge.

Collins, R. (1988). *Theoretical sociology.* Orlando, FL: Harcourt Brace Jovanovich.

Cooley, C. H. (1902). *Human nature and the social order.* New York: Scribner.

Coser, L. A. (1977). *Masters of sociological thought: Ideas in the historical and social context.* Prospect Heights, IL: Waveland.

Dahrendorf, R. (1959). *Class and class conflict in industrial society.* Palo Alto, CA: Stanford University Press. (Original work published 1957)

Dahrendorf, R. (1968). *Essays in the theory of society.* Palo Alto, CA: Stanford University Press.

Damasio, A. (1999). *The feeling of what happens: Body and emotion in the making of consciousness.* San Diego, CA: Harvest.

Damasio, A. (2003). *Looking for Spinoza: Joy, sorrow, and the feeling brain.* Orlando, FL: Harcourt.

Davidson, A. I. (1994). Ethics as ascetics: Foucault, the history of ethics, and ancient thought. In G. Gutting (Ed.), *The Cambridge companion to Foucault.* Cambridge, UK: Cambridge University Press.

DeNavas-Walt, C., Proctor, B. D., & Smith, J. C. (2009, September). Income, poverty, and health insurance coverage in the United States. Retrieved November 12, 2009, from http://www.census.gov/prod/2009pubs/p60–236.pdf

Denzin, N. (1996). Sociology at the end of the century. *Sociological Quarterly, 4,* 743–752.

Dewey, J. (1988). Creative democracy—The task before us. In J. A. Boydston (Ed.), *The later works of John Dewey, Vol. 14: 1939–1941.* Carbondale: Southern Illinois University Press. (Original work published 1939)

Dicker, R., & Piepmeier, A. (2006). Introduction from *Catching a wave: Reclaiming feminism for the 21st century.* In L. Heywood (Ed.), *The women's movement today: An encyclopedia of third-wave feminism.* Westport, CT: Greenwood.

Du Bois, W. E. B. (1996a). Darkwater. In E. J. Sundquist (Ed.), *The Oxford W. E. B. Du Bois reader*. New York: Oxford. (Original work published 1920)

Du Bois, W. E. B. (1996b). The propaganda of history. In E. J. Sundquist (Ed.), *The Oxford W. E. B. Du Bois reader*. New York: Oxford. (Original work published 1935)

Du Bois, W. E. B. (1996c). In black. In E. J. Sundquist (Ed.), *The Oxford W. E. B. Du Bois reader*. New York: Oxford. (Original work published 1920)

Du Bois, W. E. B. (1996d). The souls of black folk. In E. J. Sundquist (Ed.), *The Oxford W. E. B. Du Bois reader*. New York: Oxford. (Original work published 1903)

Durkheim, É. (1938). *The rules of sociological method* (G. E. G. Catlin, Ed.; S. A. Solovay & J. H. Mueller, Trans.). Glencoe, IL: Free Press. (Original work published 1895)

Durkheim, É. (1984). *The division of labor in society* (W. D. Halls, Trans.). New York: Free Press. (Original work published 1893)

Durkheim, É. (1992). *Professional ethics and civic morals* (C. Brookfield, Trans.). London: Taylor & Francis/Routledge. (Original work published 1957)

Durkheim, É. (1995). *The elementary forms of the religious life* (K. E. Fields, Trans.). New York: Free Press. (Original work published 1912)

Elder, L., & Paul, R. (2005). *The miniature guide to the art of asking essential questions* (3rd ed.). Dillon Beach, CA: Foundation for Critical Thinking.

Fanon, F. (1967). *Black skins, white masks* (C. L. Markmann, Trans.). New York: Grove Press. (Original work published 1952)

Feyerabend, P. (1988). *Against method* (Rev. ed.). London: Verso.

Foucault, M. (1984). Nietzsche, genealogy, history. In P. Rabinow (Ed.), *The Foucault reader*. New York: Pantheon.

Foucault, M. (1990a). *The history of sexuality, Vol. 1: An introduction* (R. Hurley, Trans.). New York: Vintage. (Original work published 1976)

Foucault, M. (1990b). *The history of sexuality, Vol. 2: The use of pleasure* (R. Hurley, Trans.). New York: Vintage. (Original work published 1984)

Foucault, M. (1994). *The order of things: An archaeology of the human sciences*. New York: Vintage. (Original work published 1966)

Foucault, M. (1995). *Discipline and punish: The birth of the prison* (A. Sheridan, Trans.). New York: Vintage. (Original work published 1975)

Giddens, A. (1990). *The consequences of modernity*. Palo Alto, CA: Stanford University Press.

Giddens, A. (1991). *Modernity and self-identity: Self and society in the late modern age*. Palo Alto, CA: Stanford University Press.

Giddens, A. (1994). *Beyond left and right: The future of radical politics*. Palo Alto, CA: Stanford University Press.

Gilman, C. P. (1975). *Women and economics: A study of the economic relation between men and women as a factor in social evolution*. New York: Gordon Press. (Original work published 1899)

Gilman, C. P. (2001). *The man-made world*. New York: Humanity Books. (Original work published 1911)

Goffman, E. (1959). *The presentation of self in everyday life*. Garden City, NY: Anchor.

Goffman, E. (1963). *Stigma*. New York: Touchstone.

Goffman, E. (1967). *Interaction ritual: Essays on face-to-face behavior.* New York: Pantheon.

Habermas, J. (1984). *The theory of communicative action, Vol. 1: Lifeworld and system: Reason and the rationalization of society* (T. McCarthy, Trans.). Boston: Beacon Press. (Original work published 1981)

Habermas, J. (1987). *The theory of communicative action, Vol. 2: Lifeworld and system: A critique of functionalist reason* (T. McCarthy, Trans.). Boston: Beacon Press. (Original work published 1981)

Habermas, J. (1996). *Between facts and norms: Contributions to a discourse theory of law and democracy* (W. Rehg, Trans.). Cambridge: MIT Press. (Original work published 1992)

Hall, S. (1996). The question of cultural identity. In S. Hall, D. Held, D. Hubert, & K. Thompson (Eds.), *Modernity: An introduction to modern societies.* Malden, MA: The Open University.

Hedges, C. (2002). *War is a force that gives us meaning.* New York: Public Affairs (Perseus).

hooks, b. (1989). *Talking back: Thinking feminist, thinking black.* Boston: South End Press.

Jacobs, R. (2006). Civil society. In J. Scott (Ed.), *Sociology: The key concepts.* London: Routledge.

Johnson, A. G. (2000). *The Blackwell dictionary of sociology.* Malden, MA: Blackwell.

Juergensmeyer, M. (2000). *Terror in the mind of God: The global rise of religious violence.* Berkeley: University of California Press.

Kagan, H. L. (2008, March). Why did my patient develop a taste for paper? *Discover,* 16–17.

Kanter, R. M. (1977). *Men and women of the corporation.* New York: Basic Books.

Keynes, J. M. (1936). *The general theory of employment, interest and money.* New York: Harcourt, Brace.

Kreisler, H. (1989). *Straddling theory and practice: Conversation with Sir Ralf Dahrendorf.* Retrieved May 5, 2006, from http://globetrotter.berkeley.edu/Elberg/Dahrendorf/dahrendorf2.html

LeDoux, J. (1996). *The emotional brain: The mysterious underpinnings of emotional life.* New York: Touchstone.

Lidz, V. (2000). Talcott Parsons. In G. Ritzer (Ed.), *The Blackwell companion to major social theorists.* Malden, MA: Blackwell.

Lipset, S. M. (1962). Harriet Martineau's America. In H. Martineau, *Society in America.* New York: Anchor Books.

Marshall, G. (Ed.). (1998). *A dictionary of sociology* (2nd ed.). New York: Oxford University Press.

Martin, E. (2007). *Jeff Foxworthy's passionate, show-stopping speech at the CMT awards.* Retrieved September 3, 2009, from http://www.freerepublic.com/focus/f-news/1821089/posts

Martindale, D. (1988). *The nature and types of sociological theory* (2nd ed.). Prospect Heights, IL: Waveland Press.

Martineau, H. (2003). *How to observe morals and manners.* New Brunswick, NJ: Transaction Press. (Original work published 1838)

Marx, K. (1978a). Economic and philosophic manuscripts of 1844. In R. C. Tucker (Ed.), *The Marx–Engels reader.* New York: Norton. (Original work published 1932)

Marx, K. (1978b). The German ideology. In R. C. Tucker (Ed.), *The Marx–Engels reader.* New York: Norton. (Original work published 1932)

Marx, K. (1994). Preface to a contribution to the critique of political economy. In L. H. Simon (Ed.), *Karl Marx: Selected writings.* Indianapolis, IN: Hackett. (Original work published 1859)

Marx, K. (1995). Economic and philosophic manuscripts of 1844. In *Marx's concept of man.* (E. Fromm, Trans.) New York: Continuum. (Original work published 1932)

Marx, K., & Engels, F. (1978). Manifest of the communist party. In R. C. Tucker (Ed.), *The Marx–Engels reader.* New York: Norton. (Original work published 1848)

Maryanski, A., & Turner, J. H. (1992). *The social cage: Human nature and the evolution of society.* Palo Alto, CA: Stanford University Press.

Mead, G. H. (1932). *The philosophy of the present.* Chicago: Open Court.

Mead, G. H. (1934). *Mind, self, and society* (C. W. Morris, Ed.). Chicago: University of Chicago Press.

Mead, G. H. (1938). *The philosophy of the act.* Chicago: University of Chicago Press.

Menand, L. (2001). *The metaphysical club: A story of ideas in America.* New York: Farrar, Straus & Giroux.

Merriam-Webster. (2002). *Webster's third new international dictionary, unabridged.* Retrieved August 3, 2009, from http://unabridged.merriam-webster.com

Mills, C. W. (1959). *The sociological imagination.* London: Oxford University Press.

National Urban League. (2009). *State of black America 2009: Message to the president.* Retrieved November 12, 2009, from http://www.nul.org/newsroom/publications/soba

Nietzsche, F. (1974). *The gay science.* New York: Vintage.

O'Connor, J. (1998). *Natural causes: Essays in ecological Marxism.* New York: Guilford Press.

Parsons, T. (1937). *The structure of social action.* New York: Free Press.

Parsons, T. (1949). *The structure of social action: A study in social theory with special reference to a group of recent European writers* (2nd ed.). New York: Free Press.

Parsons, T. (1961). Culture and the social system. In T. Parsons (Ed.), *Theories of society: Foundations of modern sociological theory* (pp. 963–993). New York: Free Press.

Parsons, T. (1966). *Societies: Evolutionary and comparative perspectives.* Englewood Cliffs, NJ: Prentice Hall.

Patterson, T. E. (2002). *The vanishing voter: Public involvement in an age of uncertainty.* New York: Knopf.

Perinbanayagam, R. S. (2000). *The presence of the self.* Lanham, MD: Rowman & Littlefield.

Perinbanayagam, R. S. (2003). Telic reflections: Interactional processes, as such. *Symbolic Interaction, 26,* 67–83.

Perinbanayagam, R. S. (2007). *Games and sport in everyday life: Dialogues and narratives of the self.* Boulder, CO: Paradigm.

Pianin, E. (2001, July 10). Superfund cleanup effort shows results, study reports. *The Washington Post,* A19.

Redford, G., & Kinosian, J. (2008). Your brain on exercise: How breaking a sweat can make you smarter. *AARP: The Magazine, 51*(2A), 26.

Ritzer, G. (2008). *Sociological theory* (3rd ed.). Boston: McGraw-Hill.

Scott, J. (2006). *Sociology: The key concepts.* London: Routledge.

Shenkman, R. (2008). *Just how stupid are we? Facing the truth about the American voter.* New York: Basic Books.

Smith, A. (1937). *An inquiry into the nature and causes of the wealth of nations.* New York: The Modern Library. (Original work published 1776)

Smith, D. E. (1987). *The everyday world as problematic: A feminist sociology.* Boston: Northwestern University Press.

Smith, D. E. (1990). *The conceptual practices of power: A feminist sociology of knowledge.* Boston: Northeastern University Press.

Smith, D. E. (1992). Sociology from women's experience: A reaffirmation. *Sociological Theory, 11,* 1.

Snow, D., & Anderson, L. (1992). *Down on their luck: A study of homeless people.* Berkeley: University of California Press.

Steger, M. B. (2009). *Globalization: A very short introduction.* New York: Oxford University Press.

Tocqueville, A. (1969). *Democracy in America* (J. P. Mayer, Ed.; G. Lawrence, Trans.). New York: Harper Perennial. (Original work published 1835)

Turner, J. H. (1988). *A theory of social interaction.* Palo Alto, CA: Stanford University Press.

Turner, J. H. (2000). *On the origins of human emotions: A sociological inquiry into the evolution of human affect.* Palo Alto, CA: Stanford University Press.

UCSC Rape Prevention Education. (2009). Retrieved September 2, 2009, from http://www2.ucsc.edu/rape-prevention/statistics.html.

Urry, J. (2006). Society. In J. Scott (Ed.), *Sociology: The key concepts.* London: Routledge.

U.S. Bureau of Labor Statistics. (2009). *Highlights of women's earnings in 2008.* Retrieved September 2, 2009, from http://www.bls.gov/cps/cpswom2008.pdf

U.S. Department of Justice. (2008). *Prison statistics.* Retrieved November 12, 2009, from http://www.ojp.usdoj.gov/bjs/prisons.htm

U.S. Department of Labor. (2000). *Changes in women's labor force participation in the 20th century.* Retrieved January 27, 2008, from http://www.bls.gov/opub/ted/2000/feb/wk3/art03.htm

U.S. Environmental Protection Agency. (2009). *Superfund appropriation history.* Retrieved November 18, 2009, from http://www.epa.gov/superfund/accomp/budgethistory.htm

Wallerstein, I. (1974). *The modern world-system I: Capitalist agriculture and the origins of the European world-economy in the sixteenth century.* New York: Academic Press.

Wallerstein, I. (1980). *The modern world-system II: Mercantilism and the consolidation of the European world-economy, 1600–1750.* New York: Academic Press.

Wallerstein, I. (1989). *The modern world-system III: The second era of great expansion of the capitalist world-economy, 1730–1840.* New York: Academic Press.

Wallerstein, I. (1995). The end of what modernity? *Theory and Society, 24,* 471–488.

Wallerstein, I. (1999). *The end of the world as we know it: Social science for the twenty-first century.* Minneapolis: University of Minnesota Press.

Wallerstein, I. (2000). *The essential Wallerstein.* New York: The New Press.

Wallerstein, I. (2004). *World-systems analysis: An introduction.* Durham, NC: Duke University Press.

Weber, M. (1968). *Economy and society* (G. Roth & C. Wittich, Eds.). Berkeley: University of California Press. (Original work published 1922)

Weber, M. (1993). *The sociology of religion* (E. Fischoff, Trans.). Boston: Beacon Press. (Original work published 1922)

Webster's new universal unabridged dictionary (2nd ed.). (1983). New York: Simon & Schuster.

West, C. (1999). *The Cornel West reader.* New York: Basic Civitas Books.

West, C. (2001). *Race matters.* New York: Vintage Books.

West, C., & Zimmerman, D. H. (1983). Small insults: A study of interruptions in cross-sex conversations between unacquainted persons. In B. Thorne, C. Kramarae, & N. Henley (Eds.), *Language, gender and society.* Cambridge, MA: Newbury House.

West, C., & Zimmerman, D. H. (1987). Doing gender. *Gender & Society, 1,* 125–151.

Williams, R. (1983). *Keywords: A vocabulary of culture and society* (Rev. ed.). New York: Oxford University Press.

Wilson, W. J. (1980). *The declining significance of race: Blacks and changing American institutions* (2nd ed.). Chicago: University of Chicago Press.

Wilson, W. J. (1997). *When work disappears: The world of the new urban poor.* New York: Vintage Press.

Zerubavel, E. (1991). *The fine line: Making distinctions in everyday life.* Chicago: University of Chicago Press.

Zimmerman, D. H., & West, C. (1975). Sex roles, interruptions and silences in conversations. In B. Thorne & N. Henley (Eds.), *Language and sex: Difference and dominance.* Rowley, MA: Newbury House.

Index

About the Author

Kenneth Allan received his PhD in sociology from the University of California, Riverside (1995), and is currently Associate Professor of Sociology at the University of North Carolina at Greensboro (UNCG). Before moving to UNCG, he directed the Teaching Assistant Development Program at the University of California, Riverside, and coedited *Training Teaching Assistants,* 2nd edition (1997), published by the American Sociological Association. In addition to teaching classical and contemporary theory at UNCG, Allan also regularly teaches graduate pedagogy courses and oversees the department's online iSchool program, which currently offers university-level courses to over 2,000 high school students per year. Allan's research areas include theory, culture, and the self. He has authored several other works in the area of theory, including *The Meaning of Culture: Moving the Postmodern Critique Forward, Explorations in Classical Sociological Theory: Seeing the Social World,* and *Contemporary Social and Sociological Theory: Visualizing Social Worlds.*

Supporting researchers for more than 40 years

Research methods have always been at the core of SAGE's publishing program. Founder Sara Miller McCune published SAGE's first methods book, *Public Policy Evaluation*, in 1970. Soon after, she launched the *Quantitative Applications in the Social Sciences* series—affectionately known as the "little green books."

Always at the forefront of developing and supporting new approaches in methods, SAGE published early groundbreaking texts and journals in the fields of qualitative methods and evaluation.

Today, more than 40 years and two million little green books later, SAGE continues to push the boundaries with a growing list of more than 1,200 research methods books, journals, and reference works across the social, behavioral, and health sciences. Its imprints—Pine Forge Press, home of innovative textbooks in sociology, and Corwin, publisher of PreK–12 resources for teachers and administrators—broaden SAGE's range of offerings in methods. SAGE further extended its impact in 2008 when it acquired CQ Press and its best-selling and highly respected political science research methods list.

From qualitative, quantitative, and mixed methods to evaluation, SAGE is the essential resource for academics and practitioners looking for the latest methods by leading scholars.

For more information, visit **www.sagepub.com**.